As I Remember

An Autobiography
by Lillian M. Gilbreth

ENGINEERING & MANAGEMENT PRESS
a division of the Institute of Industrial Engineers

Norcross, Georgia

Library of Congress Cataloguing In Publication Data
Gilbreth, Lillian Moller, 1878-1972.
     As I Remember / by Lillian Gilbreth.
       p.   cm.
     IBN 0-89806-186-5 (alk. paper)
     1. Gilbreth, Lillian Moller, 1878-1972. 2. Women industrial engineers –
United States – Biography. I. Title.
     T55.85.G6453 1998
     670'.92—dc21
     [B]   98-5577
                              CIP

Our appreciation to the following organizations for their cooperation and/or use of photographs: Purdue University Library Special Collections, Bancroft Library at the University of California at Berkeley, and the National Museum of American History.

Printed in the United States of America
Quantity discounts available

For additional copies, contact:
Engineering & Management Press
Customer Service
25 Technology Park/Atlanta
Norcross, GA 30092
770-449-0461 phone
770-263-8532 fax
Web site: **www.iienet.org**

Jacket design by Martha Benoit

Dedication

Today, we can think of no better dedication of this treasured book than to quote from another Gilbreth-related book, *Cheaper by The Dozen*, published fifty years ago.

Ernestine Gilbreth Carey
and Daniel Bunker Gilbreth

He insisted that we make a habit of using our eyes and ears every single minute.

"Look there," he'd say. "What do you see? Yes, I know, it's a tree. But look at it. Study it. What do you see?"

But it was Mother who spun the stories that made the things we studied really unforgettable. If Dad saw motion study and team-work in an ant hill, Mother saw a highly complex civilization governed, perhaps, by a fat old queen who had a thousand black slaves bring her breakfast in bed mornings. If Dad stopped to explain the construction of a bridge, she would find the workman in his blue jeans, eating his lunch high on the top of the structure and the relative puniness of the humans who had built it. Or if Dad pointed out a tree that had been bent and gnarled, it was Mother who made us sense how the wind, beating against the tree in the endless passing of time, had made its own relentless mark.

We'd sit there memorizing every word, and Dad would look at Mother as if he was sure he had married the most wonderful person in the world.

— from *Cheaper by The Dozen*
by Frank B. Gilbreth Jr. and Ernestine Gilbreth Carey

As I Remember

As I Remember

by Lillian M. Gilbreth

"Once upon a time" two couples met each other on a steamer crossing the Atlantic. All four people had been born in Germany; it was the thrill of each summer, now that they were middle-aged and prosperous, to go back home.

JOHN MOLLER AND HIS WIFE lived in New York. He and his brothers had been trained as "sugar bakers" in their boyhood days. Looking for opportunities to advance they had migrated first to Holland — later to America. They were energetic, trained, ambitious. They got ahead. They married. John married a quiet, capable young girl named Adelaide Kuhlman. The bride was a real homemaker. She lost her first few babies each named John — one after the other — for her beloved husband. But, finally, a little new one was named William for one of his father's brothers. And "John's Billy" lived, slim and blue-eyed and red-haired. Four sisters followed — Margaret (Maggie), Elizabeth (Lizzie), Matilida (Tillie), and Johanna (Hansie).

John Moller had small, snapping, blue eyes; trim, wavy, thick hair, mustache and beard. Not a dandy, he loved good materials and well-made and styled clothes. He had a well-stocked wardrobe and he enjoyed wearing it. Jaunty, well-groomed, sociable, he loved to entertain and to be entertained.

Adelaide was like a sweet Quakeress. Mild blue eyes, hair parted and drawn over her ears and coiled at the top of her head. Simple clothes, though John insisted on fine material and workmanship, modest and serene, with that peculiar combination of neatness, simplicity of desires and carefulness that deprecates gifts — cherishes them but never uses them. Instead, keeps them all carefully wrapped and arranged in bureau drawers to be looked at and admired, and given back to the beloved donor some day.

Billy in his late twenties, tall, of that type of slimness that stays through life, whatever one does, eats, etc. The red hair brown now, though the cherished mustache is red. Wiry, active, gay, cheery, a good-tempered (though hot), affectionate, generous. Loving to walk, to read, to sing, to play the piano, to go to the theater — but NOT to be taught or "educated." Wanting to select his own books, play "by ear," to be a "free agent." Never liking new clothes, rather preferring to have company than to go to other people's houses. Never being forced or coaxed or persuaded to do what he didn't like, to submit to the discipline of social life. Yet not spoiled, generous, social, beauty-loving, musical, hard-working, religious. "The best boy a Mother ever had" — "The best brother — but oh what a tease."

Billy, a bachelor, lived at home, the adored of everyone — a good son and brother. He was perhaps a bit spoiled. Not lazy about things he liked, he was lazy at school — which he disliked heartily — mostly because it kept him away from the sugar refinery that he loved. From his first visit there as a tiny boy, he knew making sugar was his chosen job. That he studied! But the best sugar makers had had little or no schooling — so it was as little schooling as possible for him. He ran away from home as often as he could. He ran to the refinery. Finally, he rebelled so thoroughly that his fiery, soft-hearted father gave in and the youngster spent full-time at the plant learning it all — research, production, distribution, accounting — on the job, all in terms of his beloved sugar.

It was fun to be independent, to live at home because one wanted to, not because one had to; to have money to spend lavishly on presents; to play fairy godfather to the little sisters. Escort, playfellow, Santa Claus — he was all of these. Girls liked him, but he had a home, comfort, adoration, freedom, even Lizzie's babies to play with — why marry?

Lizzie was her brother's favorite (he never felt congenial to Maggie) — a mixture of her father and mother. She looked more like Adelaide, but had more of John's lively disposition. Before she had married, she and Billy had a happy summer in Germany together and they had endless tales and jokes about their experiences.

Lizzie married Edward Fliedner — thin, dark, nervous, with kind brown eyes and brushed-back hair. They and their children — Eddie, Lillie and Annie — lived with Grandpa and Grandma, having a floor of their own in the big brown house on East Thirty-Seventh Street.

Maggie's marriage didn't please her father — although the Dr. Heuchling who took her to Chicago to live was a capable physician — perhaps because [the doctor] was domineering, hot-tempered and truculent. Adelaide wrote to her daughter and John knew this, though he never mentioned it or interfered. When John's Billy came home to visit (after he had moved to California), his Mother, knowing he'd come through Chicago, would say, "Did you talk to Maggie? Did you see her?" She would then sit and listen, patting his arm as he spoke, telling about Maggie's children, especially Addie, named for her.

Tillie was small and dainty and devoted to the slightly younger though taller Hansie, who looked like her father and adored him. The two little girls were the family pets and big brother's chums, to be teased, petted and amused.

The annual trip that John and Adelaide took "back home" was so care-free! Lizzie love to run the house, Billy the business. The little girls stayed at home or went to Europe too — even had some of their schooling there.

One visited the relatives; shopped ("special knitting yarn for John's Billy's socks"); told of the U.S.A.; caught up on the technical, social and clan news — and met such pleasant people crossing. "Now — take the Delgers from California — they go across every summer too!"

Frederick Delger and Ernestine, this wife, were more south German than the Mollers — and both had a passion for outdoors. Travel, scenery, birds, fish, but especially trees, plants and flowers were passions with them both. So that it must have been hard for them to leave their beautiful and beloved birthplace.

But they came to America in 1852 and went to California, about '61 — not overland, but across Panama. They lived in San Francisco for some years, he selling shoes and she keeping house. But they longed for a larger place and a big garden, so they moved across the bay to Oakland. Here they bought land, sold it, and bought more. Frederick found that he had a flair for real estate. He knew values. He sensed possibilities for beauty with development. Most important of all, he had "hunches" as to where prices would rise. He made money rapidly, saved part, invested part, but always in property — and with long-time planning in mind.

His own home place grew larger and more beautiful and interesting. He added hothouses, then conservatories with grottos and fish, a big bird house, trees, shrubs, every flower he could buy. Then came the happy thought of importing from Germany and of going back home to do the selecting one's self.

So he and Ernestine went across, leaving the children in safe hands, to buy red beech, lilies-of-the-valley, ferns — everything they could find. What fun to bring the things home and plant them. Some grew; others died. That meant going back for more next summer. Perhaps bringing loads of soil to help the plant life to acclimate itself more easily.

Frederick was large and quiet, unless he was excited. Then he could be angry, enthusiastic, eloquent. But his eyes and his voice carried even deeper meanings than his words. He spoke English fluently, although always with an accent, but he preferred to speak German, just as he pre-ferred to read and write it. His eyes were blue behind his glasses. His black hair tended to grow thin on top, his beard was thin too. He was tall and heavy — not fat. He preferred loose clothes. He was not apparently fussy about them — they looked as if he had ordered one suit and another of the same material and cut. But the material was the best and his tailor knew his job. No vivid colors or patterns, no "style," but that line and fit and workmanship that means that clothes hang well. White shirt, plain tie, dark socks, PERFECT shoes. (After all, he had made and sold them!)

Ernestine was large and ample too. Much more sociable and talkative — a lady bountiful person. Her eyes were brown as was her fluffy, abundant hair. She loved clothes — rich silk dresses, jewelry, hats and bonnets — in the lavish style of the period. Her clothes were of many colors, though all harmonizing. (Thanks to herself, or Frederick?) She laughed and chatted with everyone, going comfortably from her broken English to her fluent German and back again. Frederick used to sit quietly and smile to himself as she rambled on, but she was careful to stop and listen if he happened to choose to talk.

In there there were four children, much desired and adored, three girls and a boy — the "crown prince" after the German fashion. [Matilda, Annie, Edward, and Lillie]

Matilda, the oldest, was a responsible soul. She loved to "take charge." She learned to cook and to sew early, thoroughly and perfectly. Everything she did was done with skill and her handiwork could have graced any exhibit. She was a master craftswoman with her needle and loved to design and carry out her ideas. She was short and trim, energetic and motherly. Too active to be fat, she was plump and pretty. She had keen brown eyes and smooth hair — always like a little ship under sail.

Annie, the next daughter, was gentler, quieter and with that inner shine that promises serenity. She had, of course, to learn all the crafts too, but she never loved them or excelled at them, although what she did do was done well. Like Matilda, she loved to garden, but she did more day-dreaming than her sister. She played the piano, though not with finish; she loved to play and sing the ballads. She had soft brown eyes and soft heavy hair worn off her face with a back-comb (later in braids round her head). She was taller than her sister, though still short, and all curves though slim. She loved her family (it was an affectionate, united family), looked up to Matilda, worshipped Eddie — the precious brother — but held at the center of her heart Lillie, the baby — her special charge.

Eddie (Edward Frederick, as his father was Frederick Edward, and his son would be Frederick Edward II) looked like his mother always and had her disposition. His easy-going nature needed discipline, but it is hard to be stern with an adored, much desired, only son, especially when he is affectionate and generous. His brown eyes and build were like Annie's — in fact he was like her in many ways. But he could give himself up to his fancies more easily than she because home, duties, and Matilda's "big-sister demands" kept Annie in line.

Lillie was the only one with her father's cool blue eyes, his ability to plan what one wanted and persist in going after it. She had a good mind undistracted by dreaming, and loved to study. Being the baby, both her father and her mother petted her. Eddie, of course, teased and bossed her. Matilda, busied about many things, left the baby sister to Annie's tender care.

Each child was educated with every advantage available. As the convent schools were the finest at hand, the little Protestant girls went to them — the Sacred Heart in Oakland, then the Notre Dame in San Jose. The good Sisters, warned against proselytizing, contented themselves with showing their pupils what a comfort and guide the church is. The girls learned to sing, to play the piano, to speak and write a cultured English, to read discriminatingly, to read aloud acceptably, all the branches of sewing, art appreciation, all the basic principles of living and the social arts that make a gentlewoman. There was in education of women everywhere, less emphasis on physical fitness and mental alertness than on serenity of spirit and social adjustment — but their equipment for living served well. Each girl had some of her education in France and Germany to learn the languages, get polish and breadth of culture, and a love of travel and differing people and a certain adjustability and poise that was to prove very useful.

Eddie was to be sent to Harvard, the last word in culture for a Western boy. He did not take his preparation too seriously, for, of course, Ed Delger would get whatever he wanted.

This special summer he and Lillie would be happy at home. Matilda had married and gone to live with her Captain husband in Yokohama, where he was Captain of the Port. It was hard that her father disapproved of the marriage. Captain [John] Brown's strongly British temperament and Frederick's German ideas could not be reconciled. But Matilda, who if she made up her mind to anything was absolutely and unshakingly sure it was right, was set on the marriage and happy in it and putting it through splendidly.

Annie, just seventeen, was to go to Germany with father and mother to visit the friends she had made at school. She was a sweet, amiable, useful traveling companion. It would be pleasant too, to have her along on the visit to the Mollers in New York. The Delger and Mollers had crossed together on previous summers and been congenial shipmates. Typically, the chatty John and Ernestine carried the conversational burden, Adelaide enjoyed it all, and Frederick listened or spoke now and then (when he was not lost in his planning).

Frederick was not too anxious to visit the Mollers in New York — never caring for social affairs — but Ernestine loved the idea. Annie could help in the chatting and play with the young people.

She did more! Billy Moller, after one look at the young stranger, fell in love with her. The four parents smiled at the pretty idyll. All felt that Billy was old and responsible enough to marry. Annie was young, but so were most brides in the 70s and Billy's ten-years older would steady her. John and Adelaide were delighted that John's Billy had found such a lovely girl. Lizzie too, the small sister reveled in the romance and was happy that big brother wasn't planning to leave home, but would bring his wife to the home and family of East 37th Street.

Billy walked on air! He would follow his fiancee to Germany, be married in Hamburg, take her on a honeymoon and bring her home. As for Annie? It was her first real romance. How glad she was now that her father had discouraged the callow youths who persisted in calling and had insisted she "go along to Europe and then decide which one you want."

It wouldn't be easy to leave California — the lovely home, dear garden, Eddie and Lillie. But Lillie could visit her, father promised, and Lillie must go way to school soon anyhow.

Annie would rather have her own house, at least for awhile. But it seemed to be a Moller custom for the ones who married to bring their partners home and have a wing of the big, hospitable, old house — and life with Willie (as she called him, because no one else did) would be thrilling anywhere.

And to buy a trousseau abroad, to wear her new ring, to be married in Germany, to have one of Willie's cousins at school there (Memie Moller) for a bridesmaid, to have him bring another cousin (George) over for best man — little Annie Delger's dreamy eyes shone with excitement.

All the plans were carried through. Annie bought her trousseau, beautifully initialed linens by the dozen, down quilts and pillows, enough clothes to last years, and so much silk that a complete bolt — a misty blue-green that would stand alone — remained over to be handed down for generations. It was the day of tiny hats and flaring dresses, yards and yards of ruffles — but no bride ever worried as to how her finery was to be packed and taken home.

Willie came rushing over in May, as had been arranged. He had not checked on all the formalities — what impatient bridegroom ever does — and the delays over birth certificates, baptismal certificates, parent's consent, vaccination certificate, etc., drove him to dispair. But George was a willing and helpful best man — and of course, his German cousins could help. "Memie," the one whom Annie had agreed to invite to be

Lillian M. Gilbreth's parents —
William Moller and Annie Delger Moller (1919)

maid of honor (sight unseen) proved to be a treasure. Lovely to look at, gracious and affectionate, she and the bride were soon like sisters.

The wedding in an old Lutheran Church in Hamburg was solemn, simple and friendly. The bride and groom started their trip — happy to be leaving the relatives and friends — to be joined by cousin George the next morning, because he was lonely. Why Annie stood it, why Willie did, no one knows!

The bridal couple returned to New York and the welcome of the Moller clan. Adelaide had a beautiful locket and chain for her new daughter. John had a suite in the family home specially furnished. The groom plunged back into his work, leaving the bride to fraternize with her sisters-in-law.

It was a hard year for poor Annie. The Eastern climate was severe (after her beloved California); the home, big as it was, seemed crowded; there was no garden; there was much entertaining and going to parties. Married in May, she had escaped the worst heat of the summer, but she was not acclimated enough to avoid shivering all winter.

In April a baby came, with dark eyes like her young mother. She was named Annie Adelaide and called Addie. But mother and child both wilted as the hot weather came. Willie took them up the Hudson for coolness and a change. But the baby developed "summer complaint" and slipped quietly away — and Annie had no will or strength to live.

They tried everything — nothing helped until a Doctor suggested that she go back to her native state. This roused her. Yes, she thought she could get better there. She would go. Of course Willie would take her. Yes, but she could not bear to have him leave her — and she knew she could never, never come back.

So Willie sold his interest in his beloved sugar business, took the money along to invest, tore the forsaken little mother away from the little grave at Greenwood where Addie lay next to the little "Johns" who had died before he was born, and they started West.

The Mollers hated to see them go. Lizzie, especially grieved to lose the congenial little sister; Hansie and Tillie felt that they were giving up their big brother a second time; patriarch John mourned his depleted household, his son and partner; and Adelaide said nothing, but felt she might never see her John's Billy again.

But the California Delger clan were delighted. Of course it was sad for Annie to lose her first baby, but she would soon cheer up when she was back in her own home and another baby — a native son or daughter — would come to comfort her. Too bad for Willie to have to sell is excellent business, but there were fine opportunities to invest money and he would soon get exactly the thing he wanted.

A cozy little house near the Delger place was found and put in order — so near that Annie and her mother could run back and forth a dozen times a day. Willie decided to go into partnership with Robert Dalziel, a fine elderly Scot who had a wholesale plumbing supply place in San Francisco, and a store, tin shop, and plumbing business in Oakland. It was a satisfactory arrangement — Dalziel was honest and fair. Willie found that his training, especially the accounting part of it, transferred readily to this new business.

If he missed the East — New York, his big family, the business of which he had voluntarily and happily given so many years — he never said so. If Annie would stay well, if she was happy, if he could keep her glad she had married him — that was all that counted.

The little house was comfortable. A new baby came — another daughter, Lillie Evelyn (the "Lillie" of course for Annie's beloved younger sister).

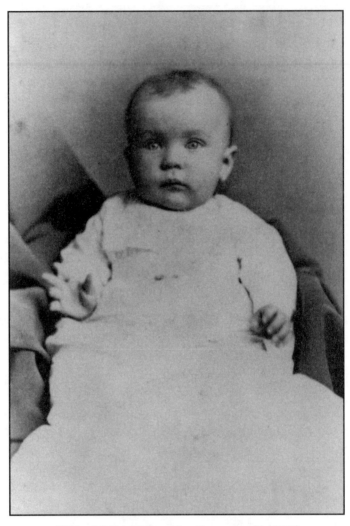

Lillian Moller (Gilbreth) at 6 months old (1878)

Lillie was not at all like Annie. She looked like her father — blue eyes, high forehead, straight reddish hair, slim, excitable — almost too affectionate and demonstrative. Quick-tempered, quick-motioned — "quick" at everything. And none too happy to be told, "You are going to have a new baby to play with — a little sister or brother."

The first little house on Telegraph Avenue was not large enough for a growing family, so they moved to one on Nineteenth and Grove Street. It was on a large corner lot that stretched from Grove Street with its shade trees and pretty homes, half-way back to San Pablo Avenue with its little shops. This meant that the San Pablo end of the garden — "the sand lot" as Willie called it because only gum (eucalyptus) trees grew there — ended at the backs of some tenement-like houses. But the gum trees were so tall that they almost cut off the view. Little Lillie could hear voices now and then and see women hanging out wash.

There was a large lawn and plenty of room for a big garden, for the house stood near the Grove Street end of the lot. It meant too that there was room for an addition if the house grew too small.

Little Gertie (Gertrude Wilhelmina, the last for dear Mrs. Neller, neighbor and friend) had come safely, just twenty-five months younger than Lillie. She had big blue eyes and almost white-gold hair and looked even more "Mollery" than Lillie. Julia McCarthy, the nurse, adored her and spent all her time fixing her hair in little "horns" on her forehead and dressing her up in stiffly starched skirts.

Her godmother also adored her and was always bringing her presents. Mrs. Neller's four big boys, two sons and two stepsons, laughed at her joy over her new little pet, but she enjoyed that and only went on thinking up more presents. Dear Mama always tried to duplicate them for Lillie, but it was hard to have so many people liking Gertie best.

The new garden was a great joy. It had so many plants and flowers and best of all were the things that smelled so delicious — mignonette, heliotrope, breath-of-heaven, sweet-briar, rose geranium, lavender, clove pink, roses of all kinds, more lovely odors than one small nose could revel in, tiny as it was.

Lillie always trimmed her hat with flowers — sticking them in the band — and crushed some sweet-smelling leaves in her hand to enjoy between sniffs as she ran through the garden or as she went out. There were so many lovely tiny flowers that seemed to belong specially to her. Everyone else thought them too small to pay much attention to. Lillie picked them for dolls' bouquets.

And now, something thrilling was to happen. Dear Auntie Brown, Matilda, Mama's older sister, was coming home from Japan.

She had had a hard life, but a happy one. Uncle John was Lillie's idol and they had six fine children — three girls and three boys. Lillie never tired of hearing about them. First came Tillie, then Annie, David, Bertie, Everett, and little Elsie — just one month younger than Lillie herself.

The two sisters wrote long letters and Matilda sent a steady stream of vases, silks, and cabinets — all the lovely wares of Japan — many as presents, some as commissions — till the Moller home was filled — for Annie, like her Mother, could never resist a beautiful thing and loved to buy. So Lillie came to feel that she knew Japan and "Auntie Brown and the Brownies" (as Papa called them) very well.

Best of all the things sent across were a Japanese couple, Toni and Stosi. Lillie was only a baby when they came, but she never forgot them and didn't need the tintype of dear Stosi holding her to remind her of all the gentleness and affection she'd had. She was the favorite — just perfect! Toni drank or did some awful thing, which meant he had to leave and, of course, Stosi had to go too — weeping to leave her "baby Lillie."

Weeping — that reminds one of poor Auntie Brown. First Herbie was terribly burned, suffering so that Auntie's hair was said to have turned white as she watched over him — as he eventually died. Then big, husky Uncle John was crushed to death in his pilot boat between two docking vessels.

And now Auntie was coming home with her children and the two bodies — to lie in Mountain View. Grandpa Delger had forgiven her for marrying against his will — after all these years — and was finding a home for her and would see that she and the children had all they needed.

They were on the steamer, almost in, when Auntie's last letter to Mama came, sent by a steamer ahead. It said that all the children had whooping cough but that Auntie had decided to come as planned. Her goods were packed and shipped, their passage engaged. But, said Matilda, surely she and the children had better go at once to their new home — and not visit at Nineteenth and Grove Street as planned — for fear that Lillie and Gertie would get the whooping cough too. "I cannot expose your darlings, dear Sister," the letter ended.

Gertie was too little to understand. Lillie, however, thought she'd die of disappointment if they didn't come. Annie was pale as she tried to decide what was best. It would be awful to expose here little girls, but oh, she did want to welcome her sister to her home. Willie decided. "Of course they must come! Perhaps the Lord will keep Lillie and Gertie from catching it. Let's go straight ahead with our plans." And they did — and the Lord did his part too.

It was afternoon when the Browns arrived. Papa and Mama went to meet them. Julia McCarthy dressed Lillie and Gertie in their very best — the new white dresses with the wide embroidery and the white stockings and shiny kid strapped slippers. Lillie had her hair in many small braids the night before and it stood up in a pleasing fuzz with a pale blue ribbon on top of her head. July had made the usual horns over her finger on Gertie's head. Gertie sat on her lap near the window and Lillie next to her, looking out. There were the carriages. First Papa got out — then a little trim lady in black. That must be Auntie Brown. Then a tall girl in a gray dress with many black bows down the front, who must be Tillie — and a little girl with lovely black tight curls, she must be Elsie. She did not seem at all shy but skipped and jumped up and down. Papa opened the door of the other carriage and Mama got out. Then a medium-sized girl with fluffy brown hair, who must be Mama's namesake —

Annie. A boy, just a little bit smaller than she, who saw Lillie looking at him and made the most awful faces, who must be Davis. Finally, a boy just a little smaller still, very neat, with his hair carefully slicked back, who must be Evvie.

In they all came and Gertie smiled at them and let them shake her fat little hand. Lillie, shy as always, hid behind Mama when she was introduced or spoken to, but ate up her cousins with big eyes all the rest of the time.

The few days of their visit were too exciting to register clear memories, but soon they were settled in their new home and then how grand it was to have one or another come over or to go there to visit.

When Tillie came, she talked with Mama almost like a grown person. She was very capable, responsible and ambitious, wanting to plan to make the most of school, to help run the house, to be useful everywhere.

If Annie came, she wanted to see all the books. She would read if she had a chance. Sometimes she would read aloud to Lillie — poetry mostly — and they both loved it.

If Davis came, he was always hungry even though Tillie carefully filled him up just before he left home. He was usually a constant visitor when the fruit trees were ripe. Papa said he never saw any human being who could hold so many cherries!

When Evvie came, he loved to look at the flowers. He usually brought some to Mama and then picked some to take home with him to Auntie Brown. And he always had one in his buttonhole. He loved to wear camellias, large as they were. Perhaps it reminded him of Japan.

Both boys liked to look in the big mirror in the hall. Davie would make diabolical faces. When Mama said, "Davie, aren't you afraid your face will stay that way?," he would grin sheepishly and stop, but as soon as her back was turned he would be back. Evvie only looked to be sure his hair

Lillian Moller (Gilbreth) at 3 years old (1881)

was right. Then we would admire his buttonhole flower, adjust it carefully, and go off content.

Best of all was when Elsie came. In the middle of the front lawn was a large palm tree. The lawn wasn't level but sloped down from the palm on all sides. There were circles and rows of tiny plants between the tree and lawn, bluets, et cetera. One could play dolls or house quietly, or one could roll down the hill. Elsie was always willing to start with a quiet play, but she was a lively piece and was soon starting a game of tag or stealing sticks — her black eyes snapping, her curls bobbing, her cheeks as red as roses. Lillie thought her the most beautiful child in the world. Oh, to be able to change blue eyes for brown, straight red hair for black curls.

Auntie was so busy that she could not come often. When she did, she brought piles of sewing or mending or insisted on doing Mama's while

Lillian and one of the Brown cousins – most likely Annie (1896)

she talked. Lillie loved her dearly. It was a great treat to be sent on an errand to her or allowed to go over to visit for the afternoon. She tried hard to fit into the rougher play of the boys — even baseball. She loved to stay for dinner even though dear pious Auntie asked a long blessing, which was very embarrassing when she prayed for "our dear little Lillie — bless her and make her a good girl."

Always a shy child, Lillie was easily frightened. If only she could have told of the things that scared her — to Papa or Mama. She never could. This was because she showed her fright so plainly that the person who scared her was afraid and made her promise not to tell under penalty.

Annie was never really strong and well after the going of little Addie. And Billy was so careful of her and so fearful that she might be tired or ill that he waited on her by inches. Maturely, Lillie observed and copied this. And, when Lillie asked Papa why he acted this way and he told her, "So that Mama won't be ill" — she began to be afraid that something would happen to her beloved mother. Probably she heard some maids whispering about her mother's delicacy, for gradually she could not bear to have Mama out of her sight. The devoted Willie, pacing up and down restlessly if Annie was late, on one of her rare trips to the city (San Francisco), did not realize that his small daughter interpreted this as fear that she'd never come back. So that even if Mama only went over to Grandma's, Lillie stationed herself at the gate to wait for her, in agony if she was delayed. When Mama took a nap, Lillie sat where she could watch her window (until the shade went up) and also watch the front door and gate so that no one came in or Mama went out.

A second fear started in her beloved garden. Mr. Helke, a kindly German with twin daughters of his own, was digging a hole for a tree. Lillie got in his way again and again and "Run along" did no good. Finally, at the end of his patience, he said, "Do run or I'll bury you in this hole." Lillie shivered with fright and turned so white that he added, "And if you ever tell any one that I said so, I'll surely do it."

Lillie never told because she had too little reasoning power and too much imagination. For years, she'd go to sleep only to dream terrible dreams and wake up to see just as horrible images on her bedroom wall — donkey's like the ones in the Minstrel Show, only gigantic, grotesque, and threatening like all the ogres in her beloved Grimm's Fairy Tales. She'd stand it as long as she could, then cry, and Papa would come and give her a drink of water. But as soon as he left, she'd fall asleep and the awful cycle would start all over again, till she would creep into Mama's bed and snuggle close to comfort and peace.

The third fright came when Lillie Marie, Aunt Lily's baby girl, died. Someone came over to tell Mama early one morning — perhaps Auntie Brown — and to ask for some white ribbon. Mama asked Lillie to give her the lovely new satin hair ribbons that she had never worn, promising to get new ribbons for Lillie later. Lillie loved the ribbons. She had had them for some days, smoothly rolled in her bureau drawer. A dozen times a day she opened the drawer to look at them and smooth them. So, she was rather reluctant about giving them up, but she did.

Auntie said, "But I do think you should take Lillie over to see her." "Oh Matilda, do you?" said Mama, "She is so young and I hate to have her shocked."

"She isn't too young to know what death is," said Auntie. "Besides, I think Sister Lillie will be hurt if she doesn't go — after all, she is her Godchild."

So that afternoon Mama took Lillie to Aunt Lillie's little house and there in a white box lay dear Violet, so pale and stiff, so different, so fearsome. Lillie felt cold to her very soul, and frightened. And then, oh, never to be forgotten horror, she saw her own white ribbons tying Violet's hair, as a part of the terrible sight. Never, so long as she lived, could she see such ribbons without a shudder. It and "tube roses" (for there were some there) were part of the terrible terror of death.

The fourth fright had come years before and was less devastating. It had happened when this same Godmother aunt was first married and brought her young husband to see her Godchild. Lillie, as always, hid behind Mama's chair. When he tried to pull her gently out, she ran and he chased her — gaily, as a game, but it was deadly earnest to her. And when he caught and kissed her, she almost fainted. Never, after that, was there any happy thrill at being chased. Even tag was an agony — the torture of possibly being caught!

The little girl who went into her teens took a burden of fear with her, carefully secreted, but real and at times shattering.

Lillie never could remember when she learned to read. I suppose her mother taught her — but she was so wild to know how, that it was such a short and simple process and neither of them knew how it happened.

She always wanted to own the books she read — so that her little library grew all the time. Mother Goose first, of course, and Puss in Boots and the "Little Folks" fairy tales. The Sophie May books — one after another. The Grimm's (in the brown two-volume edition) and Hans Anderson galloped through, then read and reread over and over again.

She had only to start a book and she *lived* in it, blind and deaf to everything. She would creep back of the lace curtains and garnet draperies and actually *be* Snow White or Rapenesol or the Little Mermaid. Grimm was romantic and thrilling, but Hans Anderson made her laugh and cry. All his characters, real and unreal, people, animals, toys, the little pine tree, came alive for her, more vivid than people and things in real life.

Next, of course, came the Alcott books, *Jack and Jill, Under the Lilacs, Old Fashioned Girl, Eight Cousins, Little Women, Little Men* — then, oh thrills, the older ones, *Jo's Boys, Rose in Bloom* — even *Work*. Mama really thought these too old, but Lillie begged so hard — she must have "whole sets." There was nothing else in the world she wanted — Christmas, birthdays, or any other time. The dear brown and green (why couldn't they all be the same color?) books made a grand showing in her bookcase.

It was probably about this time that she joined the Sunday School Library, but the books she got there were so goody-goody and so babyish in thought and poor in expression that after a short time she didn't think them worth bringing home.

I am not sure how Lillie came to read Cooper. But I remember well the big gray-blue book with all the Leather Stocking Tales, Matty Bumpo and Chigangook and the young Uncas! Next came Walter Scott, a dull red set of many volumes, none too good print, on poor paper, but magic in each one! Think of owning *all* the Waverly novels! She never did own Dickens because he was Papa's favorite English author and she could read his beautiful leather bound set with the Kruikshank drawings. She and Papa talked over each story. He liked *Our Mutual Friend* best. She liked usually the one she happened to be reading, but gradually came to the point where his favorite was her's too. Of course, she loved the romantic characters — Kate Nickleby, Florence Dombey, Little Nell. He loved Tom Pinch, Traddles, Mr. Pickwick, Macawber. They lived with this myriad of old friends until they were as real as the people they met downtown, and until dear Papa was a part of every book of Dickens to his whole family.

Because he loved Dumas too, Lillie read the *Three Musquetieres*, *D'Artagnan*, etc. Then he gave her his beloved *Count of Monte Christo*. Mother thought this rather strong meat, but it seemed to do Lillie no harm. The twaddle of Augusta Ann Evans and Marie Carelli perhaps acted as a balance.

Then came Thackeray, then George Eliot, all of each too quickly read by an immature mind, but leaving, nevertheless, unforgettable pictures of British nature and human life. In the case of *Romola* — an open door to Italy — and a great lesson.

Why Bulwer Lytton was added — all of him — Wilkie Collins — then all the new books she could lay hands on — Kipling, Anthony Hope, Harris — is not clear. Such reading was never a part of school work — just the means of living in other worlds — the refuge of an introverted imaginative child. She was never lonely or unhappy, except when she was called out of some other world to buy clothes, meet people, be a part of any social life.

Another great urge toward reading came from "hearing" books! Mama's eyes were weak. She could tat without straining them, but except on the few nights when they "went out," Papa read aloud to her, hour after hour. He had a good reading voice, and love to read aloud — dramatizing at times, stopping at the end of each chapter to discuss it.

Lillie was suppose to be asleep — or in any case, not attending — but she heard thrilling snatches of *Trilby, The Heavenly Twins, Robert Elsmere, John Brown - Preacher,* as well as *Lorna Doone,* Dickens, Fritz Reuter in his inimitable platdeutsch, and *The Schonberg Cotta Family.* Mama kept many "risque" books hidden, but it wasn't hard to find them — back of some shelf of books — and one learned to "read fast" if one wanted to finish the story. Lillie often wondered why they were hidden — she, of course, saw none of the questionable things — they were just dull, and she returned with newer vigor to her own books.

Perhaps because she was so shy and so nervous, Lillie was not sent to school at the usual age of six, and then, too, the nearest school was many blocks away — and her parents were nervous about the crossings.

Her reading went well, and mother thought she could teach her enough to make it possible for her to enter the grade of her age.

Lillie loved to learn, and especially with a gentle teacher like Mama. Her father brought home large sheets of foolscap paper from his store and Mama cut it carefully into little slips about six inches by two inches. On these she wrote lists of words to be spelled and all of the multiplication tables. Each morning after breakfast, when her chores were done, Lillie went to Mama for her day's assignment. Then out she flew through the back door to the cement walk under the linden trees. She could sit on the green bench in the sun or walk back and forth or skip and run and "sing" the words and the tables. Back and forth she went and up and down she recited them — for Mama, very conscientious, often skipped around to make it hard.

When she was sure she knew everything she called, "All ready," just like a game — and Mama answered, "I'll be there," or "Come here" or "Wait a while."

Finally Lillie stood before her — "just like at school" — and did the new work and review. Then perhaps she defined her words and used them in sentences or game synonyms — and Mama wrote out sums for "home work" — or said the might make up some. She liked that best of all, especially the addition — nine columns across and nine down!

She had other lessons too — Sunday School — which she endured because she liked neat, kind Mrs. Holmes, her teacher (with blond "water waves" on each side of her smooth part) and her nice old mother, Mrs. Gardner, who made pictures out of sea-weeds and moss and ferns and water colors.

The Bible stories were fascinating — but the lesson leaflets were infantile — and the little attendance cards, one each Sunday, and a larger one when one had four, were babyish.

Music lessons she hated — though she loved the piano. Why couldn't she play "by ear" as Papa did? Mrs. Hofeld was such a sneak — as sweet as sugar if Mama came in — cross, hitting her knuckles with a pencil, snapping at her, the rest of the time.

German she liked — mostly because she loved Miss. Teny Cranz, her teacher. Grandpa Delger thought it awful that Papa and Mama talked anything but German at home. So Lillie learned to write (the German script) and read the Gothic type, impressed that Miss. Cranz did it so beautifully. Her writing was art, her reading music. Slim, straight, with black dress, tiny white collar and cuffs and a queer cap, she was different from anyone else — a charming person, to her little pupil.

At eight, Mama thought she'd try a Girl's Private School (Snell's Seminary), but poor Lillie almost died the first morning. Mama took her and left her. The girls were of all ages, they weren't unkind, but of course they looked at the newcomer. When she was called upon to recite, her knees trembled so that she could hardly stand and she couldn't talk above a whisper.

At noon she ran all the way home and cried so hard that she frightened herself and then her mother. She begged so frantically not be sent back that the home lessons were renewed.

The next year, at nine, she went to the public school. It was in a way humiliating to be started with children who were much younger. But, of course, one couldn't be afraid of them! At ease, she soon showed she knew enough to go into a class her own age. Here she was fortunate enough to have a remarkable teacher, (Miss. Bradbury) one of a series who helped her supply her deficiencies — and use all she had.

She developed a passion for study, perhaps because its beginnings had been so happy for her.

Her only difficulties were social ones. She was afraid of boys — to the point where she would walk around the block rather than have to speak to one she knew. She was a prig; she was just the type to revel in being "teacher's pet — scrub the blackboard" — she loved to "sit in the honor seat on the platform and look on the book with the teacher." She put her head down on her desk and sobbed all day the time she got a check for standing at "attention," when the teacher had changed the procedure to "sitting" and habit got the best of half the class.

She didn't care much for going to other girls' houses — and if they came to hers, preferred to show them her books, rather than to whisper and giggle. No wonder she wasn't popular.

But her parents praised the good report cards; her teachers said she was a credit to everyone; she decided very young, that as she couldn't be pretty she *had* to be smart — so she lived in her school books as she had in her books at home.

Lillie, like almost all children, liked errands that included responsibility and did not interrupt her own schedule. Just a block on San Pablo Avenue, were most of the small shops where the family bought supplies. One turned to the left, and on the corner was Mr. Hall's drug store. There were beautiful big glass jars of colored water in the windows — purple, green and gold. They looked just like big jewels when the sun shone on them and Lillie and Gertie never tired of looking at them. Inside, to the right, was the cigar counter where Papa loved to spend a long time picking out his cigars. Lillie never realized that she saw or heard a thing of that, yet years later, standards of judgment were in her mind, and names of brands, sizes and shapes, blends, et cetera, appeared like magic when she needed them.

Then there was the counter at the rear where one went if one had a pre-scription to have made up — with all the alluring little, medium-sized, and big bottles and boxes waiting to be filled.

To the left was the long counter with tooth brushes, combs, and such things, and back of it, all across and up the wall, the Patent Medicines. Lillie loved to try to read the labels. Then there were the jars of sachet powder to sniff, all looking so colorless and alike, but smelling so divinely and differ-ent. The bottles of Florida Water to admire, and the brown, pink, and white rock candy — licorice, lemon, horehound, and flaxseed candy to covet.

A door or two beyond the drugstore was the butcher shop. Mr. Kuhnle was big, neat in his big white apron, jovial and friendly — but Lillie hated all the meat, especially the big "sides" of beef and lamb. She slid in with her eyes glued to the scales and tried not to look away before the parcel was in her hand.

If one turned right at the corner, there was the grocery store. The owner changed often, so one didn't learn his name — and one only went there in emergencies as one's own grocer was blocks down.

Next came Spencer's bakery. Of course all breads, cakes and pies were baked at home — but they had the most delicious custard cream puffs at the bakery. Lillie often bought one instead of candy. Mr. Spencer was big, thin, black and very hairy — Lillie always hoped she'd not have to see him. Mrs. Spencer was small and pale, *much* nicer to have pick up one's cake and put it in a little bag.

A few doors farther was Mr. Perry, who had the fruit and vegetable store. The little girls loved to shop there best of all because he always gave them some little thing for themselves — and an apple or orange tasted so much better if it was a present than if one bought it.

Once, on Gertie's birthday, she went to each store saying, "It's my birthday." Of course everyone said "Happy Birthday" or "How nice" — but when she said, "Mr. Perrywinkle (she always called him that), it's my birthday," he gave here a whole bag of fruit. What a thrill!

Down a few blocks was Mrs. Jones' little store where one bought all sorts of things for sewing and mending — and little toys too — besides valentines or things for other special days. First, one spent a long time looking in the windows though one knew most of the things by heart. Then one opened the door and a little bell rang and "Mother" Jones came out of her back room, behind the counter. She was short and very fat with no neck and no waist and her hair parted and waved in water waves and then pulled up into a knot at the top of her head. The store had a close, stuffy smell that was not unpleasant, and she'd smile and look at one with big starry (but friendly) eyes and ask, "And what is it today?" And first one would do Mama's errand and then explain that one had five cents or ten cents of one's own and what could one get for that. The joy of seeing, the difficulty of deciding, the pain of giving up, the rapture of taking the jacks or ball or jumping rope home!

Way downtown were the stores one went to with Mama — that was a different procedure.

Then there were the errands to Auntie Brown who was always busy but often said, "Sit down on the footstool, Lillie, and let's chat," just as if one were grown up — took the message — gave the answer — then, if one couldn't stop to play said, "And pick yourself some flowers as you go." Oh joy! Just one of each kind so as to not be greedy, but such a heavenly bunch to take home.

Errands to Grandma were best of all — but hardest to do promptly. The place was so big and Grandma was apt to be anywhere! If was fun to hunt her — and such a temptation to stay. For Grandma thought time was made to be enjoyed.

"But I have some vegetables for Mother — we must get those. And some cherries. And some flowers! And for you child — let's see if there aren't some fresh ladyfingers — and I know I've got some hard candy — and my new dress has come — and I am having chicken for lunch — and well, go if you have to, Kindchen — I'll be over tomorrow."

Staggering home went Lillie — not sure what she'd been sent for — but with beautiful returns for her errand.

There were various things that Lillie loved — one was the semi-annual visit of the "Needles and Pins" lady. She was very thin, dressed always in black, with a widow's veil. She was pale and quiet, a devout Catholic, Mama said.

She carried a pack that wasn't like a valise or anything else one knew. When she opened it there was the most fascinating collection of things to use for sewing. "The best of English pins and needles," she said. There were needles in papers and in needle books; pins in boxes — but the best in rows, oh so even, bound together. Lillie could see the needles all pinned into pinked flannel, bound into satin covers — the Christmas needle book she'd make — and the pins neatly stuck into "pin-balls." There were emeries like strawberries and tomatoes, and wax for shoe button cotton, and shoe buttons, and hooks and eyes. And Mama bought a lot and the woman said, "Thank you, Madam," and stole off.

Another treat was to go downtown shopping — to Mr. Hauschild's shoe store for "pebble goat" shoes for school and French kid for best (black, high, shining, buttoned, with tassels on top). And a shoe horn or button hook of one's own, as a present.

To Taft and Pennoyers — where one could lie on one's stomach and twirl around on the round little seats at the counter, while Mama had gloves fit — or select ribbons to tie the shaving paper pad or calendar one was making for Papa's birthday, along with "spills" of nice glossy white paper to light his cigars with.

Best of all, to Bacon's Palace of Sweets — for some candy or pink ice cream. Mr. Bacon was not fat and German like Mr. Hauschild — or thin and blue-veined like Mr. Pennoyer — but small, with blue eyes and hair that was almost pink, and a squeaky voice. But oh, his candy was delicious, and the boxes made grand pin-a-poppy shows or bureaus and furniture for the doll's house.

Another treat was to go with Mama to see Madame LePratt who did the beautiful French Laundry. She was stout and had gray hair and pink cheeks and she and Mama spoke French very quickly while Lillie admired all the frills and crisped ruffles and thought how beautiful her party things would look when they came home.

It wasn't such a treat to go see Mrs. Banforth who was English and did plain sewing, because though one never saw her husband, one disliked him heartily. He smoked a pipe — one smelled it as soon as one went into the house. Mrs. Banforth sat by her little hot stove and sewed on such *ugly* underwear, talking so queerly, with so many h's missing. One just knew how plain and simply hideous one's panties and petticoats would be, and how they would really smell awfully of smoke until they were washed, and always, in one's imagination. Thank goodness she never did buttonholes, "You know Sister Matilda likes to do those," Mama said. You'd be able to take the things over to dear Auntie Brown who would just snap them in, while she'd look the garments over, sniff, raise her eyebrows and say to you, "Well, I suppose she needs the work!"

A great treat was to go to see Mrs. Nicoli. It was Cousin Annie Flo who took one there. Mrs. Nicoli worked for one of the big furniture stores of the city. She could bring home pieces of plush, velvet, satin, or silk left over from draperies, upholstered chairs, et cetera. Her house was crowded (Papa said "cluttered") with things she had made of them. Pillows, curtains, drapes, quilts — it was fun to sit quietly and look around or walk carefully through — just drinking it in.

Best of all was the chance to select pieces to take home. Lillie just loved Mama's crazy quilt made of them. She had been allowed to make a square, joining the pieces with fancy stitches, herringbone, featherstitch, button-hole around circles drawn with a thimble. Even some patches were embroidered with flowers, monograms, et cetera. And she was starting a doll's quilt of her own.

Almost the best treat was going on Sundays, with Papa and the small sisters, to Lake Merritt. Mama was tucked in for a nap, Papa filled his pocket with cigars, got his hat and cane, and they set off. The streets and stores looked so different on Sundays. There were weeping willow trees by the lake — and they could sit under them and play — or listen to Papa's stores about when he was a little boy in New York.

They went home a different way, by the house with the morning-glories. Lillie almost died to pick one, but Papa said, "They aren't ours, my little girl!" And when Lillie looked forlorn, he added, "You can remember them, dear, and always keep them that way." And there were always the flowers waiting at home, to be smelled and picked and enjoyed.

Grandpa Delger's house had a white picket fence all around it and a hedge inside that. People thought that was so no one could see in; perhaps that was one reason it was there. Another was that he loved to imagine that he was back in his beloved Germany, and it was harder to do this if he saw Oakland.

When you went through the front gate, you saw the big white wooden house. On each side of the front steps were red geraniums, each in a glazed pot, and the pot in a dish. There were two pots on each step and all pots and plants exactly the same size — a lovely sight. There was frosted glass in the doors. When the door opened you saw the big, wide, cool hall, with the staircase to the second floor in the distance.

To the right one went to a big porch all glassed in, with vines and trees next to the glass, so that it was like being outside.

To the left was the parlor with mirrors in heavy gilt frames, black horse-hair furniture, wax flowers under glass domes, some of Auntie Brown's exquisite tapestry work ("Joseph presenting his Father to Pharaoh") and oval paintings of Grandma and Grandpa when they were young. Best of all, were two wonderful music boxes. One was in an inlaid box — a large gilt roll with little pins that revolved as it played. The other was even larger, and had little bells and drums. It was a never-failing ecstasy to stand watching and listening to them as they played the sweet German folk songs — the very same ones that Mama played and sang and that Lillie herself was learning to play — "Ween ich Komm," "Aanchen von Taura," Kommt ein Vogel," and "Freut euch das Leben." Sometimes Grandma would tell her of beautiful Switzerland, where they were made — high mountains, lovely meadows of wild flowers, little chalets. And they would go into the hall to look at, and listen to, the cuckoo clock that came from there too.

Then on into the big double dining room — with the pantry where limitless supplies of ladyfingers and cup cakes and jams and jellies were waiting and (if Sing were out) out into the kitchen to his pantries where the gardeners brought the fruit and vegetables every morning. Grandma had probably made the rounds of the daughter's homes in her big, low carriage that very morning, with the whole back of it filled with all these very things, for she was like a Goddess of Plenty, only happy when she was giving.

From the dining room one went down the side stairs into the garden. On this west side of the house always grew big, most carefully cultivated flowers. Sometimes it was carnations, sometimes pansies, no matter how many Grandma picked, there always seemed to be as many left.

And there was the magic conservatory. When she opened the door the most delicious smell in all the world crept out. Soft, green moss was everywhere — and pots of gloxinia, red and blue and purple — and many-colored coleus — and one's best beloved, the maidenhair ferns, the coarse ones like those that come with "cut flowers" — and the fine ones that one saw nowhere else. One could hear the little waterfall splash in the rookery — and few steps and there one was, standing before the pool, the goldfish skimming about! Or if one wished, through the aisles of the potting sheds — out into the garden. To the vegetables, the fruit trees, the currants, and raspberries, and gooseberries.

Off to the little arbor with the green iron furniture, there Grandma often had coffee, past the big aviary where bright birds flashed through the trees, down the long paths to the rose garden, off under the big shade trees where Grandpa's favorite lilies-of-the-valley bloomed.

No one but him ever picked them. In spite of his rheumatism he went out in the early morning and gathered them lovingly, so that no plant would be hurt. When Mama got the bunches he sent her, she smiled tenderly and arranged them so carefully that Lillie came to love them best of any flower. After all — she and they had the same name!

One summer when Grandpa and Grandma went to Europe, the Moller family "kept house" at the "Place." Then the little girls came to learn every inch of it. Before that it had more mystery and surprises. After that it was a second home, but always impressive, grand, different — austere like Grandpa, gracious like Grandma, bountiful like both of them.

As a baby, Lillie had been baptized in the Presbyterian Church. All four grandparents had been Lutheran — and her father and mother had been brought up in that church, but there was no English Lutheran Church in Oakland at this time.

Her first memory of church was going to hear Dr. Sprecher preach. He was thin and dark. He always started to preach very quietly and spoke very softly. But as he went on he became excited, the words pouring from him, and he paced up and down the pulpit, gesticulating. Lillie could seldom understand all that he said, but she loved to watch him and to listen to his beautiful voice. She loved the church too. It was large and gracious; it had a big choir and a great, wonderful organ; everything about it was beautiful!

As she grew older, the Lutheran Synod decided to start and English Mission Church in Oakland. They found a shabby little building, a group of people who were interested, and a minister who was willing to come to them.

Lillie's father was the most prosperous man in the new congregation, so he was expected to ask the preacher and his wife to stay with him, until they could find a home.

There was much work and excitement, getting their room ready. It meant that the little girls had to double up and that things had to be moved from other rooms, to make that room more attractive.

It was late afternoon when the Graifs arrived. He was a tall, very pale, thin man, his black hair and whiskers making him look even more white. She was short and puffy, looked much older than he, wore very thick-lensed spectacles, and what Lillie was *sure* was a wig! Though why would anyone choose such a big, fussy, untidy-looking one? They had a lot of hand luggage and a big green parrot in a big brass cage, that made hor-rid noises and looked as if she hated everyone.

At supper that night, Lillie'd disgraced herself. Papa, in talking about someone, said, "He raised Cain," and she, anxious to show how well she knew her Bible, piped up, "Why didn't he raise Abel too?" No one laughed — and Mama looked at her with sad eyes. She felt so sorry that she kicked her chair leg, swinging her feet out in larger and larger circles until Mr. Graif said, "Someone seems to be kicking me," — and that was she! And she knew that Mama would have to talk to here in the "Blue Room" in the morning, and she hated that more than anything in the world.

Papa felt that she was old enough to help the struggling little church by going with Mama and him to *all* services. And that she might use her training in music to play the little organ.

That might have been fun — but it was squeaky and never in tune — and everything was so ugly. The church itself was so plain and bare, the hymns, words and music, so jingly. Mr. Graif's preaching was so flat and uninteresting — and the members — almost none of them spoke English correctly and without an accent.

These were good honest people, Papa said, and he never, ever before had asked her to do anything — so she tried to do what she could, willingly — but oh, what a terrible effort it was!

Some of the visiting preachers were interesting. Dr. Hockinson from Sacramento had gray hair, flashing brown eyes and a way of speaking that made people feel as they did when they sang "Onward, Christian Soldiers." Dr. Barnitz, when he came on from the East, was a ministerial Abraham Lincoln, tall and shambling and slow, but with a smile and a sense of humor that made one love to hear him or to have him come to visit.

Poor Dr. Unangst, from Africa, though, was one of the ones one dreaded. He was big too, and older, and always cold. The family almost smothered and roasted to try to make him comfortable, yet he sat and shivered.

There was a sweet old lady from the San Francisco church who came to visit too. Her name was Mrs. Myers. She had lovely gray hair, parted, and in ringlets. She sang very loudly and very high — with a quaver now and then — and knew endless stories of the Lutheran Church.

Dear patient Papa bore most of the burdens, financial and other, uncomplainingly — but finally ingratitude, criticism, and lack of cooperation were too much for him.

Lillie was happy the day that he decided they would "take out their letters." That meant she could go to the big, lovely Congregational Church? Yes, Papa was willing. Oh, it was even more beautiful than the church of her little girl days. Carpets, stained glass windows, flowers, a gorgeous organ and choir — and Charles R. Brown, with his flashing eyes, quiet gestures and speech, yet moving eloquence. She sat entranced, drinking it all in.

It was a thrill too, to have Mr. Brown ask her to take a class — to go to the Teachers' Meetings he led — to try to keep her eight small boys quiet and interested — to be a member of the expanded choir, where there were Oratorios — and listen to the beautiful contralto of Mrs. Nicholson peal out.

One could only give a little — but one could receive so much — be a part of something gracious, in a group of gracious people, freed of all irritations, ready to be lifted up!

The first doctor whom Lillie remembered was Dr. Warren. He was a kind old gentleman with white hair and beard and pink cheeks. He might have been a lovely person to know when one was well — but oh, how one dreaded his coming when one was ill! In the first place, he seemed to believe that it helped to cure one to keep one hot. He shut the windows; he piled on covers; he wouldn't let one have any water to drink. As one, of course, usually had a fever, one grew just unbearable hot! Oh — and he also "shut out the light" in case it should hurt one's eyes. Next, he gave horrid tasting medicines — *always* castor oil, bitter syrups and pills, so that one was scared into getting well so that one could give up taking them. If Lillie felt sick, she kept it to herself as long as she possibly could. When she did get caught and Mama said, "Let me put you to bed, dear — and send for Dr. Warren," she always said, "Yes, I'll go, but please don't send for him." "If I must," said Mama, Lillie ran to the window to get all the light she could, drank all the cold water she could hold, and prepared to fight the medicine. She developed a real technique in throwing up oil and being unable to swallow pills, till Mama's worry made her give that up.

But it was a happy day when Dr. Warren was succeeded by Dr. Burdick. He was a near neighbor, tall and distinguished looking, thin, with a long white beard. He was a "homeopath" and oh, how the little girls did love him and his medicines. They were all small sweet pellets and even the drugs they were saturated with didn't spoil their taste. And the doctor brought extra bottles of pills with no "tinctures" for good little girls who let him take their pulses and look at their throats and tongues.

He believed in light, fresh air, and all the water one wanted; it was almost fun to be sick. He was interested in all sorts of things — sciences, even astrology. When Freddie was born with two crowns on his head, he said, "He will travel in two worlds," and took down the exact time that he was born, so that he could have his horoscope cast.

When [Dr. Burdick] died, the whole family mourned him — and sent for Dr. Hill, another homeopath who carried on the same pleasant practices. Lillie dreaded going to the dentist even more than having the doctor. No wonder — for the first one she had went gradually blind, poor soul, and neither Lillie nor her parents realized that the pain she suffered was not being exaggerated by a sensitive and imaginative little girl, but was caused by instruments misdirected, slipping, not under control.

When she finally went to good Dr. Timmerman, fiancee of her beloved Miss. Hilton, to find skill and gentleness, she went resignedly through years of reconstruction. But she never lost the nervous tension that made every visit and ordeal.

Most interesting of the men appealed to, to care for the family's health, was Dr. Li Po Ti, a distinguished Chinese physician. Grandpa Delger, who tried every school of medicine and every remedy, had heard of his cures and insisted that Mama try him.

So Lillie went with her through the strange, fascinating sights, sounds, and smells of old China Town, up some narrow stairs, into a small room, up to a very thin, wrinkled, old Chinese who seemed to have all the wisdom of the ages! His hands were veined and had long painted nails. He felt one's wrist delicately, looked at one, asked no questions — sat and thought!

Then he made some beautiful letters with a queer pen and queer paper. And one went into another room and waited until another Chinese gave one some flat packages. When one opened these at home, they had dried leaves and herbs and licorice and other roots. And one cooked these and they smelled awful and tasted awful, but did one good. And as one drank them, one thought of China Town and longed to go back —and Dr. Li Po Ti — and knew he'd say wonderful things if he would only speak. Maybe Mama would take one again! If only Gertie or one of the others could take the medicine, it would be a perfect experience!

Lillie could never remember life without Gertie. They were devoted to each other, though they very often disagreed. Neither was selfish, but Lillie was jealous of affection and of things. The two little girls were two years apart, not enough for Lillie to feel motherly. And Lillie had a great sense of property — her things were untouchable, especially her beloved books.

When Lillie was four, the next little sister came. Lillie could always remember going into Mama's room and seeing the tiny head with long, thick, dark hair, lying on Mama's arm. This baby was named Ernestine — for Grandma Delger — but called Tiny. The two older girls forgot all their quarrels over joy in the new baby.

Two years after (Lillie was six) came a dark-eyed little sister, Elinor Matilda, named for Auntie Brown and Aunt Tillie. Papa was overjoyed to have a daughter with his Annie's eyes. He called her "Nori" and could deny her nothing. She was a plump, smiling, placid, quiet child, always happy to be petted.

When Lillie was eight and going through the agony of trying to fit into school, then staying out another year, Josephine Elizabeth came, named for a school girl friend of Mama's and for dear Aunt Lizzie. When Lillie went in to see her, she smiled at her, with sparkling brown eyes, and she thought, "This is *my* little sister."

Mabel, the last of the six girls, came when Lillie was ten — another little blue eyes — this one with golden hair. Lillie had begged that she be called Constance, here latest love as a name, but it was Mabel Johanna for Aunt Hanna. And she was Gertie's baby.

By this time Willie must have thought that his chances of ever having a boy were slim! Though he never acted disappointed as the babies came, or as if he had one girl too many.

The family built a new house in a lovely neighborhood on "Lawyer's Hill," Prospect Avenue. This is Twenty-ninth Street, between Telegraph and Piedmont Avenue. Auntie Brown had moved her house on upper San Pablo to a home only two short blocks from the Mollers. The new neighbors were cordial and congenial — the Earls, Davis, Borlands, and Olneys. Moving was a great thrill.

Another, to Lillie, was entering high school. But the third and greatest of all, to them, was the coming of a baby brother, the first boy in the family, the first Moller grandson.

He was named Frederick John for his grandfathers. He was dark and looked like his mother; he was everyone's idol.

When he came, Mama called the two oldest daughters into her room, and said, "Girls, I shall be very busy with this little brother. I am going to give Josie to Lillie and Mabel to Gertie to help bring up. You shall each have a room and a crib next to your bed for your little sister. Shall you like that?" And, of course, they did.

A few years later little Billy Jr. came — a pale, thin, delicate little fellow. He cried so pitifully that Lillie would get up at night and walk with him, rock him, or cuddle him for hours. He grew well and strong later, and able to hold his own with the rest.

The last of the family, Frank, named for the Delger uncle, came when Lillie was at college. He was dark like Fred, the most active of the nine.

But to Lillie, her Josie was the smartest, the prettiest, the most attractive of all. Josie had only to make eyes at her and she gave her whatever she wanted. She had such sparkling eyes and brown hair with sunny glints in it that curled all over her head. She was such fun to dress up! She was such a delightful mischief! Take the day that she hid in the jelly closet, eating her favorite strawberry jam, saying in a high little voice that one could hear all over the dining room, "Eat fast, Josie, Lillie's coming."

Take the time when Mama went East with Papa — to see his family — leaving Lillie to keep house — and Josie refused to take a bath. Auntie Brown, appealed to, came over and said, "Josie, if you don't get undressed, I'll put you in the tub, clothes and all." "I won't," said Josie. In she went — surprised, but still smiling. What a baby!

A strong family spirit grew, year by year. It was rather a clannish family. Papa felt that home was the place to be — that no girl should sleep away from it. He missed any child who was away from a meal. He loved to look around the big table and see each boy and girl in his place.

Year by year the bonds grew stronger — almost too strong, perhaps — for one was homesick when away — preferred the family to anyone else — welcomed guests, but preferred having them to going elsewhere.

Lillie could not remember when she was too young to hear the bells and whistles sound the New Year in. She often tried to stay up until after midnight — did not always succeed — but the first sound of the celebration found her up and at the open window.

Papa and Mama always preferred to be at home for the holidays — so that they were there to say "Happy New Year" and then tuck her back in bed.

On New Year's Day every lady had a reception. Papa, of course, must be away most of the afternoon making calls, but Mama put on her best dress and the little girls helped her receive the gentlemen who called, and to pass the refreshment. Gertie was always at her ease, and did a fine job, but it was an agony to shy Lillie — who had to be kept busy all the time to be contented.

Valentine's Day was seldom a happy one. Every room in school had a box where all the Valentines for the teacher and the pupils were deposited to be distributed just before school was out.

Mama did all that she could to help. She selected pretty valentines for Lillie to put in her class box. She secretly had a few put in for Lillie — trying to conceal her lovely handwriting by printing the name. Lillie always recognized these, but never said so because she knew that Mama wanted her to think she was popular. She wasn't — poor lamb never got any cards from her schoolmates and came home reduced to tears over the "comics" that some of the boys thought it fun to send to the little bluestocking. Oh, those comics — what atrocities they were! Lillie hated the gaudy colors, distorted figures, horrid captions, and cheap paper. Yet she could never resist looking at them and feeling desperately hurt by them.

Easter, on the other hand, was unmitigated joy. On Friday, one had hot cross buns — oh, so delicious. On Saturday, one dyed hard boiled eggs with dyes. On Sunday morning, one had soft boiled eggs — served from the china "hen on the nest" that only appeared that one day of all the year.

Then one hunted eggs — and was given the best one. Chocolate eggs with one's name in white icing — beautiful creations of crystallized sugar, with a peep-hole and a lovely scene inside. There were Easter cards, too — bunnies, angels, and crosses.

One wore one's newest, starchiest, white embroidered dress, and the white Leghorn hat with wide ribbon streamers and a wreath of forget-me-nots or little white or red daisies with yellow centers. And the church was lovely with flowers, and large choir, and the Easter music. It was a perfect day!

May brought Lillie's birthday — and all the birthdays were events in that household. Weeks before, one made a list of the presents she would like to have. Early in the morning, the whole family walked in with her to see the gifts all arranged on a table. Mama was so thoughtful that any on the list one could not have had been crossed off. So everything that one expected was there — and other things that one hadn't known one wanted until one saw them. Usually one great thrill — perhaps a ring or a pin — which was a complete surprise. When evening came one put everything away — except the chief treasure. One slept with that under one's pillow, so that one could revel in it, quietly as soon as one woke up.

There was always a birthday cake — sometimes just a family dinner with all one's favorite dishes. Now and then a party — Lillie didn't care for these — there was too much excitement, and it was such a responsibility to see that everyone had a good time. It was better to snuggle down with the new book — a year older!

The Fourth of July was a hateful holiday — Lillie hated every bit of it, except putting up the big flag and wearing the little ribbon one that Mama had kept in a drawer of her black and gold Japanese lacquer cabinet all the rest of the year.

Even before one got up there were noisy guns — pistols — crackers and torpedoes. Papa always bought some and Lillie had to pretend she enjoyed helping him set them off because he enjoyed it so much. But she hated it — and the Roman candles of the evening even more.

She might have enjoyed the late evening fireworks if she had not been so desperately afraid they would set her house on fire. Papa always stayed at home and kept every pail and bucket in the house full of water in case of an emergency. None ever came!

But Lillie, as she crept with relief into her bed a night would think, "Isn't it grand that there won't be another Fourth of July for a whole year!"

With Thanksgiving, the great holiday events of the year began. It was usually a perfect autumn day — not, of course, the sort of day the New England poets wrote about, but a clear cool California day.

All the family who were old enough went to church in the morning. Before they left, Lillie was allowed to help set the table, with the best linen, china and silver. It was decorated in yellow and orange — usually a pumpkin, perhaps oranges and bananas. Lillie always made the place cards, with verses (which she did fairly well) and drawings (which she did very poorly). She loved to paint and crayon, and decalcomania, and do spatter work. Each year she tried out something new.

There was always a turkey for Thanksgiving, and mince pies. Lillie had had a happy time helping make the mince meat and was always disappointed that she couldn't taste all the delicious things she had fixed — separately — raisins, currants, and citron — she wished she had eaten more of them instead of carefully saving them for pie.

Papa said grace — in German:

> *Komm Herr Jesus*
> *Sie unser Gast*
> *Und segne was Du uns besheret hast.*

It sounded so much lovelier than in English — where they had forgotten to translate the part about "be our Guest."

Papa never forgot that Lillie preferred dark meat, and liked the neck best of all. "Just like my Mother," he used to say.

In the evening they all played the "thankful game." It was wonderful to see how long a list one could make of the things one was thankful for.

All December flew, as one thought of the Christmas holidays. Mama's birthday was December 24th — so the festivities started the night before, when Papa and the children set her birthday table. Papa always hung his favorite framed photograph of her over it, with a wreath around it. There was a beautiful birthday cake from the bakery — a pound or a sponge cake, with white icing, and on it in pink script "Happy Birthday to Mama." The children almost died of joy, to think it was from them — and oh, how hard it was to keep from breaking off little pieces to taste. Each child brought his present — not wrapped, but placed in the very best position he could find. Lillie had probably crocheted one of her enormous woolen shawls. What did Mama ever do with them? And all the others had made things too — blotting pads with calendars on them, circular flannel pen wipers with pinked edges, needle books, pin balls, or things they longed for themselves like pencils and many-colored blocks of paper. And, of course, vases of flowers — as many as the table would hold.

Papa always dashed out the last thing to buy his present. Even the children knew that he had a terrible time selecting one and that finally the sales-person just sold him something. A big cut-glass bottle for perfume, a hand-painted porcelain box with gilt legs for — nobody knew what — a brush and comb, all filigree.

After that was put in place the children went to bed knowing that Papa, impatient to show his surprise, would tease Mama until she went in to look at the table.

Next morning, each child dressed hurriedly, ran outside to make a little bouquet, then gathered in the group outside Papa and Mama's door to sing, "Happy Birthday, dear Mama, Happy Birthday to you!" She would cry, "Come in." And in they would all pelt, to kiss her and give her their flowers. Then they would run to inspect the birthday table until she came, in her favorite cashmere wrapper, and Papa in his blue velvet "smoking jacket."

She tried so hard, poor darling, to act surprised, and Papa looked so guilty that the children had to say, "Never mind — we know you saw the table last night — we don't care." And Papa would say, "I will never do it again." And everyone would say, "Of course you will — you just can't keep a secret."

Lunch was a quick, simple meal — soon over — for there was so much to do for the birthday party. This came in the afternoon — with Grandma, Auntie Brown and Mrs. Neller for company. The children loved to set the tea table, to help fix the salad and sandwiches — and sniff at the coffee, gaze at the ice cream freezer and gloat over the cake.

They didn't even want to be at the table — but get ready for their own tea party — with cambric tea and all the birthday cake and ice cream they could eat. Papa usually joined them, not to be cajoled into joining the "Kaffee Klatsch" in the dining room.

By five, everyone had gone — and Papa and Mama had disappeared into the parlor, where Santa Claus was trimming the tree and fixing the presents. The children got as near to the door as they could — all one could hear was whispers. Unless they cried "Santa Clause, blow your horn!" Then *he did!* And what a thrill that was! Each child had sent him a list of the presents she wanted, always read to and edited by Mama. Would he bring the things? Would he remember who wanted which?

When Santa had the tree finished he blew a very loud blast on his horn, and then Papa came out and said, "He's gone, children, he had so much to do that he couldn't stay — he said 'Good-bye and Merry Christmas.'"

The children went way to the other end of the house and lined up — the smaller ones in front, and Lillie at the end — and they sang:

> *Merry, merry Christmas — everywhere*
> *Cheerily it ringeth through the air*
> *Christmas bells — Christmas trees*
> *Christmas odors in the breeze*
> *Merry, merry Christmas — et cetera.*

[Then the children returned to the parlor door.] Papa and Mama flung open the door and stood watching while they filed in. The tree was so lovely   gilt ornaments and tinsel — bonbons, candies in white paper with colored fringe, strung cranberries and pop corn — tinsel — gilded walnuts — lady apples — the chains of paper rings the children had made — the lovely ornaments and little dogs Auntie Brown had send from Japan (which disappeared every New Year, mysteriously, to appear on next year's tree). Best of all, there were real candles, of many colors — the only light in the room!

The children sang softer now — Luther's hymn sung to the music of "Home, Sweet Home" —

> *Away in a manager,*
> *No crib for his bed* — et cetera

Then Papa put on lights and they could see plainly all the presents heaped under the tree. Always new dolls — and new outfits for the old ones. Perhaps doll carriages — or beds, complete with mattress, pillows and covers. One year a doll's house — complete. And packages, beautifully wrapped. It was a thrill to sit in a big ring, while Papa read the tags. He always waited until the package was open, the giver thanked, and the gift admired. He and Mama never failed to be surprised and to like their gifts. "Just what I wanted — how did you ever know!"

Mama had her birthday table and each child had a table or shelf or stand, to display her gifts. Papa just piled his up! The final thrill was to open the "New York Box" — from Grandpa and Grandma Moller and the Aunties — socks for Papa, which his mother knit every year for her "John's Billy" and presents for Mama and the girls that had all the glamour of New York.

And, at the very end often — a little sort of prize for the child who had done something special — once, a gold pin — little leaves with coppery dust on them — enchanting — "For Lillie, for keeping house while Papa and Mama went East" — and a little girl sobbing with surprise, pleasure and excitement.

Then everyone put the last touches to her display, while Papa put all his gifts on, or in his pocket — and clasped his books and beloved box of cigars tight — wandering off to enjoy a final smoke.

Christmas Day was more quiet. The big family reunion, with all the cousins, had been at Thanksgiving. But there was the one o'clock dinner — goose, perhaps — and always plum pudding — with holly center piece and some more of the girls' place cards.

Then, the ecstatic dive into the new books!

As Lillie grew older, she took more and more of the Christmas responsibility. It was she who trimmed the tree and arranged the presents, shutting everyone out, and reveling in becoming completely exhausted. Poor little self-made martyr — she sternly repulsed everyone who offered to help — and shopped, wrapped, labeled, trimmed, like a whirlwind.

Mama was never strong and was glad to shift the job to willing hands. Papa always preferred to sit by her, smoking peacefully if he could. But the younger sisters would love to have helped. No indeed — they must be a part of the group to be surprised.

Mama was sorry to see every Christmas Eve celebration end in a storm of tears — the reaction of fatigue — but Lillie enjoyed even those — probably — as a part of the holiday excitement.

All week long friends ran in to call — to be shown the tree and presents, to be persuaded to sample the hard candies, the ribbon candy, et cetera. To pull the snappers, to eat marzipan and tangerines.

Then, the day before New Year's — the children got out the well-worn packing boxes — dismantled the tree — and put all the permanent ornaments lovingly in place.

The tree itself must not be thrown out — it deserved a better end. So, Papa made a lovely bonfire of it — that it might go beautifully — and Lillie thought of her beloved Hans Anderson's Pine Tree and its history.

Each year the traditions deepened and became more dear — until the Christmas season came to mean not only a lovely, enchanting time, but a pageant — every detail of which was repeated ever December.

"Merry, merry Christmas!"

~ ❦ ~

Even as a child Lillie loved rhythm — which wasn't surprising, as her father was musical and her mother loved music, too.

One of her first memories was of riding on her father's shoulder, during Blaine's campaign for the presidency, carrying the wax lighter with which Papa lighted the gas light in the front hall, and singing, "Blaine, Blaine, James G. Blaine, lit the gas with his golden cane."

Almost every evening either Papa or Mama would sit down to the piano. Papa played only by ear and mostly Stephen Foster. He loved "Way Down Upon the Swanee River" most of all. None of his children ever heard it all their lives through but he or she saw him sitting at the black upright piano, slim, blond, with his head thrown back — happy to be with his family.

Mama played a greater variety of things — a Minuet of Beethoven, Handel's *Largo,* some waltzes and polkas. In one of these she had to cross her hands. The little girls were always thrilled by that. In another — it was probably "Listen to the Mocking Bird" (with variations) — she did all sorts of trills, and a long run that went down most of the piano. She had a sweet voice, too, and sang the lovely old ballads — "Nellie Grey," "Annie Laurie," and the rest. Lillie loved these, but never could hear the pathetic ones without crying. Two songs made her so sad that she could not bear to listen to them:

> "When the silver tints the gold
> And together we grow old"

and

> "When you and I are old, Maggie"

Papa and Mama saw no hardship in growing old together — silver wedding, golden wedding, were their dreams. But Lillie saw only her beloved Mother preparing to leave her!

They all enjoyed singing patriotic songs together — the national songs and the Civil War songs. And the German folk songs that were in two black volumes that Mama had bought in Germany. Sometimes Lillie herself played the accompaniments — only she could not transpose, so if the song was too high Papa came back to the piano and played chords in the proper key.

Often he would dance with the little girls, while Mama played — waltzing beautifully to the "Beautiful Blue Danube" or other Straus waltzes.

Later Lillie went to dancing school. First to Miss. Daroshe, who had a small class and put great emphasis on deportment. She did not teach aesthetic dancing — or solo dancing (only social) — at least, if she did Lillie never studies these. But she admired her friends who did — the steps they took, but especially the fancy clothes they wore.

Her music went on, under a more kind and gracious teacher than Mrs. Hoefeld. She never memorized music rapidly — perhaps because she was such a quick reader that it was hard to discipline her to keep at a piece she could play easily and well, until she could do it without the notes.

She was invited to join a little musical society. It was agony to a shy child to have to play for others, but this only happened now and then. And at each meeting there were little souvenirs — small musical instruments to wear as charms, or paper boxes to hold little candies, and always delicious refreshment.

One winter she joined a class in gymnastics. It met at the Turnverein, and all the little girls wore navy blue serge bloomers and white middy blouses, black cotton stockings and black tennis shoes. She hated it! It took so long to undress and put on the gym suit; the drill was so reg-imented; the Indian club and dumb bell exercises were rhythmic, but stiff; the climbing, running, and jumping too strenuous. It was all ugly and hateful!

Another winter she had a happy time studying Delsarte. This didn't seem to get anywhere, but it was easy and graceful, and it was fun to make one's hands flutter like birds or butterflies.

Most of all, she enjoyed lessons in elocution. She couldn't remember when Mama had not recited poetry to her — "Wimpie Little Whimpie" first — then, "Oh, who can pierce the future dim" (she thought is was fuchsia) — then, "If I had known in the morning."

Of course she tried to memorize and recite, too. In the elocution class she learned to say "The Leak in the Dyke," "Curfew Shall Not Ring Tonight," and some poem about:

> "Mabel, little Mabel, with face against the pane
> Looked out across the night
> And saw the beacon light
> Atrembling in the rain"

Voice and hands — swung out with the Curfew bell — or trembled in the rain — this was the most satisfying rhythm — so far!

Lillie and her sisters were brought up within a framework that is interesting not because it concerned one family, group, or community, but because it was common to most homes of the time. It may sound rigid — it was really a source of security and serenity.

As for religion, God was the great Father. He loved mankind. The *Bible* was His word, revealed to holy men, who loved and served the *Bible*. Prayer was talking to Him — one did not know how He would think best to answer petitions — but one knew it gave one comfort to pray — and that one owed thankfulness for all one's blessings.

The church was the place built by man to honor God — where people met to sing and pray and meditate, listen to the preacher, go away quieted and ready to undertake the work of the week. Creed wasn't especially essential. The Lord's Prayer, The Ten Commandments, The Beatitudes — these were the things one tried to follow. Most of one's rules for living were based on these.

As for home and family — the home was the center of life — one was expected to stay in it, unless one left for school, travel, or short visits. The parents expected to look around the breakfast and dinner table and see all their flock. And to see each head on its pillow every night. Some parents carried this so far as to expect every child at 8 o'clock Sunday breakfast — no matter how late the party the night before — and even if the poor sleepy youngster crawled back into bed after breakfast — until one o'clock dinner. No child even thought of asking to go out on a school night, or on Sunday night.

Father and Mother made all decisions. Some homes were run by patriarchs, some by matriarchs — some had decisions "within the gate" made by Mother, and "without the gate" made by Father.

Believing as all did that life was a blessing and a privilege — and that "Honor thy Father and thy Mother" was the commandment that most concerned the child. It was expected by everyone that the child would do what he was told, promptly and gladly — and that he would be kept busy, since "Satan finds some mischief still for idle hands to do."

Everyone had a tremendous respect for education — for books, for teachers. Of course it is true that teachers were usually invited to dinner when father was away, and the pupil needed a little help in getting better work. But to be a teacher — especially in a college — a Dean — a President — was a high ideal.

Men were thought to be stronger then women — more capable in industry and business — incapable of doing any work in the home, except the things a mechanic or worker in the Building Trade would do. The women of a household felt it a disgrace if one of the men had to do any housework or care of the children. Father was often the disciplinarian; of course, he was the "provider"; he sometimes checked the bills and handled the banking — that was all.

Boys did chores — where these were needed. Only if a mother had no daughters did she call on a son to help with housework, or wheel the baby. Even then he was disgraced!

Men and boys took off their hats to women, actually off their heads, not just tipped — and kept them off if they stopped to chat. They were expected to give up their seats to women, old or young, in street cars and buses, et cetera, whether they knew them or not.

A gentleman never smoked when walking with a lady. He never smoked in her home (even in his own home) without asking permission.

Marriage was considered sacred. Separation was allowable — even divorce if the offense was flagrant — but remarriage was frowned upon, and seldom happened until years had passed.

Mourning was universally worn — according to very exact regulations. Widowers and widows remarried, and if there were young children this was condoned. Though it was considered in better taste for a widow not to remarry.

Public opinion frowned on marriages between people of different races, religions, social strata. If was considered nicest for a woman to marry a man five to ten years older than herself. If the man was much older, she might be called "An old man's darling" and if much younger a "Cradle snatcher." Disapproving friends whispered, "He will soon look more like her son than her husband."

There was a theory that opposites attract one another.

Long engagements were not uncommon, but were frowned upon. A young man was expected to ask the girl's father for her hand and to explain his financial status and his plans. It was usual to expect that she would have "what she was accustomed to." And, of course, that she would contribute only household linen, etc., and *not* be expected to take any economic responsibility — much less a job. If she had one (it was likely to be that of a teacher) she gave it up.

If it were necessary, because of a man's death or illness, for his wife to work, she took roomers or boarders, did dressmaking or sewing, et cetera, without losing caste.

Decent women dressed quietly — did not smoke in public or private — did not swear — drank only very moderately (sherry, et cetera) in their own homes or at friends, *never* in public — used no cosmetics of any sort. Lillie heard her mother say, "A lady should only appear in the newspaper three times — in the Births column, the Marriages column, and the

Death column." A lady's aim was to be inconspicuous. She rose for breakfast, unless she were ill, and dressed completely. She might wear a wrapper instead of a house dress. Her hair was well groomed. She did not wear house clothes on the street or street clothes at home. She was expected to complete her toilet before she left her own room — and to return there if she needed repairs. She was *never* suppose to touch her hair, face, clothing, in public!

She was expected to have her hat and gloves on before she opened her front door — even in a hurry, she had everything complete, before she went out the garden gate! (Lillie had often buttoned Mama's last glove button there and put the glove hook in her purse.)

For evening she wore the low gowns that were fashionable, but head, throat, arms and hands were carefully covered on the street or in the cab.

When dressing, she wore a long kimono, or a short "combing jacket" even while slipping on her dress — and she undressed under her wrapper or her nightgown.

Girls were taught all these things. Also, never to raise their voices in public — never to even glance into a barber shop or a club window — to keep her eyes in front of her when she walked — to "speak when spoken to" — to listen carefully — to treat older people with great respect.

Many topics were never spoken of, except in whispers. Divorce — the coming of a child (even the whisper was "Did you know that Mrs. Smith was expecting?").

Chaperonage was universal. Chaperons were older women, who sat on a strategically placed sofa — all evening long! Some intrepid parents allowed their daughters over eighteen to go to a party with a masculine escort — but only if they knew the daughter would be most carefully chaperoned after she got there. More conservative parents insisted that a chaperon accompany the escort.

All girls came home directly after parties — which started early and were over by midnight.

No "protected" girl went out after dark, even a short block to mail a letter.

An engaged girl had more privileges. She could go with her fiancee, of course (she never went anywhere with anyone else) to a concert, theater, hotel dinner. Many never went to "public restaurants," vaudeville, or on a train trip with a young man until after they were married.

Mothers told their daughters that fine, worth-while young men had no use for girls who were not carefully brought up. They might ask such girls to parties, take them to theaters, but when it came to marrying, they would select some good daughter who had spent most of her time helping her mother and was thus trained to be a good wife and mother.

The daughters looked around, and saw that many of the wives they knew hadn't much beauty or charm to recommend them. In any case, some of them, at least, believed what they heard and made no effort to meet or please young men.

Some of them, perhaps, dreamed day dreams about a Knight who would come riding, rap at the door and say, "I hear a lovely, worthy and duteous maiden dwells within — I claim her as my bride!"

Of course it wasn't easy to stay quietly at home while other "bolder" girls went pleasuring. But one could console one's self by thinking, "She may be having a gay time now, but she will be sorry later on, when she is a forlorn old maid, with nothing to amuse her except memories — while I, who have been patient and obedient, am having a well-deserved good time."

In many a home, especially if there were boys, or they were younger than their sisters — no young men ever called. The kindest of fathers and mothers would have thought it poor form — "chasing" — to have asked any. If any presumptuous male did ask to call, the girl would have to say,

"I'll speak to Mama." If she did, Mama would say, "The right kind of young man would have asked me," or "You are too young, yet, dear," or perhaps, "And what did *you* say, dear, that led him to ask you?"

If he were allowed to come, the parents were about, he must be introduced, the younger children came in — any one to "play propriety."

Some of all these furnished the framework in which the average girl lived. In some ways it undoubtedly was restricting. But in many it gave measuring sticks, standards, even ideals. There was far less of questioning. Of course, if one *did* insist on questioning, it was rather disturbing to everyone — especially, perhaps, to the questioner.

In the grammar school and in high school there was a great gap between Lillie's life. Undoubtedly moving to another part of town, and having a new home and new neighbors were a part of this. The new home was much farther from the center of town — instead of walking to school she had to take a street car. This was disturbing. She had always had a keen sense of the value of time, and the great importance of being prompt. It was not easy to calculate exactly how long the trip from home to school took. A run down the hill — that one could time — but the cars ran irregularly. And the several blocks that one had to walk at the other end of the trip were through crowded business streets — where one had often to wait at crossings. Getting home on time was not a matter of so much importance — though she had her studying carefully scheduled, too. She had little to do at home these days, except the spring preserving and holiday preparation — and this could usually be fitted into weekends.

When the new house was built, the "tower room" on a corner, with a big bay window, was specially designed for Papa and Mama, but they did not find it adapted to their needs, so they moved into a room next to it and gave the tower room to Lillie and Joey! What joy she took in it! Her own wash stand, neatly screened; a big closet; wall space for all the cases of her beloved books; and a big work table, in the bay window, where she could study.

The neighbors were lovely, cordial people. There was a boy in Lillie's class at school, but she was afraid of boys, and this one started of badly by laughing at her when she fell off the plank into the raging stream that a heavy rainfall left in the gutter, as she was crossing it with her pile of books, coming home from school.

The two girls — Ethel and Agnes, who were nearest her age were older, not so much in years as in social life — and such chums that, kind as they were to her, Lillie felt like a "third party." She did of course ask schoolmates home, as Mama suggested, but never as many as the younger girls did. They had neighbors their own age too (the Earls), as did the small boys.

The truth of the matter is, Lillie was a born student — an introvert by inclination — and having been allowed to stay so, she lived most happily in her books. Added to this was a determination to stand high in her classes. That would have made her keep at her studies even if she hated them, but she loved them so that marks and credits came to be secondary.

During these years of her life, it was her teachers, and not her friends, who meant most to her. She loved some of them as persons — it was a great thrill to make bouquets and take them to them. One, Elsie Lee, became her ideal — as she stood, tall and serene, in slim black skirt and spotless white blouse, her hair pulled back from her high forehead, her eyes shining with enthusiasm, reciting "Self-reverence, self-knowledge, self-control" et cetera. There was nothing of the "crush" in these affec-tions. Here was leadership, in scholarship, a group that opened doors.

She went from text books to reference reading — and that, or course, carried her to the Public Library and to the reference books at home.

Her cousin, Annie Florence Brown — Annie Flo — several years older, and some years ahead in school, was a real inspiration. In her little room, Saturdays, she read Emerson and "Trial and Death of Socrates" and "From Milton to Tennyson" aloud to her younger cousin, and fired her imagination with great deeds and great words.

Most of the drive Lillie got went into "studies" — science, history, mathematics, languages, English. Some went into writing verse. She had always loved to try her hand at this — now she was encouraged by having some of her attempts published in the school paper, "The Aegis."

She graduated with a record of all A's for her senior year. Quite a thrill, as was also writing the class poem! Unfortunately, the graduation night was a nightmare. The girls of the class had all agreed to wear a simple colored figured dimity. In spite of Mama's protests, Lillie insisted her dress be as prescribed — and was in an agony of bashfulness to find every other girl had succumbed to the usual elaborate white.

The ice cream — her favorite vanilla with fresh strawberries — for her family "after the exercises" party was a failure, as the strawberries froze as hard as stones. And, a slight cold developed into a feverish flu. Only the poems in "The Aegis" offered consolation!

From the first that Lillie could remember — the day that the Browns landed from Japan — the two families had been almost like one. Mama and Auntie Brown spent all the time they could arrange together. The children went back and forth — they always celebrated Thanksgiving together, and it was only when the little Mollers got numerous that they decided to spend their Christmas separately.

Lillie never felt quite so close to Aunt Lillie and her family. While she was a little girl, Aunt Lillie, many years younger than Mama, spent a great deal of time at school in Europe. She and Mama corresponded all the time — big, thick letters went to and fro — but, of course, these did not bring her Godmother any closer to the little girl — though it did to her mother.

When Aunt Lillie came back she was very German, in her looks and in all that she said and did. It seemed only a short time to the little girl until her aunt was engaged — and then married. The new uncle, Harry Trowbridge, was young, kind, and handsome — but his shy little niece was afraid of him. They had a pretty little house, across from Grandpa Delger's and near Mrs. Moller — but Aunt Lillie was busy, at home or at Uncle Harry's drug store, so Lillie did not run in and out, as she did at Auntie Brown's.

When the Trowbridge babies came, Lillie Marie (Violet), Delger, and Henrietta, they were of course much younger — and Lillie had babies at home if she wanted to play with them. After the two girls died, Delger went to Europe with his mother, and when he came back, he too was very German, so that it was years before he came as close to the Moller-Brown families as he finally did!

As years went on, the Trowbridge marriage did not work well. Harry was the social, emotional type — Lillie the intellectual. She finally decided on a separation — and prepared herself with tremendous effort and enthusiasm for medical school. It was a real achievement, as she had never had any pre-medical training, and most of her schooling had been abroad. But she disciplined her excellent mind to do the job, entered fully equipped to do the work, made a fine record, and graduated near the head of a large class of men and women.

While there she and a fellow student, Swazey Powers, brother-in-law of Carl Grunsky, the engineer, became attached to one another. She secured a divorce — and the marriage proved an extremely happy one. They lived in New York, then Vienna, she studied with Freud, and prepared herself to practice psychiatry, according to his theories.

Delger remained in the West, went to the University of California, became a beloved member of the clan.

Because Lillie was a very conservative, priggish little person, the divorce and remarriage —which disturbed but did not estrange the family — came as a horrible shock to her. She felt it a "disgrace," and for years did not write to, or wish to hear about, her Godmother. It was really only after her own marriage that they became friends again (though it was doubtful if Aunt Lillie knew of her attitude). Then it was chiefly because Aunt Lillie and Lillie's husband admired one another immensely and were very congenial. Also, probably Lillie had more sense as she grew older.

Uncle Edward was the member of the family least seen and least understood by the children. As a young man, he had gone east to college, and Papa had been sent by Grandpa Delger to help him out of some dilemma. The little girls never knew what happened — only that Grandpa and Papa were estranged, and that it was a great grief to their mother.

They knew that Uncle Ed must have misrepresented something — and that he, not their beloved father, was wrong. Papa never said anything — he never even tried to separate Edward from Annie. In fact he always welcomed him to the house. It was only many, many years afterward that Edward said, "Willie was absolutely right — I want to beg his pardon." Even then, Lillie never knew what the difficulty had been — she, like her mother, grieved most that Grandpa died without knowing that Papa was not to blame.

Eddie used to bring his best girls to the house — beautiful young creatures who enchanted the children. But they had never seen the girl he married until after the wedding. Margaret Prior, the new "Aunt Maggie" was a gay, radiant person, with a captivating way. She wore a fashionable dress and a black velvet toque, with a pink velvet crown. Lillie thought it was the most beautiful costume she had ever seen — and she loved Aunt Maggie on sight. It was one of her greatest treats, once in a long while, to go to San Francisco to visit her and Uncle Ed — and later Pearl and Freddie.

None of the other families ever joined the Moller-Brown holiday groups, but there were visits back and forth and a clan feeling.

The grandparents were neither of them well — in their later years. But even before that there was no clan gatherings there. Each child made his visits — taking now one, now another grandchild. But the groups were really decentralized — it was only if anyone was criticized or in trouble that the entire family rushed to defend or to help.

As early as Lillie could remember, Papa took trips "Back East" to see his family. They continued to live on East 37th Street, although the Fliedners moved to Bedford Park, out near Bronx Zoo — then a lovely country district, with flowering shrubs and wild flowers.

The first trip that Lillie remembered was when Elinor was a baby. Papa, Mama, and the four little girls went. They had a stateroom and were very comfortable. There was only one difficulty — getting fresh milk for the baby. Papa would dash out at stations to try to get this at the lunch rooms. Once the train almost left without him. The lunch room had run out of milk and sent him to a house across the street. Such a time as the little girls made when they thought he had been left behind! Instead, he jumped on the last car and it took him some time to walk forward to the sleeper where they were.

Tiny loved the porter, and was never tired of watching him make up the berths. Mama used to hold her when night came, and after the baby was settled, and sing:

> "Mr. Porter set the table, set the table, set the table
> for my Tiny Tim."

The older girls had dolls, paste, paper, pencils, and decalcomania — and made endless paper dolls, mats, and picture books. Lillie loved her paint box and colors most of all — and tried to do careful work, in spite of the motion of the train.

Grandpa and one of the aunties met them in Albany — probably Aunt Hanna. Grandma and Aunt Tillie were busy getting the last touches on the house, and dinner. It was a happy visit. The children loved the house — so different from any they had ever seen. In the basement were the kitchen, a sitting room and behind the kitchen a little garden with a lawn in the center and lilies-of-the-valley under the trees.

On the ground floor was the parlor and the big dining room and pantry. Also the dumb waiter — a great thrill! On the next floor was the big family living room, a passage-way full of cupboards, and Grandpa and Grandma's room. Above this, the two aunties had their rooms, each with its dressing-room big enough for them to use as bedrooms when they gave their rooms up to guests. The floor over this had bedrooms, too — it wasn't used much since the Fliedners left. The attic must have been over this — though possibly the maids slept in the basement.

The next trip Lillie made was with Papa. Mama couldn't leave home, and Lillie was proud to be allowed to go. They went not only to New York, but to Boston, and to visit the Glenwood Range factory, as Papa was their agent for Oakland.

Lillie loved Boston. She got Papa to take her to all the historical places she had read about, especially to the homes of the New England poets — and her beloved Louisa May Alcott. How glad she was that she had read Emerson and Thoreau — and could recite Longfellow, Whittier, Lowell and the rest.

She never got tired of the winding streets. They stopped at the Parker House, walked through the Common, admired the State House, went to Cambridge to Harvard College. It made so many books come alive!

Going down the Hudson they talked of Washington Irving and of J. Fenimore Cooper. In New York they went downtown, saw the street where Papa was born; went to Central Park to watch Grandpa and the aunties horseback riding; crossed Brooklyn Bridge and visited Rosa's; went to see Tishjohn and that family; and went out to Bedford Park to see Aunt Lizzie and her family.

Auntie let Annie stay at Grandpa's while Lillie was there (to keep her company) and the two girls became devoted friends.

Annie was Grandpa's pet — he called her Puckie (from "Puck" in *Midsummer's Night Dream*). The little girls had a wonderful time with him. Breakfast was their favorite meal — delicious hominy, fresh hot hard rolls from Cushman's with Grandpa moving one's roll from one's plate to his if one wasn't looking, and pretending that he wanted all the milk.

Going home, through Chicago, Papa and Lillie took a walk over a drawbridge. While they were looking at the sights the drawbridge was opened and stayed so, so long that they missed their train and had to stay over another day.

Lillie thought that was fun — she loved the Congress Hotel and all the excitement of Michigan Avenue — but Papa was anxious to get back to home and business and never did enjoy having to change his plans.

When Lillie was fifteen — in 1893 — the year of the World's Fair in Chicago — she went East again. The father of a friend of hers, Mr. Conrad Rued, invited her to go with him and his daughter.

Mr. and Mrs. Rued were both Swiss — there were two daughters, Paula (Lillie's friend) and Lulu, and a small boy "Connie." Both girls had lovely brown hair, beautiful teeth and smiles. In fact, Lillie thought them entrancing. They had been to the best class in "fancy dressing" and often danced in costumes in exhibitions. It always impressed the quiet, bookish, shy Lillie that Paula like her! She was so full of mischief — such a favorite with the boys. She was very ill with fever, once, and had to have her lovely hair shaved. Anxious to get her back to school, her mother had a wig made for her. It was very life-like — and probably no one would have noticed it. But every time a teacher turned his back, Paula snatched it off — then put it on again before he saw her — to the great amusement of the class. Lillie wore her hair braided and wound into a bun on her neck. Elsie Brown, who sat back of her, loved to pull out the hair pins, much to her embarrassment. So she specially admired Paula's savoir faire.

Papa planned to take Lillie East on his visit to his people, but he could only make a short stop at Chicago. Mr Rued had business there, wanted a companion for Paula, and thought the Fair worth a long visit.

It was a great thrill to Lillie to get so many new clothes (though she never cared much for clothes, and was called "Mrs. Noah" by her family). She wanted to do Paula credit.

It was a revelation to see how easily Paula met people, and how popular she was with everyone — including young men. There were several in her father's organization who called at once — and invited the girls places. Lillie was grateful to quiet, conservative Mr. Rued, when he made their excuses — but Paula, of course, was dejected.

The Fair proved a great thrill. The girls went to the educational exhibits in the morning; to concerts and shopping trips in the afternoon; and to the Midway and other amusement places with Mr. Rued at night. Everything was fascinating. There is never anything, later, quite like one's first World's Fair!

The Rueds left Lillie at Grandpa Moller's in New York. Annie came to stay with her and the days flew, until the one when father was expected. It was evening — Lillie had not gone to meet him, but was helping Grandma prepare the home welcome. The carriage drove up while she was doing an errand upstairs. As she ran down the last flight, she heard Papa say, "I've brought a friend with me. May I bring him in?" And

Grandma replied, softly, "Of course, John's Billy." "But she'd rather he had come alone," thought Lillie. Papa went outside again and brought in — Little Joey, Lillie's beloved baby sister!

It was one of those moments of surprise and pure joy that do not come often, and that are never forgotten! The whole visit was a happy one, but that welcome was best of all.

There was a return visit from Grandpa, Grandma and the aunties — which everyone enjoyed, but which meant a great upheaval. Everyone was moved out of his or her room — it was odd to sleep somewhere else; not to be able to find any of one's things; to have so many people at table; so much entertaining; such continuous excitement.

Out of their own home, it was in some ways easier to study one's relatives. Grandpa seemed more sociable and lively than ever — always ready to go places and to see people. He liked festivity; a little claret at dinner; Whist every evening; a sip of sherry or port before he went to bed.

Grandma seemed even quieter than in her own home. She sat and smiled, her eyes on her boy. She loved to hold the baby, or have the children pull their little footstools near to her. She liked to see them industrious, and helped them learn to knit or admired the patch quilts and all the other handiwork.

The two Aunties, of course, were lovely and sociable, glad to fit into any plans; renewing friendship with Aunt Lillie (with whom Tillie had gone to school); to be watched and admired, in their fashionable New York clothes.

It was always a very great satisfaction to Willie and Annie that their families were so congenial. It made having them as visitors so easy.

It was a great advantage to the children to have near relatives across the continent. Not only did it mean the visits, but added interest in geography. This extended across the sea, for there were relatives in Germany, too.

Fortunately the family all felt that having Grandparents who were born abroad was an advantage — not a handicap — that it brought one a heritage of tradition, history, interests, which one would otherwise not have had. A mother who was a "Native Daughter" — a father who was a New Yorker — four grandparents who were German by birth, American citizens and loyal sons and daughters of the U.S.A. What more could any child ask?

Many times, while she was at High School, Lillie had thought of the possibility of going to the University of California. Annie Flo was there, and Everett (E.J.). David, who came between them in age was at Stanford and Elsie hoped to go there, too. Tillie had not gone to college, as she felt she should keep house — as Auntie Brown was keeping house for Grandma Delger, who had had a stroke and needed her.

Mama was sympathetic to the idea — she always supported any plan to cultivate one's self. Strangely enough it was Papa — always so quick to give any child what she wanted — who opposed the idea. His reasoning ran like this, "Your mother, aunts, grandmothers, never went to college, they are cultivated gentlewomen. Your place is here at home, helping your mother and learning to be like her. You can devote yourself to your music, read a lot, travel perhaps. College is only necessary for teachers and other women who have to make their living. No daughter of mine will have to do that. I can support them — I want to!"

Lillie followed and concurred to the extent of not taking all the college preparatory work. She had only one year of Latin. But as the years went by — and she got more and more pleasure out of study, and saw what college meant to her cousins — her longing to go grew, until finally Papa relented, said, "Try it for a year," and hoped that would be enough.

It was not simple — for the University hesitated to admit anyone with a condition — and of course she had one in Latin — in spite of her record of "Straight A for her senior year."

It also meant giving up her music, for John Metcalf, her excellent teacher (he was a composer of note, composer of "Absent," et cetera) refused to keep her as a student if she went to college. "You could play well — if you devoted full time to it. You'll do mediocre work at college *and* your music if you attempt both," he said.

Lillie gave up her lessons very reluctantly. She never memorized music easily, as she did poetry, but she was good at sight reading. Besides, she had hoped to write music for some of the verses she loved to write. Mr. Metcalf had written some for her "Sunrise," which was published. It was a thrill to have one's name on the words — but how much more thrilling it would be to have one's name as a composer, too! She made up her mind *never* to lose such facility as she had — and to go on, ahead, as soon and as far as she could.

August came and college opened. Annie Flo and Susie Belle (Culver) helped her register. Ethel Olney, who lived across the way, invited her to the Theta house. But Papa, like his father before him, was strongly opposed to secret societies of every kind — and Lillie was too anxious not to give extra excuse for his opposition to college to want to accept any such invitation!

Freshman year was very heavy — especially the first semester, where under the careful tutelage of Mr. Price, who passed on his love of classics to his students, she studied Cicero and Virgil to pass off the condition.

That done, the second semester brought the thrill of being invited by Prof. Louis Syle, of the English Department, to take a small part in the Eighteenth Century play he was putting on at Charter Day (March 22). Of course Lillie knew that she was only asked because she was Annie

Flo's cousin — and Annie was to play the "lead." But there were only a few Freshmen in the cast, and they were much older.

To go to rehearsals with Annie Flo, to meet Alice Marchebout, Aurelia Henry, Arthur Elston, and the other seniors — to have a white wig and several costumes — it was all wonderful!

The experience did wonders for her! To look in the mirror on the great night and see that, made up in costume, she was actually pretty; to be able to forget herself in her part, and move, speak, *live* a great lady; to find that she could act — gave her an assurance that she needed very badly.

Prof. Syle was a wonderful coach. A person of rare cultivation, who thought his period — the eighteenth century — the most sophisticated and finished. He threw his fiery spirit into making his annual Charter Day Play an appeal to the college audience to appreciate the beauties he saw in these old comedies. He awakened in the immature hobble-di-hoy youngsters, who were his actors, a love of him, of the play, of the period, that transformed them, for the time, at least.

Bound to show what she could do, this trial year, Lillie kept up her studies. Among them was German — under dear old Professor Putzka. He happened to be a friend of Papa's — they played billiards together. When he told Papa that his daughter was a fine student, it was a great help! The play helped too. So did the fact that Lillie tried hard to be useful at home! He first "endured — then embraced" and became happy and proud that his "Firefly" was at her beloved University of California.

The other three years of college seemed to fly past. One great thrill was the winning of a prize, from the magazine, for a set of sonnets about Yosemite Valley. This meant a little recognition, a great thrill to the family, meeting some congenial people on the campus, and a closer contact with some of the faculty. This last was what counted most, for the University was growing, many classes were large, and anything that made a professor interested in one was a help to an ambitious student.

Lillie took only the required mathematics and science — and never got far enough in either to get to the fascinating stage. And she had very little history — a real lack, though not so serious as if she had not had a thorough, though elementary, course at the high school.

But she did have much of the work for undergraduates in Philosophy, History of Philosophy, Logic, Ethics, Kant. A major in English included aesthetics. Considerable French and German, and enough "Education" to get a teacher's certificate.

Best of all, was having fine men, and leaders of thought, as teachers. Men who cared for their subjects — and their students. Who left in the minds of all who worked under them deep impressions that were to last always. To have heard Gayley recite ballads, read Shakespeare, expound Literary Criticism — was a never-to-be-forgotten experience. Even a monotonous job, like being a member of a class who indexed one of his books, was worthwhile. To have read *Laocoon* and Aristotle's *Aesthetes* with Lange; to have seen Montague's keen mind present logic; Moore's high idealism discuss ethics; to have heard French read as Paget read "Hernam"; and German as Seugger read "Faust"; to have sat hours in the library, followed on with some thrilling idea that one of these men had presented, then carry books home; to read as late as one dared and start again as early as one could — all this made the months and years fly by.

Three of the four years Professor Syle had plays — and Lillie (now Lillian, for she decided that as her Godmother, Aunt Lillie, had dignified her name, she might do so also) had a part in each. There were great events in her life.

She made new friendships, too. Some started in the summers at Cisco — the Browns and the Stones — strengthened as the young people saw one another on campus. Some came through meetings at class. There were assets in being a hard student — lazy boys as well as girls caught one's car going to college, or came to call, to get a translation done quickly. It was really a brave youth who called on the oldest of a family of nine! The

Lillian (third from left) in Goldsmith's comedy, *The Good Natured Man*. Performed at Berkeley in 1899.

younger children could lie in the upper hall and listen — or crawl half-way down the stairs and perhaps see the caller in the big hall mirror. Lillian, always shy, was in agony!

Being in Professor Syle's plays brought pleasant contacts. Lillian was invited to several fraternity houses — most often to Phi Delta Theta. This was a specially pleasant place to go, as some of the alumni and upper classmen were very kind to the girls invited by the younger boys. It was a studious crowd, too, where brains, even in a girl, were not a great handicap.

Lillian would never be a social light — she had not the looks, poise, small talk — but she wasn't the constant wall flower she was sure she would be — probably because she was reconciled to being one, so didn't worry. If one enjoys being an onlooker; is content to keep herself company; if no one asks her to dance; is a good listener; admires pretty girls and good dancers — it is surprising what a good time one can have.

Lillian wanted all the education she could get — travel, meeting interesting people, a job to do. She wasn't sure what it would be — teaching, perhaps — and some far-off day, perhaps to be a dean in a Woman's College. She did not think it likely she would ever marry — as she was not pretty or attractive. In any case, she would try for an interesting job — to which she would devote such time as she could be spared from home. For she knew it had cost her parents something, to let her have so much time for school-ing — and that she was *needed* at home. Her lovely mother was too deli-cate to undertake chaperonage — and the younger sisters were invited often and she could supply it. Also, the housekeeping was a job she could handle and really enjoy. She liked the planning — the responsibility — using the skills housekeeping calls for. In fact, only her books called her from such things. It was always a discipline to leave them for anything.

She enjoyed, too, coaching her brothers and sisters — especially in algebra, which she went over with each one. It was such fun to be con-sidered wonderful.

She still had far too little interest in clothes, or in her appearance. To be clean, neat, inconspicuous, seemed enough. Brains were what counted! Or so she thought. Probably because she had some to offer!

There were two important happenings for a senior who has devoted himself to study — one is the announcement of Phi Beta Kappa list; the second is the choice of the Commencement speakers. Lillian hoped to have the first honor. It never occurred to her that she would have the second.

But the list came out — and her name was not on it! The fact that no girl's name was on it might have consoled her — but it did not. She heard, from a reliable source, that she had tied with one of the boys, but that someone had said, "He needs it more" or "It will be more useful to him." True or not, this did not comfort her. She had wanted "The Key" — had worked hard for it. It was a bitter disappointment not to get it. Fortunately her family knew nothing of this — so she did not have the added ordeal of breaking the news to them. She bore her disappointment quietly. Of course she had no dream that she would be elected to Phi Beta Kappa — her own University of California chapter — some years later!

Often, in her life, it seemed that unhappiness and success came together. Perhaps this is so in most lives! President Wheeler sent for her and told her that she had been selected as one of the three commencement speakers. The other two were both men, one to represent (as she did) the academic students — the others the students from affiliated colleges.

This — in the eyes of her family and friends — was a great honor. Lillian felt it a responsibility. She thought deeply — trying to find a subject — and finally selected "Life — A Means or an End." It is to be feared that a sense of humor and the light touch were not her strong points — at this point in her life, at any rate. But Dr. Moore, her advisor, approved her subject and the way she presented it — and so did President Wheeler.

He sent for her — she had been one of his students in linguistics, though not really adequately prepared for the work, so it was a treat to talk with him — and advised her to be "womanly" in her presentation. "Don't wear a stiff dress, wear one that is soft and has ruffles. Don't scream. Don't give an oration — read what you have to say. And not from 8.5 x 11, but from small sheets of paper, easy to handle. Don't try to imitate a man — speak as a woman," he said. And so kindly that Lillian was fired with a desire to do a good job, as he felt it should be done.

The whole commencement week is filled with festivities. Class Day, reunions, parties, teas, and open houses — she was in a dream until Commencement Day.

It was the usual lovely California May morning. She had a big bunch of lilies-of-the-valley — her favorite flower and a part of every great event of her life. Her "soft dress with ruffles" turned out even better than she had hoped and was becoming — under the black gown. Her family all gathered to back her up. It was before the day of commencements in the stadium. The exercises were in Herman Gymnasium. It was not an attractive building, but friendly, and not so large but that she could see her family and friends.

At last her turn came — President Wheeler gave her a smile of encouragement as she passed close to him on her way to the reading stand. Thanks to the excellent training of Professor Syle, and the Charter Day Plays, it was easy to forget herself and say what she had to say effectively.

President Wheeler looked approval as she finished and went back to her place. Her family beamed. The Alumni luncheon under the oaks, with dear Annie Flo, was like a dream. And in a few hours "Commencement" was over.

Lillian graduated in 1900 from the University of California–Berkeley.

But it was good that the people whom she cared for most said she had done a good job. Perhaps the thing that touched her most deeply was when her beloved Dr. Charles R. Brown — the pastor of her church — said to her father, after church the next Sunday, "Lillie ought to be in the pulpit taking my place." Of course she knew that was his gracious way of saying that he thought her speech had been good! But how much more tactful, to say it to her father rather than to her. And how pleased dear Papa was! He felt that her time at the University had been well spent.

Her mother was of course pleased, too, though she deprecated the newspaper publicity — and especially the photographs. There was no change in her feeling that a lady did not appear in the newspaper. But she said, "If it *had* to be there, dear, I'm glad it is in such a dignified way." And Lillian knew she was proud and happy that her "big girl" had gotten through creditably.

As for the sisters and brothers — a joy to one was always a joy to all! They made such a fuss over her that it was good to put on a home dress and get back to home tasks!

Perhaps it was because of the Commencement speech that the family agreed with Lillian that it would be a wonderful thing for her to take her Master's Degree in the East. Professor Gayley had advised her to study under Brander Matthews at Columbia.

It sounds naive, but neither he nor any of the other faculty people with whom she talked knew that Professor Matthews refused to take women students. Because of this, he could not give graduate work — but he was independent and informal — liked to sit on desktops and talk as he pleased — and preferred teaching men.

All of this Lillian heard after getting to New York, securing a room at the dormitory (which was then a part of Barnard College), and going to Columbia to register.

But she found wonderful courses to take — comparative literature with Professor Woodbury, psychology with Dr. Thorndyke, music with Dr. McDowell. Every hour was a treat! And the big library an even finer place to work than the one on the U.C. campus.

Woodbury was quiet and scholarly and spoke in the same graceful, polished sentences that he wrote. He was equally at home in the literature of all ages and countries — one sensed great vistas, through the pictures that he painted, and longed for time and strength to explore them. One came away from his seminars serene and uplifted.

Thorndyke was like a strong wind. A person of tremendous vitality — physical and intellectual — he had no use for fussiness and no patience with pretense. He would ask questions — quietly — that made plain just the value of what he said. He encouraged the shy, quizzed the assured, flattened out the pretentious. But he was a leader as well as a teacher of all who were in earnest. And once his student, you remained so all your life, and could carry your little failures or successes to him, sure of encouragement and appreciation.

McDowell, already marked by his approaching great illness — from which he was never to recover — was a restless genius. He wandered, or strode, around the room while he talked — pulling shades up and lowering them again; sitting down at the piano to play a selection that illustrated what he was saying only to stop suddenly, after a few minutes, as if he had forgotten what he wanted to do. He would toss his lion-like head — start off on a thought — stop, begin again. But the class sat hypnotized, whatever happened, recognizing a master.

One never realizes what one's home means to one until one leaves it. Lillian was terribly homesick. There were only a few graduates in the dormitory — and it was considered wise to have each share a suite with an undergraduate. Lillian drew a Freshman who was unattractive, odd, and extremely untidy. It was not a happy combination.

Everything here seemed so different from the West. On her various visits here she hadn't noticed this, but now, as she was settled down for a college year, it impressed her greatly. Going one day to a grocery store, she asked for "Two bits worth of Gheradelle's ground chocolate." "I don't know what two bits is — I never heard of Gheradelle's — and we don't carry ground chocolate," said the clerk — and the homesick shopper longed to take the first train West.

The great consolation was the kindness of all the Moller family — kith and kin. Lillian wanted to meet all the cousins she could. There were many, for Grandpa had been one of six brothers, and all had settled in or near New York and had families.

Lillian got a list, asked all about her age to tea, and was thrilled to see what a fine lot they were. They came to see her — entertained her — seemed to enjoy the family meetings (for many had not met one another).

Another joy was visiting the Armand Millers — he was pastor of Grandpa's church — his wife was as gracious and hospitable as he, and the three handsome young sons treated her like a big sister.

All was progressing well, when cold weather came. The California girl, not acclimated, not warmly enough dressed, studying long hours and not paying enough attention to rest and food — caught cold — then had a severe attack of pleurisy. It was miserable, being ill in a dormitory, with a roommate so untidy that mice scratched around her tea set and cookie jar, and knowing one's beloved work was getting behind.

But tragedy was to follow. For "the Aunties" — Tillie and Hanna — sorry for her, and worried, wired her father, and he came on, by the next train — surprised her, didn't listen to her arguments, but packed her up and took her back to "God's Own Country!"

Dear good man! He felt it was the one thing to do! But, while she regained her health immediately, she mourned and grieved for the uncompleted work. To have had one's dream come true — to live in it — and then to lose it — it did seem more than she could possibly bear!

The few months at home, after leaving Barnard, only convinced Lillian more than ever that she wanted to go on studying. She would have liked to start at once for her Ph.D., but Professor Gayley, under whom she planned to work, advised an M.L. first. It meant writing an extra thesis, if one went on to the Ph.D., but it also meant that , if one did *not* go on, one had accomplished a definite stint, in the year's time.

It was good to go back to the U.C. campus that August — to register for some courses in education and philosophy, but to devote most of one's time to English.

Under Professor Gayley's guidance, Ben Jonson's *Bartholomew Fair* was selected for intensive study and the thesis subject. But Lillian went at it with the same technique which had so impressed her in Gayley's course in Literary Criticism — the play being the result of the time, place, and "moment." This meant wide reading — in history, geography, world affairs — before one settled down to the "moment." Being of the type who easily "live" in the thing on which they concentrate, Lillian soon felt she was more Elizabethan than 1901 American.

She imagined she could see and hear the life in London — the theater, the audience, and the play. Its roughness, frankness, lack of reticence, which would have been abhorrent to her in real life, were all part of an exploratory age.

The thesis was no masterpiece, but it did show careful research, keen interest, and that aliveness that comes from being a part of what one attempts to describe.

She had had time to do other things — to read modern literature, to join an "Art Club"— and read and discuss books on painting, legends, lives of saints, all similar things that would prepare one for visiting the great art galleries and museums.

And time too to get to know more people, and to see more of her and the family's friends. She had still much more talent for listening than for small talk. And she was so unobservant that, when the conversation turned to things people had seen, her mind wandered off to the world of books. She came to care more for how she looked — due partly to persistent efforts of her style-conscious Mother and sisters, partly to expert saleswomen who knew the family and were glad to help a customer who gave herself so willingly and completely into their charge, took what they advised, and was happy with it.

Lillian's
Mother's excellent taste meant that she looked well and appropriately dressed. But she did not at all appreciate the importance of clothes, or their influence on other people and one's self.

She bought a hat, once, which the family milliner selected, and the family approved. She was persuaded to look at herself in it, and realized that it looked well. But somehow it never seemed to look so well after that first day. So, after many wearings, she took it back to the millinery shop one day, and said, "Do you know, I thought this was becoming when I bought it, but I never have since." "Well, Miss. Moller," said the milliner, "It would help if you'd wear it right side to." She took it off, made a cross X in white thread in the front, and set it back on at the correct angle. Of course, after that Lillian could get it on front forward, but she never did get the slant right.

Through her friendship with Alma Brown, starting in Cisco days and going through college, Lillian learned that there were other things to spend money for besides books. Alma had charge accounts, and went happily through Taft and Pennoyer's, buying gloves and hand bags and all sorts of things; through Smith Brothers for the new novels and the popular Gibson drawings; to Sanborn's for big bunches of violets; to Bowman's for sachet and equ de cologne; and endlessly to Lehnhardt's for oyster cocktails, ice cream and big boxes of delicious candy. Carmels were their favorites!

Saturdays they went to "The City" — to the matinee or the light opera at the "Tivoli"; with lunch at the "Golden Pheasant"; and hot chocolate after the matinee before the lovely trip across the bay — home. Henry Miller came every summer, with a galaxy of stars, an excellent stock company, the fine old plays, and many new ones to try out — Miller himself, Frank Worthing, Blanche Bates, Margaret Anglin, Margaret Dale — in "Brother Officers," "The Only Way," and a long line of successes.

Life was rich and full and happy. Not romantic or aesthetic, but satisfying and interesting — with no worries over the present or future.

Like every other studious boy or girl, Lillian had, all her life, looked forward to a trip to Europe. Naturally, with four grandparents who came from there, and parents who had spent happy days there — a "tour" was presented to her as one of the great events of one's life.

Her parents would have loved to take the whole family abroad for a year (a thing which they did later). But at the time there were too many small children and the trip would have been financially difficult, too.

But every child in the family grew up preparing to travel. "When you go abroad, you will need French, or German, or a knowledge of history, or art, et cetera."

In the summer that Lillian took her Master's degree, a fine opportunity to go abroad presented itself. Miss. Minnie Bunker, a teacher of Latin and Greek in the Oakland High School, and a specialist in, and lover of, art, was trying to find three congenial young women to go abroad with her.

She had been over many times before — knew Greece and Italy, as well as England, France, Germany and Switzerland — was really the perfect leader of a group who wanted to use a trip as an educational project. Intelligent, stimulating, interesting, alert, capable — she know how to handle every possible situation, with ability and tact.

A member of the First Congregational Church, Lillian knew her only slightly, but admired her very much. The third member of the party was to be Eva Powell — a life-long friend — for she and Lillian had gone all through school and college together and were very congenial. The fourth, Mary Barker, she did not know so well, for she belonged to a slightly older and much more "social" group. Her aunt, Miss. Henrietta Simpson, had the next room to Annie Florence, in the school where they taught. The father, Timothy Barker, was a grand old pioneer, who kept temperature and other data — year in and year out. Mary, like her mother, was tiny, a brilliant conversationalist, loyal, and interesting.

The four met, the parents worked out the financial arrangements with Miss. Bunker, the tour was carefully planned, and the decision come to that they would sail from Boston and meet there a few days before leaving.

Eva and Lillian would go first to New York — which Eva had never seen — to visit the Mollers, and get to Boston a little ahead of the time scheduled for the meeting. Mary would visit some relatives en route, then others near Boston — might join the others just before sailing time. Minnie (Miss. Bunker) would visit her relatives in Boston, and gather her three charges together there.

Getting ready was very exciting. Lillian even (at last) took an interest in her clothes — though of course even more in the guide books, et cetera, she was taking along. Her family and friends, and Eva's, saw them off at the queer old 16th Street Station where all such overland trips started. It was great fun to "show the ropes" to Eva, who had never been East before. In the twenties as they were, the two girls were excited to be "traveling alone" and the trip across the country was too fast to suit them.

They had a lovely visit in New York, staying together at the Martha Washington Hotel, being entertained by the family, but free to sightsee when and as they chose.

Then they went on up to Boston and to the Parker House, where little Lillie had stayed with her father years before. Here again, they had a happy time sightseeing. Mary had not yet come, but Miss. Bunker was at Boylston Street visiting her two aunts and her cousin — the Gilbreths — and expecting her brother Fred to come down from Maine to see her off.

Lillian knew a little of these relatives of Miss. Bunker's. They came from Fairfield, Maine — near North Anson, where Miss. Bunker's family lived. "Aunt Martha" — left a widow in her early thirties — had taken her two girls and a boy first to Andover, then to Boston. One daughter had died, the other, a musician, lived in Brookline with her husband and small son and daughter. [Martha] lived with her son — Frank — a construction engineer — as did her sister, Caroline, "Aunt Kit," an artist. Miss. Bunker often visited them on her trips East. She would stay at their home rather than at the hotel with her charges. They were not likely to see much if anything of her before the day of sailing. Then they might meet the aunts at the steamer.

So they made their plans along these lines, and started off in the evening after dinner, to go through the public library — but especially to study the Punis de Chauvennes and the Abbey pictures.

The girls were enchanted with the Abbeys; not only as pictures, but as telling the Grail story. They were deep in discussion of them when Miss. Bunker, who had their schedule, having helped them plan it, found them there and —almost sorry to be torn away — invited them for an automobile ride in her cousin's new car.

The car proved to be large and beautiful and Minnie's cousin Frank, big and jovial. The girls were taken over to call on Aunt Martha and Aunt Kit, at the comfortable apartment on Boylston Street. Aunt Martha was the finest type of New England woman, tall and stout — she wore dresses of her own design, carefully made and of beautiful material. Aunt Caroline, much thinner, with lovely curly hair of the typical family rust color, looked the artist that the many paintings on the apartment wall proved she was. It was quite evident that family ties were very strong, and that Frank was the center of the family life. Minnie's brother Fred was coming down from North Anson to visit with her before she sailed, so she, Frank, and the two girls took a short drive, and then went to the station to meet him. In was North Station and Minnie ran eagerly into the train while Frank opened the hood of the car to gloat over his engine and exhibit it to his guests. Neither knew much, if anything, about engines, but both admired enthusiastically, though it is doubtful whether their host was much deceived or in the least impressed. Fred Bunker, when he appeared, might have been Frank's brother — with the same slanting Bunker eyes that most of the family had, much less hair, considerably stouter, but the same jovial way and the same business ability visible through the joviality. The two men — now side-by-side on the front seat, for Lillian had moved back with Minnie Bunker and Eva — wore similar well-tailored suits of fine material, though the Boston cousin had more style and was a bit less conservative in his choice in design and color. There was another drive, a snack somewhere, and the girls were back at their hotel and talking over the adventures of the day and the relatives of their chaperone.

Sunday morning found them up early and enjoying the delicious currants, coffee, and rolls of the Parker House, then off to church, and back for an early dinner. This had only been ordered when Mr. Gilbreth appeared — sending in a card which said, "F.B.G. and the Buzz-Wagon." Eva, more sensible, proposed sending him word they had not had dinner. Lillian, however, felt sure that the proper thing was to countermand the order and go at once, without mentioning that dinner had been omitted. Back to the apartment to pick up Minnie and Fred Bunker, and then off for a ride which went on and on, not only through Boston, but through the beautiful suburbs on a perfect June Sunday. It was a new experience to be shown the Boston of the present. Only if one asked, was one shown the homes of the New England writers who had been so vivid a part of

Lillian's life. Minnie, of course, insisted on seeing Harvard, and the other schools and colleges, but there host's interest was all in buildings, preferably new ones, and many of them those which he himself had built or was constructing. With her usual adaptability, Eva enjoyed everything and made notes in her mind as to what could go into her diary and the voluminous letters which she sent home. Lillian tried desperately to understand what she was seeing, to make intelligent comments, and especially to concentrate and be observant, for she knew well that her two worst faults were daydreaming and being interested only in the things in her own field. It was surprising but a bit dismaying to find so many things of which she knew nothing — a strange vocabulary, difficult to understand and practically another language, which she not only did not speak, but had never heard of. It was even more shattering to be asked questions about similar projects in her own state, city, and neighborhood, which she had never seen, and about which she could not remember to have heard. No courteous host neglects checking on his guests' interests, and trying to shift the conversation to their fields, but it was quite evident that comments on the literature and history of Boston, while listened to politely, were another language and another area to her host.

Late in the afternoon the faithful car, which had hurried over rough roads as well as smooth and climbed in and out of construction projects — more like a mountain goat than an automobile — broke down! None of the first-aid offered by the host or his cousin was effective. A new tire seemed the only answer. Meantime, as was even more unusual then than it is now, youngsters appeared from all quarters and swarmed about, hindering the first-aid work — not only by their presence as they came closer and closer in larger numbers, but by their frank and caustic comments on the car and on its driver.

No big sister in a family of nine could possibly be unacquainted with ways to catch and hold the attention of the young. So it was not a hard job for Lillian to get the group out of the way of the workers and to start off on the perennial favorite of the Moller youngsters — Hans Christian Anderson's *Tinder Box*. It was a little embarrassing, in the middle of the story, to find one's host seated in the background listening with the children. That probably meant that Cousin Fred had volunteered to go somewhere to phone for a tire and that Minnie and Eva were having a chat in the car. There was only one thing to do and that was to carry on with the story and to try to prolong it until the tire should come back and be in place. Much practice made this not too difficult, especially as the host disappeared again, so that finally as the sun went down the car was ready for another start, and the children could swarm around to wave it farewell.

Long experience in handling emergency situations enabled the host to furnish a welcome invitation for the party to wash up, from the friendly janitor and his wife, in one of the buildings he had erected. A late supper, with groans from the men on discovering that the girls had had no dinner, finished an adventurous day.

Lillian was a bit overcome by the compliments from her host on what seemed a very small achievement in taking the children out of the way and wished as she fell asleep that she had spent less time on literature and more on science and current events.

Monday was a sightseeing day, made exciting by the arrival of the fourth member of the party, Mary Barker, who had traveled extensively and was a well-informed companion. Her marvelous sense of humor and the vitality and amusing exhilaration packed into a tiny body made everyone enchanted that she was to make the trip. With the evening, the entire Bunker-Gilbreth group of six joined the three girls for a dinner party at the Parker House. Anne Gilbreth Cross, Frank's musical sister had come in from Brookline and proved a stimulating addition to the party. It was a marvelous dinner, and Frank was in his best form. As a dinner companion he proved to have much more interest in other things beside construction than he had evidenced on the Sunday trip. He had read much about Egypt and seen every museum that had material on that country, both on his trips to London and in the Eastern cities where he had worked and visited. He was interested in the transmigration of souls and in the possibilities of people having met in previous lives. He was inter-

Lillian Moller (1904)

ested in the influence of the past on the present, but his real passion was
for the present and for the future and for the things which he hoped to
do with his life. It had been a full and interesting life, especially in the
work area, for it was quite evident that he lived in and for his work and
rested only long enough to recover from work and get back to it. It was not
possible, of course, even in a prolonged talk — necessarily interrupted

Frank Bunker Gilbreth (1890's)

while one talked with other people — to get much idea of ideals and attitudes, but it was evident that the whole family shared the New England ideal of making the most of one's self and giving the most to the world.

Very much an introvert, inexperienced in many things, rather lacking in a sense of humor, Lillian found it difficult to cope with a man whose experience was wide, who was highly extroverted, and who loved to joke — and who especially liked to tease anyone who proved teasable. He was kind enough to recognize her difficulties, but could not resist allusions to a future where she might write up his experiences — which left her entirely at a loss as to how to reply.

The next day was of course filled with packing and planning; with rather an anxious half hour because the car and the host, who had promised to take the girls to their steamer, proved to be late. There had, it seems, been unexpected work to attend to, speeding to make up for lost time, a pursuing policeman, a ticket, and a few other things to account for the delay. Everyone was safely deposited on the steamer but with little time for conversation or good-byes. There host, however, promised to meet their incoming steamer in November and the ship sailed — after days that seemed like a happy dream.

The four travel-mates had a large, airy, comfortable cabin, but they spent most of their time on deck. It was a very foggy crossing, which meant that Lillian could spend most of her time drowsing in her steamer chair and living over every moment of her stay in Boston — a thousand times. The other travelers concluded that this sleepiness was a form of seasickness and let her alone. Miss. Bunker, feeling deeply responsible for the emotional as well as the physical welfare of her charges, tried many times, and very adroitly, to find out how deep an impression her cousin had made on Lillian, but her customary shyness and reticence stood her in good stead. Finally, wanting to make sure that no attachment was developing, she said, "I hope that you did not take anything that Frank may have said seriously! He is always gallant to ladies. You heard him say that his Mother has made the rule 'No Jewess, no dwarf, no cousin, no widow!' Each of these restrictions refers to an experience where she has saved him from what she considered a mistake. He is completely devoted to his Mother and Aunt, has a perfect home, unlimited devotion, everything done for him, his sister's two beautiful children to enjoy. Besides, as you must have seen, he is devoted to his work. He was once deeply attached to a beautiful girl who died, and her memory means so much to him that he will never marry."

Now, nothing is so discouraging to a romance as a dead, adored rival! Of course Lillian had no way of knowing that Miss. Bunker had invented this one as a protective device, but she did sense that there really was no such person, so let her day-dreaming go on for the duration of the ocean voyage. But by the time the steamer landed in Liverpool, she had made up her mind that such foolishness must stop. If Mr. Gilbreth did care for her, he would meet her steamer in New York, as he had said he would do. If he did not — well, it was all a mistake, and a doctorate and a deanship were still possible. She must enjoy and profit by Europe as she had planned to do. Eva had an attachment, which meant that she wrote voluminous letters and would watch for the mail. Mary was debating within herself whether to accept a very fine offer or not, and profiting by the opportunity the trip gave her to clarify her feelings, meet other people, and make up her mind. Minnie Bunker was looking forward to revisiting beloved spots, and some new ones, and to making the trip as worthwhile as possible to the three girls. Lillian resolved that she would not concern herself with the future, but just live in the present and enjoy every minute of her trip, knowing that she would have days crowded with wonderful experiences, if she would take all that Miss. Bunker, and the things they would see, could offer.

It is true that this "present" would be colored for her by the past — for it was Scott's country, Burns' country, Shakespeare's, Ben Johnson's, Dickens' — that she was to visit during the first part of their trip and the country of poets, historians, and other writers that she would visit all through her stay in Europe.

They went direct to the Lake Country and spent their first night in England there. Miss. Bunker knew it intimately, could supplement the guide book, as she could in every country visited. They went on through England, and Scotland, making every day count, with a time and place schedule, and the equivalent of lectures, on history, art, and literature. Miss. Bunker was a very human, as well as a very intelligent teacher. She planned for museums in the morning, excursions in the afternoon, plays or concerts at night, with time for shopping and for rest. Most of the things the four did together, but of course Lillian with her bookish and studious bent, wanted more museums than the others did. That, too, was arranged. Fortunately for her, she was dragged to shops and fashionable restaurants, only to discover — to her own surprise — that she had latent capacities for enjoying both that she had never suspected!

When they were ready to cross the channel, it seemed to her that she could not tear herself away from Great Britain. Each day had been a series of thrills — Grassmere, Edinburgh, Ellen's Isle, Canterbury, Stratford-on-Avon, Westminster Abbey, The British Museum, the Tate Gallery, the Old Curiosity Shop — and many, many more! The high moment, perhaps, was when she stood in the Abbey and saw the stone with the inscription, "O rare Ben Johnson!" That tied back with her thesis on the *Bartholomew Fair*, and far-off California, and the dinner at the Parker House when Frank Gilbreth had said, "I don't know anything about Ben Johnson or Samuel Johnson, but I know all about the Johnsons who are prize fighters and builders!" She did not long for either Berkeley or Boston, but she did long for leisure to re-read everything British she had ever read, in the light of all these new and stimulating experiences. The rest of the trip was just as exciting — Holland, Belgium, France, Switzerland, Austria, Germany, and Italy. The stay in Holland was very short, and of course the art galleries were the chief attraction. It was marvelous to find the cities so beautifully kept up and encouraging to find that her father's beloved "Fritz Reuter" enabled her to understand a little of the morning paper. Brussels was a transition to Paris, with the shops competing with museums, and the thrill of seeing handicraft and the applied arts beautiful enough to compete with the fine arts. Even the lace exhibited in the shops was, much of it, worth to be in a museum or to become an heirloom. The point-lace handkerchief and bertha, which joined the Scotch plaid woolens and the Liberty silks in the travel bags, had stowed away with them memories of lace-makers working with bobbins and needles, as well as of happy Belgians strolling through their beautiful streets and parks.

There is only one Paris and only one first visit to it! Fortunate the traveler who has an experienced guide who is at the same time an understanding friend. Every succeeding visit profits by the careful use of time and energy in the first one — with just enough time off to revel in the small and large shops. Every hour of light was spent driving or walking in the suburbs of the city and in looking at the masterpieces of every sort. How richly all the time put in, in studying the history of art, the guide books, and the carefully made schedules, now paid for itself — and oh, how one longed for more time and more energy!

Off to Switzerland, and the stereotyped tourist experiences — there not so much living in the past as trying to get all the pictures possible of the beautiful mountain country. Lillian left the others to dash up to Berlin to visit the Moller cousins. All three of the daughters of one of Grandpa Moller's brothers had married Germans and settled in Germany. Tillie was in Lubec, and too far away to be visited, although she and her officer husband wrote hospitable invitations. Abbie had married a merchant in Frankfort, and there was a short stop there with her and her husband, and the boys. But the real visit was made to Emma and her husband, Adolph von Tiedeman. He had been a guest at the family home in Oakland on his way back from one of his trips to the Orient, for his father had been secretary to the Great Bismark, and he himself had done important work as a German officer in the Orient. Small and slim, with nerves exhausted by illness, he was a cordial host, but a difficult one. His beautiful blonde wife seemed quite accustomed to his dictatorial ways. When he said, "Emma, play!," she would drop everything and go to the piano. The little daughters were quiet and friendly. The one boy, Christian, gave promise of being like his father, but was subdued when he was at home. The whole household tiptoed about whenever Adolf was there, but became merry and almost noisy when he went to his office. Lillian had a touch of his imperious nature, and the typical officer technique, when she appeared the evening they were to go to the opera in a conservative evening gown, to be sent to her room to put on a light blouse, long as to sleeve and high as to throat, and a black skirt, as "only light ladies wear evening dresses to the opera!" She conformed outwardly, but fumed inwardly, and resolved that no girl of her generation would marry a German, and above all, a German officer!

But when she met the rest of her party in Munich, and enjoyed the Hofbrau and the parks, and met the friendly, home-loving Bavarians at work and at play, she saw another side to the national life, and came to love the country and the people of her grandparents.

Of course the high spot to the Munich stay was going to hear a Wagner opera. The group was fortunate in that they were there while *The Ring* was being played, and had the wonderful experience of seeing it in its entirety and hearing the thrilling music for the first time sung as it should be sung, with singers and audience in complete accord, and giving themselves without reservation to the experience.

Thanks again to study, to Mr. Metcalf's careful supervision, and to hours spent with the piano, one listener got so much that she felt the entire trip would have been justified by that all-too-short stay in Munich.

Vienna proved to be an equally thrilling experience, for the city was still gay and beautiful. Here the shopping contingent of the group took charge, for the time for going home was drawing near, and it was necessary to order some new clothes, if they were to be bought at all. Minnie Bunker felt sure that Viennese styles were equal to Paris, and prices much lower. While Lillian got only a few things, she did enjoy the process and had almost more fun out of the purchases of the others than her own. Mary especially had a large budget, excellent taste, and great patience with the endless fittings and alterations. There were trips to the museums and through the old parts of the city, afternoon chocolate in the parks, and theaters in the evenings — and the few days went by all too rapidly.

Then came Italy, and a repetition of the experiences of England, for here, much of the material in the history of art came to life and the readings in history and in fiction made Rome, Florence, Pompeii, and every hour of every day an excursion into the past.

The four traveling companions got on to their boat almost surfeited with experiences and completely tired out physically — far to sleepy to mind the short days and the rough weather. This lethargy, of course, passed, and the excitement of landing in New York — being met and going home — made them speculate and plan, in between making and checking lists for the customs, writing up diaries, and making sure that no one and nothing had been forgotten. Mary did not expect to be met, but would spend a day or so in New York with the others, then on to visit relatives on her way home. Eva expected her father and mother, and Lillian expected her father and mother, and the two young sisters whose turn it was to make the trip East. Travel, like other experiences, was fairly and carefully apportioned among the various members of the Moller family. Minnie Bunker said she expected no one, but she and Lillian both shared the remembrance that Frank Gilbreth had said he would meet the boat, although they said nothing to one another about this.

The final day arrived, and the hour for landing, and the boat slowly edged its way in to the pier. The four traveling companions stood high on the deck looking for the welcoming group. Yes, there they stood, the Powells and the Mollers and Frank Gilbreth was with them. It was he who stood at the gangway to shake hands as each one came off, and the whole party was soon on its way to the various hotels where they had planned to stay. Mr. Gilbreth mentioned casually that he was not allowed to carry luggage because he was just recuperating from an appendicitis operation. His infrequent post cards addressed impartially to all the travelers had said nothing of this. Many years after, he told Lillian that he had thought of writing her a long letter before he went to the hospital, but had decided that if anything happened to him it was better not to have complicated her life.

He walked along now teasing the small Ernestine and Elinor Moller because, he said, they wore Western shoes. They could not imagine what this meant. It was only because they had a certain type of stitching, which he knew was used only on shoes shipped to the West, but the little girls feared he thought their feet were large!

Eva went with her parents to their hotel; Frank Gilbreth to his Club; Minnie to the Bunker cousins; the Mollers to the Holland House; and Lillian to Martha Washington, where she had promised to stay with Mary until she left on her way home. There was, of course, a reunion dinner, and the entire party went to the theater to see *Ben Hur*. Before the evening was over, Lillian promised to go to the Metropolitan Museum of Art with Frank the next day to see the Egyptian wing. He had persuaded the family to prolong their expected visit to Boston — to show the little girls who had never been there all sights — to include a little sightseeing with him.

He was very late in keeping his appointment the next day because he had stopped in to see Mary Barker, and had had a long heart-to-heart talk with her. This, perhaps naturally, infuriated Lillian, who very nearly canceled the date; but the museum trip finally took place and was a good bridge back to Boston and the talk on Egyptology and transmigration of souls!

After that, Frank went back to Boston, the Moller family paid the usual family visits, and it was several days before they, too, went to Boston, and the comfortable Westminster Hotel. The stay in Boston was short, but full of the usual travel sightseeing for the Moller parents and the small girls. This left Frank and Lillian free to do some sightseeing of their own. She felt very much interested but slightly embarrassed to visit his office, meet his partner, serious Mr. Bussell; the handsome and good-looking Hamlin; the slim blond Brooks; and above all, the small dynamic Anne Bowley. The last seemed the indispensable member of the organization — one of those little, hard-working secretaries who could do anything from extend a note at the bank to keeping her boss's crowded schedule in order. The big new hat with the fluffy chiffon veil and the Vienna suit

— while the last word in imported style — seemed inappropriate and foolish in the busy office, and even more out of place on the construction jobs. But, after all, there was so much to learn, and everything was so interesting, that clothes were, as usual, a "slight thing to mention." Mrs. Gilbreth and Miss. Bunker entertained at dinner, and the party went to see *The Wizard of Oz.* It seemed a pity that the only combination of seats Frank could buy meant that two were separated from the others — but nobody seemed to feel that that presented any difficulty!

Just before the Moller's train left for the West, Frank dashed in, in great excitement, to say that his contract for a job including a trip to the Northwest to see the project, had been signed. He hoped to meet the Moller party in Chicago for a short reunion, and would perhaps see them again in California. As he had for several days spoken as if this was a foregone conclusion, Lillian was a bit puzzled — until [he explained] his belief in what he called "Premature Truths." These, he said, often became *real* truths if you believed in them hard enough — the trip to Seattle being a case in point!

Chicago proved windy and sleety — but he appeared according to schedule, and Lillian was a bit surprised that her Mother made no protest when he suggested taking her to see *Florodora* that evening. Absurd as it may seem, it was the first time she had ever gone to the theater unchaperoned. A shopping trip, to purchase her escort some heavy shoes in a little Regal Shoe Store, as he had come unprepared for such weather, and the first of many stops to look into camera-shop windows, with plenty of opportunity to plan for the reunion in California, made the short day a satisfying one. There were a few hints that a trip to Seattle could be made via Oakland — but she paid no attention to these, as, with the last lap home, all the friends and attachments there became increasingly alluring. A little time on the train and at home before the strenuous and insistent visitor arrived would be a great help!

He did arrive, according to schedule, and telephoned over to the Moller home. Mrs. Moller, who answered the phone, was a little surprised to be told, "This is the white rabbit." Lillian remembered a chat about *Alice In Wonderland* and surmised correctly that the visitor had been reading it and was letting her know this. As his stay could be only a short one, he came over at once, and endured with great nonchalance and apparent enjoyment, the more or less surreptitious inspection by all the sisters and brothers. It was fun to share the beloved job of trimming the Christmas tree, and to arrange to go to the Christmas football game, the family Christmas dinner, and a sightseeing trip to San Francisco the day after Christmas. Frank's cousin, Abbey Bunker Weston, and her family had claimed him as house guest and this complicated scheduling a little, but not to any serious extent.

Christmas dinner with the Brown cousins was rather an ordeal — but all did their best to act as if a guest at their family dinner was a usual occurrence, and Annie Florence, as usual, took over the entertaining with zest and with success.

December 26th proved a perfect California winter day, and the excursion a complete success. It was humiliating to Lillian to know so little of the engineering and construction developments which her guest saw everywhere and concerning which he asked innumerable questions. But Old San Francisco — with its enchanting Chinatown, beautiful Golden Gate Park, the Cliff House, and her best beloved view over the Pacific — were in her own territory. They went to the Museum in the Park, and saw the octopus and had a dispute as to how one pronounced the word, in which he was — as usual — right! Out at the Golden Gate they decided that, in spite of the fact that he had a life filled with strenuous work ahead; felt that he could never leave his Mother and Aunt; and had innumerable responsibilities to face and problems to solve — she would not only be willing but glad to share these experiences. It was a different city they went through as they got on the little cable-car and went down the long hills toward the Ferry, and Oakland, and home!

The family was blind, or pretended to be; the Bunker cousins generous; and there was time for short intensive planning before he took the train and started East. Daily letters full of hard work, and intensive effort to put it through, went westward and equally long letters — but much more full of daydreams, and wishful thinking — went East. Frank's diary notes, as well as his letters, show that he was never too busy to keep in the foreground of his thinking, plans for the wedding that was to take place as soon as he could arrange it. The solitaire from Tiffany's came presently, and by April it seemed time to announce the engagement. That was an exciting day for the Mollers, for the engagement really was a surprise to all but the immediate family. On April 14, Lillian — dressed in a brand new point d'esprit dress, with a big bunch of her favorite lilies-of-the-valley — set the photograph of Frank, which she had extracted after a tremendous amount of pleading, up on the mantel, just behind where she and her mother would receive the guests. She put on her ring, and her new Octopus pin with green emerald eyes, and prepared for the excitement of surprising the guests. The surprise was very evident, and in some cases not too complimentary — as when one of her favorite teachers, Miss. Hilton, almost sank to the floor and murmured, "At last my prayers are answered!" She was sure that if Lillian married at all it would be a long white-bearded philosopher — and she seemed to find Frank's young strenuous face attractive and reassuring.

After that the hope-chest preparations could go forward even more vigorously, for of course Lillian's Mother had the fine old-fashioned idea of dozens of everything — all hand-initialed. The fact that she had been six times a bridesmaid and brought up in the community meant a lovely collection of engagement cups and a series of showers and parties.

The usual trip with the younger children to Cisco was a much needed rest. It was not until the children were back at school that the wedding date was set and then with the understanding that it might have to be changed, for Frank's work was most demanding, and his schedule very uncertain. The Moller plans were completely made, of course, that being the family custom for all plans — and great was the relief when the bridegroom was finally on the train for the West. He concealed his amazement and dismay that he was expected to be there several days before the wedding, even though this cut short the all-too-brief honeymoon. Lillian's Mother had set her heart on having the wedding on a Wednesday because "that was her lucky day." This meant to poor Frank going to Church the preceding Sunday; visiting all the relatives on both sides; and an extension of what he quite frankly regarded as a terrific ordeal.

Lillian's Father, always cordial, and her oldest brother, offered to take her to Sixteenth Street Station to meet her fiancé, but when Cousin Minnie Bunker decided on joining the party, she decided that she would rather meet him when he arrived at the Prospect Avenue home. It could not be a private meeting, however, as Minnie came along with him, and added to the ordeal by insisting that the entire family join hands and dance around the engaged couple on the lawn. Frank thought this amusing — Lillian's thoughts she kept to herself!

It was a great thrill to exhibit her fiancee to her relatives and friends for the first time. The list was long, because only the family were invited to the wedding, because otherwise Grandma Delger could not have come. He stood this well, especially taking lunch with Grandma Delger in the beautiful old home. She made a party of the occasion, with all available delicacies at hand, and even champagne for a toast. She had checked with Lillian as to the bridegroom's taste. The latter remembered having written shortly after the engagement for information on questions the family asked, like, "What Church does he belong to?" "Is he a Mason?" and certain questions of her own. One answer had been, "I like everything to eat but onions, and everything to drink but glue!"

Far too excited to eat much, Lillian made no great hit that day with her hospitable grandmother; but the guest, having always a fine appetite, and an appreciation for good food, made a most favorable impression. When the champagne was served, and white-ribboned Lillian took only a sip or two, grandmother looked disapproving. When the guest spoke and demonstrated his appreciation, Grandma was enchanted and said, "He's the fellow," — and a favorite he remained from that time on. He had thought everything he had seen in Oakland and San Francisco "Fairyland," but the Delger place seemed to him the most enchanting he had ever seen and he wondered how his bride could possibly be willing to tear herself away from it and from the beloved family and home on Prospect Avenue.

The day of the wedding proved long and distracting. Frank, unaccustomed to the necessity for making travel reservations long ahead, waited endlessly and impatiently at the Southern Pacific offices in San Francisco. He never did succeed in getting the type of reservations he wanted. The Moller family, accustomed to being ahead of time, became a little upset, especially dear Josephine, who was to be maid-of-honor and who feared that the thrill of a lifetime might be denied her. When Frank finally appeared, she raced down the steps to meet him, having spent most of the afternoon watching from an upper window. She was a great favorite with her brother-to-be, who always called her "O Yuki San" and he was both amused and touched by her anxiety. Finally the family assembled and the two guests whom the bride and groom had invited — Alma Brown for Lillian; and Ethel Olney, the near neighbor and friend, for Frank. He had selected her as his guest, as none of his own friends were near at hand. There was some commotion when Everett Brown, who was to be best man, arrived wearing a black tie, and found the bridegroom wearing a white one. But Frank's collection of haberdashery was always extensive, so that that alteration was soon accomplished. Dr. McLean came to perform the ceremony as Dr. Brown was in the East, and it was discovered that he and the bridegroom had not met. Dear Grandmother, slowed by her lameness and excitement, delayed the wedding, but at last was safely seated in her place of honor, and the party started down the broad hall stairs. Frankie got out of step and insisted that they back up and start over again. Frank always claimed that he and the minister exchanged nothing but nods, which meant on the one hand, "Are you the victim?," and on the other, "Yes, I am." Also

Frank and Lillian's
wedding (October 19,
1904) at her parents
home in Oakland,
California.
L to R:
Annie Moller
(Lillian's mother),
Josephine Moller
(sister and
Maid of Honor),
Lillian, Frank,
William Moller
(Lillian's father),
Ernestine Delger
(Lillian's grandmother),
and Everett Brown
(Lillian's cousin and
Best Man)

that he measured the distance from the place where he stood to the nearest window while waiting for the bride, and calculating just how long it would take him to escape. The ceremony went through smoothly, the sister maid-of-honor and bridesmaids and the three brothers and the one cousin ribbon-bearers doing their parts smoothly. The supper went through smoothly also. "O Yuki San" caught the wedding bouquet to everyone's satisfaction. The travel clothes were donned and the bride and groom set off for San Francisco and the St. Francis Hotel. The bride was annoyed to have their carriage directly next to Uncle Ed and Aunt Margaret's on the long ferry trip across the bay, but the bridegroom was finished with his ordeal and enjoying everything immensely. The suite at the St. Francis was beautiful with flowers. Champagne having been refused by the bride, the bridegroom happily ordered beer and rejoiced at his transformation from guest into host.

All his thoughts were on getting back to work with his new partner and making all the progress possible toward the goals he had set. He took everything in his stride. The nervous waiter, who dropped the heavily loaded breakfast tray because he had evidently never served a bride and groom before, was calmly sent for more supplies. Brother Fred who appeared at the Sixteenth Street Station in Oakland to wave good-bye for the family, was invited to come East at once. The entire Moller family had been whole-heartedly adopted and their birthdays and anniversaries entered in the diary which never left him, and which had programs and records of every sort crowding its pages.

The fact that a drawing-room had been available, and that family friends had the next section as far as the Sierras and were obviously interested in the bridal couple was no hardship to him. He started in immediately to discuss plans. "Of course we want to work together, I don't know a thing about your work, so you'll have to learn mine. So, I'll start right in to teach you now. I think the first thing you had better learn about is Masonry. You did a good job indexing *Field System* and I don't for the life of me see how you did, when of course you don't know anything about anything in it, but you soon will know everything about everything. Well, let's get at the masonry. 'Bond is the relationship of joints in masonry.' Here, let me get a pencil and some paper and I'll show you exactly how that works."

The pencil and paper were seldom out of his hands. Even in the dining-car he drew sketches of the passengers, all looking at the bridal couple, with little dots and arrows leading toward the table. He jollied the steward; ordered just those things the chef turned out best; tipped easily and effectively; never missed anything going on inside or outside the train!

He had brought an Atlas with him and marked every detail of the trip upon it. There were a few happy hours at the Garden of the Gods in Colorado and then on to the World's Fair in St. Louis. Lillian had been fortunate enough to be at the World's Fair in Chicago, and remembered vividly the things she had seen there. This was an entirely different experience. Of course the Fair itself was different, and Frank supplemented the art and other exhibits she wanted to see with intensive study of the Science Buildings and of every phase of construction. They tried out many types of restaurants and tea rooms, some so gay they were a new sensation to the California girl, who had seen very little of night life. One served salad and chicken in the French fashion, and there they planned for trips abroad. All too soon came a telegram from Bowley in the Boston office that Frank was needed at once. In the hurry to getting off they forgot to check their trunk and the poor bride arrived at her new home with only such clothes as were in her traveling bag.

Frank had had little time to give to selecting and getting ready this new home, but his faithful Mother and Aunt Kit had done a fine job. They had found an apartment on West 94th Street, near the river and west side subway station. It was long and narrow — a good-sized living room on the street — bedrooms opening off a long, narrow hall — and an adequate kitchen and dining room, to meet the taste of the two New England housekeepers. They had sufficient furniture to outfit it adequately, so that really there was no room for anything the bride brought. Her things were carefully stored for later use. Her place was set at the head of the table for the first meal, but she could see so plainly that

Frank Bunker Gilbreth (1904)

Mother Gilbreth missed her usual job, that she immediately insisted that she resume the carving, the serving, and all the other things that she enjoyed so much. It became evident that Lillian really was not needed, so far as housekeeping was concerned, and would have ample time for what Frank wanted her to do. This was — to work with him.

Lillian Moller Gilbreth (1914)

Leaving her to her new in-laws, he had to dash off on the sleeper to Boston. The next morning, she and Aunt Kit rescued the belated trunk, and she tried to settle her things and plan her schedule. Neither her training nor Frank's business made it feasible for her to work with him at his office, so she must try to do what she could at home, and be ready to go with him on any trip where it might be easy for him to take her. She must try, too, to find out which jobs in the home would gladly be delegated to her, and to do these the very best she could. She was heartily welcomed — both as daughter and niece — yet of course she knew that every member of the household faced difficult problems of adjustment. Frank's first absence was short, and never was a returned traveler more heartily welcomed. In his eyes, apartment and all the arrangements were perfect, as was every member of the new family. It must be the job of the three women to keep him feeling that way, constantly.

He did realize that his wife must be kept busy, and spent every free minute trying to teach her about the work, giving her his ideas and plans, and outlining how they could put into writing the "Systems" which made his business so successful. This was an absorbing job. A publisher had asked to print *Field System* and it became evident that a series of systems covering his work would not only be useful within the organization, but might be profitable if turned into books. He was deep in every branch of concrete construction, including concrete piles, and patents were constantly to be applied for, possible uses written up, photographs collected, lantern slides made, and so on. Advertising was another absorbing problem, and everything conceivable came from the office, home, to be talked over by the new partners. As always, Frank had to travel a great deal of the time. He had a wonderful philosophy, which meant that you made decisions slowly and carefully, using the parallel column to set down pros and cons. When you had once made the decision, you went ahead steadily, not stopping to moan, or to wish you had decided on something different.

A houseboat was bought and anchored at Port Washington, and with it, one of Frank's dreams came true. He was entirely happy on it, and loved keeping it full of guests. Sometimes these were very helpful, sometimes they made a great deal of work, and poor Lillian was too inexperienced to life-on-the-water to know how to take the job easily. The entire Moller family went to Europe as an educational project, and Lillian scarcely knew whether she was more homesick for California or for them!

But Frank's work went well, in spite of many worries incident to its large and rapid expansion, and his prestige increased constantly. Lillian found much to do in helping to organize the material which went into speeches and papers, for technical meetings and universities — and into the advertising and systems as well. Besides, it was her job to keep up with current events and books, not only in the technical field, but in general. What a satisfying assignment that was! Really it was not fair to call it work at all!

She had trips with Frank to visit Anne and her family; to Boston; and one happy trip to Montreal. It was always a thrill to see her husband off at Grand Central Station, or wait for his train to come in. Sometimes this was late at night, when he was most rested, after a chat with friends or hours spent making notes and plans. Sometimes it was early in the morning, then he was invariably the last passenger off and terribly tired because he had been the last one to bed. She had never seen anyone with such ambition, such drive, and such vigor. If she were to keep up at all, she must learn to rest and relax when he was away, in order to be an adequate companion when he was at home.

It was of course a tremendous thrill that a new member was to join the household. Frank had decided, with his usual knowledge of exactly what he wanted, that they would have six boys and six girls. This seemed an easy undertaking to a person who had practically been an only child most of his life, but was a little appalling to "the oldest of nine!" However, she was all for doing anything he wanted, and he was sure that the same principles of efficiency which worked out on the jobs should make the running of the household and the bringing up of a family easy. The Moller family sent over most of a layette from Europe, including a christening robe and all the undergarments that went with it, very long, very elaborate, with many infinitesimal hand-run tucks put in by the devoted sisters. Lillian herself made enough garments for half a dozen babies and spent happy hours fixing up the crib and wishing the small person who was to occupy it was lying in it. She came, on the ninth of September — California's Admission Day — with loud yells, and to a

Lillian and baby Anne (1905)

hearty welcome, to be named Anne Moller for her maternal grandmother and Aunt Anne Cross. She was a fine, healthy, blue-eyed, gold-
haired baby, with a will of her own, and wonderful techniques for getting
her way. Her father had had little experience with small babies and

regarded her not only with affection, but with keen interest. All his theories of education and rearing were to be tried out on her. She loved him, on sight, but screamed at him as lustily as anyone else if she wanted anything. Her adoring Mother and aunts sat unprotestingly when he dumped her in her bed if she roared, and closed the door! It is to be feared that they spoiled her the rest of the time, although the two older women were the soul of tact and never interfered. From his wide reading and well-stocked memory, Frank drew all sorts of theories for experiments. He walked in one morning and said to the small girl's mother, "I read somewhere that if you put a very young baby into the water, she will swim. Do you mind if I try it out?" His mother and aunt protested, but his wife consented to the experiment, provided the trained nurse could be at hand for first aid if that was needed. In a few minutes he was back from the bathroom to say, "She sank. It wasn't true!" But the small daughter was none the worse for the experiment.

Through some undiscovered occurrence, Lillian had a bent coccyx for some months and dragged around until her capable doctor patched her up. In the meantime much of the pleasure of wheeling her baby and showing her off was spoiled by the fact that no matter how comfortable and sound asleep Anne might be when she was put in the carriage, no sooner was she on the street then she screamed so lustily that kind old ladies would stop and ask what her mother had done to her. The baby grew and prospered, but Lillian got thinner, and finally an attack of jaundice disturbed everyone and Frank snatched her up in April of 1906 to visit with Auntie Brown and the Brownies while he did some business up and down the West Coast. It was a very happy visit, in spite of the fact that the Moller family were abroad, so were not in the dear old home, for Auntie Brown and Frank proved to be very congenial, to the point where he proved to be the only person allowed to drive her steady old horse.

The California earthquake and the fire which came after it proved a milestone in the family life. Frank dashed out to San Francisco at once and found so much work to be done in his line and had such success in signing up contracts that he decided to move his family out immediately.

Mother and Aunt Kit were not entirely convinced that they wanted to go — but it soon became apparent that he would be unhappy if he were separated from them that they put their own wishes aside. They planned to visit Anne and then go West as soon as the home was found and ready. The Mollers hurried back to handle the slight repairs needed on their home, and Papa, who had retired, happily re-entered business to solve new and important problems and make adjustments and expansions in the work which the earthquake and fire brought.

Lillie found a house in San Francisco and the small Anne adjusted herself easily and quickly. Her father was still busy with her education, during the short time he could be at home — putting marks around the place in the closet where his bed room slippers belonged, and other marks near his bed, and teaching her to get them for him and put them away. He insisted that there be no baby talk. He tried to insist that her mother talk German with her, and he persisted in having her do everything she could for herself. She was a young and fluent speaker, and a born arguer, so she and her Daddy had some wonderful times together.

Mother Gilbreth and Aunt Kit came on, but quite naturally disliked the climate; the torn-up condition of San Francisco; and all the strange surroundings, shops, friends, and foods. Lillian reveled in her own family and friends, though it was not easy to see all she wished of them. The worst trial for all of them was that Frank had to be away so much of the time. Probably no one appreciated how hard it was for him. He had always been foot-loose, and had had really no family responsibilities which tied him down at all. Widespread as his work was, there had been only one headquarters, and he personally could be there enough of the time to make all important decisions. Now, he had demanding responsibilities, two headquarters — one on the West Coast and one on the East — and the necessity of delegating not only much of his work, but some decisions to people who were not accustomed to this. Even the fact that his wife was a native daughter and his daughter born on California's Admission Day, did not make him completely persona grata to the local-minded Westerners, or give him all the facility on getting materials and labor that a native son had. If he was in the West, the Eastern jobs suffered, and his Eastern organization either made decisions which he did not always feel were wise, or kept after him to make decisions himself which he felt were their responsibility. If he was in the East, the Western organization — devoted as it was — missed his master-mind, and slowed down or made mistakes which took time to correct. Added to this, although he never complained or mentioned it, must have been the fact that no matter how absorbing the work, he was homesick when away from his home and family, and knew that they — not always so silent — were homesick and not very happy when he was away from them. Undoubtedly the fact that the usually beautiful city was a wreck from earthquake, fire, and reconstruction — which made getting about on foot or in any other way difficult, and beauty spots hideous — had much to do with the fact that the year was not highly successful in anyone's estimation.

The one completely happy event was the coming of a second little daughter, Mary Elizabeth, born December 13, 1906. Her father was away when she came, but came hurrying back, bringing a diamond so much larger than Lillian's wedding ring, and the ring with three stones —which had been the present when baby Anne came — that the entire household was in an upheaval! There never was a sweeter, lovelier baby. Like many second babies, she was much more peaceful than her older sister, and seemed entirely unspoiled by grandmothers and aunts on both sides of the family. The trained nurse who had been in the house for some time before her coming — because of her father's absence and of the difficulty of getting about — was a sweet and lovely person who brought calmness and good nature everywhere she went. Mary had blue eyes, but lighter blonde hair than Anne, with a cowlick in the front — which no amount of brushing could ever make lie flat. Anne adored her, and could not wait for "my baby" to be big enough to walk and to play. Sundays became happy days, when the entire family were bundled into the big car and drove down to the ferry, to be carried across the Bay and drive on up to Grandpa Moller's house. There Frank could toss balls with the boys, the two elderly ladies could sit in the sun, and Lillian, relieved of all responsibilities of every sort, could draw a long breath between the end of one week and the beginning of another. This made the decision which was inevitable, hard to make. This was, to move the family back East. The San Francisco jobs had been completed quickly and well, and nothing remained there but what the organization could complete without Frank's supervision — while work on the East Coast was steadily expanding. Problems of distributing his time and attention became more and more acute. Besides, Grandma and Aunt Kit were homesick for New England, and Anne, and the children. So back they went, this time not to 94th Street, where the apartments were too small, but to the beautiful new Hendrick Hudson, on Riverside Drive and 110th Street. Aunt Kit never saw this apartment, for she died during her visit with Anne. She had had for many years diabetes. Her own uncomplaining nature, the strong feeling for Christian Science which Grandma Gilbreth had, the fact that she would have died rather than worry Frank — meant that no one had realized how ill she really was. Through the years that followed, Lillian wished that she had known that that disease affected one's nerves and one's disposition, as well as ones digestion, and been more patient, inwardly as well as outwardly, with the devoted aunt, who concealed everything when Frank was at home, but often was unable to do this when he was away. Grandma missed her beloved sister, but always took the hardships with fortitude and serenity and settled down to enjoy her son and his family and to contribute in every way that she knew.

The two little girls were well and happy and companionable, but living in New York and on Riverside Drive was no easy thing. Dressing them up in the pretty clothes which the California family showered on them, and taking them out on the Drive for air and exercise meant that one was in and out and up and down continuously. But Frank's work went well and he took much pleasure in his membership in the American Society of Mechanical Engineers [A.S.M.E.], and the friendships which started there. He became interested in the Taylor System, and Scientific Management, and read and re-read everything that Mr. Taylor had written. He enjoyed having Levor Tillotson, one of his British friends, visit him. He gave talks on his experiences in San Francisco, and the earthquake, and on his construction jobs there. The partners were busy in the evenings and on his Sundays at home, in writing *Concrete System* and getting it into press. But the great thrill in this area was working on *Bricklaying System,* which was in some ways the finest thing Frank ever wrote. There was nothing about bricklaying that Frank did not know, and little, if anything, that he could not do with his own hands. It was a joy to write everything down as he remembered it, to make countless drawings of different types of bonds, and to make trips with his wife to see interesting brickwork wherever it was to be found. He started gathering, then, not only the material which appeared in *Bricklaying System,* but material in this field which accumulated all through his life. No diary was ever to be without pages devoted to it. There were friends to run in, including the devoted Alice Dickson; many of Frank's old and new business friends; — but the happiest time was when the children were asleep and the partners could spread out the rough drawings, and first drafts, and gradually perfect material, the galley sheets, the page proofs — as *Bricklaying System,* month by month, was assembled and criticized and developed.

On the 5th of April, 1908, a third daughter, Ernestine Moller, joined the family group. The months before her coming had been cold and wintry, and when Lillian made her first trip to the roof, after the baby came, she thought that nothing ever was so beautiful as the blue sky and the green trees and the river. Ernestine was an enchanting baby and it was a joy to pack her up when she was about six weeks old and take her out to show to the California family. How fortunate that Frank had to make a trip at that time! The diary notes are full of "worked on *Bricklaying System,*" "dined with relatives and friends," "visited University of California library" and so forth. The two other little girls were safe and happy with Grandma.

The new little "Ern" lay happily in her basket wherever she was put, and the days were not long to enjoy all the good times. Even the fact that Frank was anxious and worried, with many problems on his mind, could not spoil her pleasure. It was not easy to close up the San Francisco business — to place the men, handle the finances, and refuse opportunities to remain that offered. Also there were problems involved with the new interest in Scientific Management, which seemed to be pulling both partners away from construction and into the Management field itself.

Nineteen hundred and eight was in many ways a hard year. Hugh Kershaw, a very dear British friend and representative, died of typhoid; various lawsuits proved troublesome; work was either too plentiful with not enough people available, or not sufficient to keep everybody busy; but the home was happy and the children grew splendidly.

Nineteen hundred and nine started happily, with visits to Philadelphia and Boston; correcting the final proofs of *Bricklaying System;* and a visit to Buffalo Bill at Cody. In April came word that the bitter enemy who had made the California situation difficult, had died of smallpox. In July, the beloved *Bricklaying System* finally appeared, to be welcomed almost as happily as a new child, and sent to a list of friends, which reflects the diversity of interests — Dodge, Taylor, Thompson, Gantt, of the Management group — Bruce of publicity — Professor Johnson of Harvard — Albert Wiggin and George Coleman, boyhood classmates — many professor friends at various colleges where Frank had spoken, and many, many others. Technical paper after technical paper was written by the partners and presented and printed. Frank's versatile and creative mind busied itself not only on his jobs, but in plans for the efficient house and in helping run a smooth and happy family life.

In September the family moved to Plainfield, and on November fifth, Martha Bunker, the fourth little girl, made her appearance. She was later than expected, and her mother and nurse had made many a rapid trip around the neighborhood hoping to hasten her arrival. She came with considerable difficulty, but she was worth the wait. She had blue eyes like the others, but lovely red curls, and became on sight the idol of her grandmother, for whom she was named. The three little sisters welcomed her with great enthusiasm, and as the next summer came, her high chair on the porch was the center, not only of family, but of neighborhood life — for the Netherwood neighbors proved very congenial.

Next door on one side lived the Fenners — Dave was a Gantt man — and the one little girl about Anne's age. She was very pretty and always exquisitely dressed and Anne looked at her clothes enviously. One day she came in and asked why she could not dress the way Betty did. Her Mother tried to explain, but finally got annoyed at the diversity of questions and said, "Anne, we believe that brains are better than clothes!" "Andie" disappeared and her observant Father said, "I am afraid she has gone next door." Sure enough, back she came to say, "Betty's Mother thinks clothes are better than brains." It took a little adjusting to straighten that out!

Through the gardens on the left, lived the Lawrences, quiet Frank and lovely Margaret, with their two small boys. Margaret was the daughter of Mr. Ransom of the Concrete Group, and one of Frank's fiercest competitors in that line, but that never interfered with the friendship.

Through the gardens the other way lived Bill Cooke and his wife Helen. Bill's family had the pew in front of the Mollers in the Congregational Church for many years, and it was a real treat to have neighbors who knew the California friends.

Life went happily for the family, for Grandma liked the neighbors and the pretty little house. Lillian did not make much progress in women's social affairs, because she had neither the time nor inclination for bridge. But the writing of books with Frank and the happy life with the four baby girls was very satisfying. Business life became increasingly difficult because the construction work had more and more peaks and valleys, and all the difficulties which happen when the personnel changes from the worker all the way up. Southern Europeans were taking the place of the Northern Europeans who had furnished the early stock and the careful craftsmanship in the building trades. This inevitably resulted in a different status for the business and in the professions associated with it. Lillian regretted the amount of time her husband spent with people whose business practices and intellectual and social interests were so different from his. It was not a question of the dignity of labor, but of working with people whose ideals, attitudes, and customs were alien to his, and those of the group in which he had been brought up. His schedule was more and more crowded and the work more and more exacting. It was not the work, of course, but the worries, which were exhausting. Problems in

Lillian and her four oldest daughters –
Anne, Mary, Ernestine, and Martha (1911)

financing; in getting patents; in fighting patent infringements; in checking on personnel procedure in the office and out on the jobs; in continual travel; in trying to flatten out the peaks and valleys so as to provide constant employment — left all too little time for writing, and for investigating the Scientific Management which held such a satisfaction for him.

This was compensated for by the fact that the two partners found more and more things which they enjoyed working on together, and by the satisfaction that Frank's plan for running the home and family on the Family Council idea worked well. The little girls seemed to enjoy Daddy's ideas and made out their work sheets and filled in their charts very happily.

Lillie had been the second and oldest survivor of seven girls who came to the Mollers before they had three boys — Frank had been the one boy of a family of three. So in his plan for having six boys and six girls, he reconciled himself, and certainly seemed satisfied that his four first children were girls. Now and then he would say he was sure he would never have a boy. But as he had previously said that he had been sure he would never marry; and then as he had said he was sure he would never have children, nobody took his premonitions very seriously. In fact nobody ever knew how much he had hoped for a boy until Frank Jr. was born, March 17, 1911. Then he whole-heartedly repeated what Grandma said had been his father's performance when he was born — telegrams, telephone calls, and letters to everyone — distribution of cigars — and all those things which the proud father usually reserves for celebrating the coming of his first son!

Dear Uncle Jimmy Dodge telegramed from Philadelphia, "Greetings to Patrick's sufficiency." Frank was firm in saying his son should not be named for him, as he was entitled to a name all his own. But the small boy's proud Mother felt that "Frank Jr." was the only appropriate name and everyone started to use it at once, Daddy subsided, more gracefully than might have been expected.

The writing of books went on, *Motion Study* in 1911; and the *Primer of Scientific Management* the same year. Both were in their ways milestones — the first as establishing the name for the most characteristic Gilbreth work and presenting much of the material that was to follow, in its first draft form. All its illustrative material was in the bricklaying field. It grew out of one chapter of *Bricklaying System,* and presented unsolved problems which led to the series of books which followed through the years. The writing of it, like that of *Bricklaying System,* was a labor of love, and a great source of inspiration to both partners. Like all of the other books which bore Frank's name, it had a waiting and an eager publisher — who pushed the printing through as rapidly as possible.

The *Primer of Scientific Management* indicated a close and happy relationship with Fredrick Taylor and the Scientific Management group. Mr. Taylor, after much urging, had written some articles which were published later in book form as *Principles of Scientific Management.* These included an appreciative account of some of Frank's work. The publisher of these articles was deluged with questions. Mr. Taylor felt that he did not have time to answer them. At his request, they were turned over to Frank, who incorporated the replies in the *Primer.* This was written longhand, in what was practically one stretch. Frank sat at his work table, in pajamas, with Lillian supplying food at appropriate intervals and easing his arms by specially made little wool pillows, according to his directions. If only all of life could have been as free from stress and worry as the all-too-few days spent at home! There was sufficient equipment for work there to keep Frank busy and happy, and he was able to concentrate so completely that outside things were not allowed to interfere. It is possible that the stress of business and professional life was a tremendous drive — but he really never needed drive of any sort, except his ideals and ambitions.

In the midst of this highly-keyed and emotional type of living, came the most dreadful calamity the family was to experience for many years. The two older girls had been taking more and more part in community life, going happily to Sunday school and to dancing school with the small neighbors. Grandma Moller and the aunts sent beautiful white dresses, and hairbows, and sashes, and the blue-eyed, rosy-cheeked, blonde sisters had a lovely time dressing up and coming back to tell all they had learned. Out of the sky — no one knew where — they developed diphtheria. Anne had it very lightly and threw it off very easily. With Mary it went differently. She seemed to have no resistance, and in spite of day and night fighting of doctors, nurses, and parents, she could not throw it off. Lillian was quarantined with her, while her Father agonized outside. Near the end he insisted on trying his techniques, but it was no use. It was a shattering experience, because neither parent had ever been through anything similar, and Frank for the first time in his life faced a situation which he could not master. Added to all his sorrow and loss, was the shattering knowledge that he had failed, or thought he had failed in a project nearest his heart. He was not the type who could take grief easily or articulately, or who could reconcile himself quickly to illness and to death. Never from that day on could either parent find the relief of speaking freely of the experience, and never could he answer the question, "How many children have you?" without stopping to calculate. It was an experience which an understanding psychiatrist might possibly have adjusted, but it was not adjusted, and it left a permanent scar.

Coming as it did in the midst of trying to decide whether to continue in construction work or to go into the management field, it probably hastened the decision to go into the latter type of work. There were many determining factors. Lillian had been working for a long time on her Doctor's thesis for the University of California. It was to be called *The Psychology of Management* and as her field work had to be done in the East, the University of California had made special provision for waiving the rule that one's last year for a Doctorate must be spent on the campus. After the thesis had been completed and practically accepted, she was informed that the Committee declined to go through with waiving the rule. It was of course impossible for her to plan for a year's residence at Berkeley; so the decision was made to publish the thesis and get the degree at some other institution. One of the technical magazines did publish the thesis, using the chapters for articles. Frank shopped strenuously among book publishers. He resented the fact that, while the manuscripts that had his name and were in the construction field were competed for eagerly, this one upon which both partners had worked as they had upon the others, which included psychology along with engineering, and was to have his wife's name, found no ready market. Finally, Mr. Walton, a Macmillan man setting up his own firm, accepted the manuscript, provided the author's name should have only initials and the publicity should not include the fact that it was a woman. This disturbed feminist Frank more than it did Lillian. Next came the job of finding a college willing to give a Ph.D. degree on "Applied Management." Many of the large universities were not interested. Brown University, at Providence, was.

Due to his new interest and work in the area of Scientific Management, Frank had renewed his acquaintance with John Aldrich, the managing executive of the New England Butt Company, a small but very progressive factory in Providence, Rhode Island, making braiding machines. Mr. Aldrich was anxious to have the entire Taylor System introduced into his factory and was interested in having the Gilbreth Motion Study applied and developed there. The beloved sister, Anne Cross, and her husband, and two children, lived at Anne's Music School, which had been an influence in the cultural life of the city for many years. Anne was an active and enthusiastic member of the Art Club, to which representatives of both the Town and Gown belonged. A move to Providence seemed the appropriate solution to many problems.

It was not easy to find a place to live. The family was fortunate enough to rent the house of the Professor of Greek and Archeology, while he was off on his holidays. The children had a whole new area in which to ask questions, because of the busts of Greek and Roman heroes all over the house, and the many pictures and photographs of the classical world, in the Golden Age and now.

Then half a house was located at 71 Brown Street — just a block or two from the college, and a few more blocks to Aunt Anne's. Grandma was of course enchanted to be back in the New England atmosphere, and near her beloved daughter. She had visited there so often that it was almost like going back to Boston.

Frank found the problem of handling New York affairs rather difficult. He was removed from the possibility of daily visits. This presented difficult transportation problems, but travel was never any burden to him, and nobody had ever worked out better techniques for handling it. The house was too small to include an adequate office or laboratory, but sister Anne gladly turned over a large and very satisfactory room at the Music School, which he named "Taylor Hall." It had its own entrance on the side, plenty of seats and blackboards, and storage space, and was ideal for meetings. The children could have a small backyard and the whole Brown campus to walk on and enjoy. There was a Sunday school close at hand and a little dancing school almost across the street, with fine possibilities both at private and public schools.

As for Lillian, sister Anne would tell her where to find some domestic help. College girls might be available to walk with and teach the children in the afternoons; the family friends would be glad to welcome her; and Brown University was so near, that, as Frank said, she could go to class and if a child fell out of the window, catch him before he landed on the ground. She tried to set up her life adequately in all its various areas. There were a few unavoidable delays, as several of the children developed diphtheria, although there were no other cases in town and no evidence of their having brought the disease with them or having a carrier in the family. The attacks were light and were chiefly difficult to handle because of the terrific emotional factors involved. Even the little girls had to be protected from being frightened that another one would be snatched away. Probably the intensive nursing and solicitude did little harm except to tired bodies and emotions.

Through one of Aunt Anne's students, a fine woman named Mrs. Cunningham came, first for day-work, and then as a permanent member of the household. The heavy work was delegated to Thomas Grieves, who was remote kin of hers, and who came in as handy man and also became permanently attached to the family. Mrs. Cunningham was of British background, stable, serene, and competent and able to get on with everyone from Grandma to the baby. No amount of work, responsibility, clutter, or children underfoot seemed to disturb her. Best of all, Grandma might cook or do anything else she pleased, yet hand over any part of the job which was non-creative or boring, and be free to spend as much of the time with daughter Anne as she chose. Tom was a different proposition. He was of Irish descent, with a marvelous sense of humor and great versatility, but with an unfortunate history of "Jack of all trades and master of none." He was a one man's man, and everything went beautifully as long as the master of the household was at home. But the moment he left, poor Tom wanted to make decisions, to drop any work if anything more interesting suggested itself, to forget things on one shopping trip in order to be sent on another. But the children adored him, and he was never anything but exemplary when they were around. Grandma, though she scorned his shiftlessness, and refused to have him launder her clothes, or have anything to do with her room or possessions, forgave him everything, for the sake of the children.

Frank made a fine job of taking these two helpers into the Family Council and making them feel that they were a part of the Family Project. This applied to the operating of the work plans and schedules — and to family relations, and the educating of the children to the responsibilities they were supposed to assume, the work they had to do, and the records they were required to keep. His achievements as organizer and maintainer of the household and home projects were equally remarkable with those in the fields of industry and business.

A great help at this time was that the college girl, Helen Douglas, who fortunately was found easily, was enormously interested in the project. She listened spell-bound while Frank explained his aims and his attitudes and the techniques he wanted used. Every afternoon she took the older girls walking if the weather was fine, or read to all old enough to listen if the weather was unfavorable. Anne, especially, drank up every word. Her fine character, tireless patience, and beautiful serenity with her young charges, undoubtedly did much to enrich their lives. She was clever enough to prevent upheavals which might have happened when she had to be away, by asking if she might train in a few classmates to substitute for her. She did this adequately that the children felt no jolt, but enjoyed the changes in personality. "Helen's redheads" were known all over Pembrook College and in their neighborhood in the East Side District.

The relations with Brown were quickly established and very satisfactory. As *The Psychology of Management* had been published, a new thesis was set up, to be called *Waste in Teaching* which aimed to put the material from industry at the service of the educational group. At the same time Lillian would be able to get the new material in psychology and education and make this useful to management in the business and industrial fields. President Faunce was interested; Professor Colvin of the educational psychology; Professor Jacobs in education; and Dean Barus and many others proved cooperative. There was no need to hurry the project, and this had its advantages.

As for Frank, he was freer in many ways than he had been for many years. While the worries of closing up his constructing work were demanding and furnished some long-term problems, these would all become increasingly less pressing.

The work in the Management field proved even more engrossing, stimulating, and creative than the partners had dared to expect. What was more, there was much greater chance than there ever had been of their working together, and even more need to do this, since the new work was an integrated application of the findings of engineering and psychology in the industrial fields. They had a tremendous amount to learn in Scientific Management, and the days and nights that had been spent in the intensive study of the pioneer writings of Taylor and his followers more than paid for themselves. So did the faithful attendance at the meetings of the American Society of Mechanical Engineers, and the many new contacts which grew out of Frank's membership there. Among the friends and neighbors in Providence were not only John Aldrich of the Butt Company, but William Dart of the Brown and Sharp group, and above all, John R Freeman, the great civil and mechanical engineer, whose interests in photographs, in earthquakes, and in transferring management principles to techniques and even to forms made him and Frank congenial companions. Of course the most useful asset the partners had in the new work in the field of Management was their own special material on Motion Study. The fact that Frank had discovered this neglected area of work and had invented the units, methods, and devices for making the necessary measurements gave him a unique service to offer his clients. This the partners appreciated and, whatever else had to wait, never neglected the opportunity to develop, expand, use, and apply their Motion Study Methods.

Of course it was not possible for Frank to spend all of his time in Providence, but the job at the Butt Company did demand a great deal and it was surprising how much concentration — of your most interesting job, your home and family, and your satisfying friendships —into a small town, contributes to a satisfying work program. With this in mind, Frank planned to move his office there as soon as possible, and to specialize on work which did not mean so much travel. There were various things which mitigated against this — one was his background and experience of expanding, delight in travel and diversity, and ambition to achieve leadership. Another was the fact that interest in and opportunity in Scientific Management spread geographically, as well as through industries and business, in this country, abroad, and all over the world. World events, management events, family events, and his own temperament, were to take him far, but there were happy days at the plant, evenings at work at home, or at meetings in his own Taylor Hall and early mornings and weekends with the children at home or on excursions and little trips.

In the midst of these, another son joined the family — Bill — William Moller, born December 18, 1912.

He was born at 71 Brown Street, in the little house, proved to be small and blond and lively, was named for Mother's beloved Father, and certainly gave indications of being a Moller in looks and temperament. Every new baby was the idol of the family and especially Grandma Gilbreth's idol, but because Bill was so little and so delicate-looking, she took him to her heart at once, as did Helen Douglas. Frank was always good natured and happy, and not a bit disturbed by having the center of attention some one besides himself, and the little sisters were too motherly ever to resent a new baby. This was fortunate, as Bill took plenty of time and attention. His little slim body held an indomitable spirit and he crawled, walked, and climbed with indefatigable persistence. There was nothing he would not try and nothing he would not dare. Frank was his Daddy's pal and pride and hope, and went along on trips whenever this was possible. Bill occupied himself with giving full-time occupation to the family at home.

The older girls were by this time starting at the Lincoln School and never was there a more happy experience. Their father deprecated the fact that they were not at the public school, for he was a born democrat, so far as family and school as well as citizenship relationships were concerned. But their Mother was glad to have them taught by a gentle-woman, and hearing the speech and vocabulary of cultivated homes during those first impressionable years. When it came time for Frank to start school, the whole group was moved to the nearest good public school. Fortunately, by then, Andie was old enough to shepherd the crowd, and the school they attended was excellent. Never were youngsters more adequately prepared for school experience than these were by their father. He anticipated difficulties; he taught methods of solving problems; rather than working out solutions and handing them over. Above all, he made every subject so fascinating that every child took an open and an interested mind with him to the subject at hand. Parent-Teacher meetings were as carefully entered on his schedule as technical meetings, and any request to speak for the school had priority over any other invitation.

One of his chief pleasures was turning learning into a game. He had always believed that interest was essential to learning and had thought through his own experience, at school and outside school, in the light of the principles which the partners' reading in psychology and education made evident. He did not agree with all the material in books, but he checked it carefully by his own experience and his wife's — used everything that he got — and tried to fit his own experiences which did not check with the theory into such findings as he had accepted. He had found some of the experiments made with him — such as learning the metric system before he learned the complicated systems of weights and measures usually taught in the Boston schools — very profitable. It was interesting to see how the boy, who had been a student in the school where practice teachers were trained, had profited not only by the material taught but the techniques used in the teaching. He bought wooden models of pyramids and cones which could be separated into sections, and taught the children the fundamentals of geometry. He bought a cup and a wooden model of a sphere and taught them something about physics. He had large copies of a chart of squares printed and taught them all of the rapid calculation one could do by memorizing the squares of numbers from one to one hundred. He had no inhibition about taking them with him not only on pleasure trips, but on work trips when this was possible. He spent every possible minute on excursions pointing out interesting things and training them to be observant. When he came back from a trip, his pockets, briefcase, and suitcase, were full of things he had picked up everywhere that might be interesting to them — bits of fabric and metal and cotton from the shops, all kinds of gadgets, time-tables and maps — these he would bring out at the dinner table and pass around and ask, "What do you think this is?" If the discussion demanded reference books, these were close at hand, for he had had them moved into the dining room. If the table became crowded, there was a set of nesting tea-tables close at hand to take the overflow. The one criterion of table talk was "It is interesting?" and the most blighting criticism often supplied in a piping voice by the youngest was "Not of general interest!" All kinds of experiments were encouraged and when Bill attempted to feed himself with two spoons instead of one, operating like a clam-shell bucket, his mother and grandmother, who thought it a fine opportunity to teach table manners, were stopped until he could determine for himself whether it was an effective procedure or not.

Of course, there were complications at school when the children challenged information, or insisted on supplying it, starting always with "My Daddy says!" and ending with "My Daddy knows!" — but he was never too busy to straighten these out, and the teachers, like the household helpers, and the devoted Helen and her group, gladly co-operated in the project.

Frank's diary at this time showed lectures for the N.E. Butt Company group at Taylor [Hall] and visits of Mr. Taylor, Mr. Brandeis, and others of the Management Group, to Providence; trips to Dartmouth to lecture there; frequent visits to the Engineer's Library; and conferences with Miss. Margaret Mann and Dr. Craver; papers for the American Society of Mechanical Engineers; visits to the Dodges in Philadelphia; work with Doctor Howell on the New York Hospital motion studies; and to the Mayo Brothers' at Rochester.

On April 1, 1913, pioneer stereochronocyclegraphs of Lillian were taken in the home laboratory and Frank was as much thrilled with this new technique as he had been with the early Micro-motion study. In April, he went to see Professor Johnson; then to New York to talk with Will Irwin and Norman Hapgood. He conferred with Mr. Ball, the editor of the *Sunday Providence Journal* on articles for that conservative Sunday paper; and went to Andrews Field at Brown University to make Micromotion studies of track meets and baseball games. He supplied Robert Kent with cyclegraph material for his magazine, took the stereochronocyclegraphs to Philadelphia to show the Bancrofts; photographed some football; described his cyclegraph techniques to Mr. Taylor and Morris Cooke; and dashed back and forth from Philadelphia to New York to Providence to Boston. His notes show that he had been reading Pepys' diary and Boswell for he says, "Coming over on the 633 from Providence I did find my classmate, "C," who once did kill a man who tried to rob him and also on the same train was "D" who looks, with his hat off, exactly like an ostrich before it is hatched!"

The spring went happily, for not only was the installation at the Butt Company coming on splendidly, but the research in Motion Study techniques gave limitless material for magazine articles and new books. It was a thrill to both partners to find the Motion Study techniques so serviceable not only in business and industry, but in surgery, in the sports, and in the home. All the practice accumulating seemed to fit together and furnish an increasing number of rules for Motion Study, and these rules, as the partners followed them out into an increasing diversity of fields of application, gave such interesting experiences that days were not long enough to enjoy them. Certainly, in this period — if ever — they were having work which was play! In every city were cordial, inspiring friends, and every mail brought new opportunities. Even the places and times scheduled seemed extraordinarily satisfactory, with spring American Society of Mechanical Engineer meeting in Baltimore; and an opportunity to take micromotion pictures of the Giants at the baseball game; May thirty-first in New York; and — best of all — a chance to be members of the American Society of Mechanical Engineers' party which was to join the Verein Deutscher Ingineur in Germany for a series of meetings.

The previous trip which the partners had made with the American Society of Mechanical Engineers, to England, had been stimulating and interesting, perhaps because of the companionship of many of the Management Group. As they planned for this one, Lillian thought over these experiences. The Dodges and their family had been there, also Frederick and Mrs. Taylor, and the meetings in London and the excursions through a few industries had been — to her — something completely new! The only part of England which looked as it had on her previous trip was Stratford-on-Avon where she and Frank went primarily to see his old friend, Josephine Preston Peabody, get an award. She had been touched to see the time Frank took to select one perfect rose to send to his friend as an appropriate tribute and to recognize a love for the beauty and perfection — which he acted in his daily life, but seldom spoke of. Lillian had noted, too, how easily and quickly he met people of all kinds, and how at home he was in every industrial and social situation, and of course it had been pleasant to visit with the Kershaws and the Tillotsons, and to have her first glimpses of British home life.

This trip to Germany was to be much more complicated and required much more planning. Baby Bill seemed well, but was still very thin, and light-weight, and she could not bear to tear herself away from him, even though Aunt Anne, Grandma, and Helen would lavish every attention upon him. Frank was determined she should go on the trip and quite willing to take the baby along. They started off and the experiment worked beautifully. It had been decided not to take a nurse because of the extra expense, and to take as little luggage as possible, as Frank was sure an excellent nurse and anything necessary could be easily acquired on the "other side." Two other small babies made the trip, each accompanied by a trained nurse, and mountains of luggage. Both trained nurses immediately took to their beds with sea-sickness and the mothers had not only the babies but the nurses to look out for! The small Bill in the three-piece gray knit wool "Teddy-bear" suit which his father had selected for him, and in the bureau drawer stuffed with pillow which his father fixed for his bed, seemed perfectly content. His mother, too busy with him to be sea-sick, enjoyed every minute of the trip, and his father perched him on his arm and took him everywhere to be made much of by engineers; sailors; the entire personnel of the crew and passenger list. A cable to friends in Berlin brought a trained baby-nurse to the pier to meet them. Sister Clara was German and Dutch, with probably a touch of Japanese, and not only competent but extremely good looking. She took over not only her small charge, and all his problems, but his father and mother as well. It was a little appalling to Lillian to have him and the luggage and Sister Clara vanish in a taxi, but when their own taxi arrived at the hotel, Sister Clara had pre-empted the best of the available rooms reserved for the party; had certified milk on its way from the nearest supply place; the bags unpacked; and everything in order! Only a certain number in the party could expect outside rooms and private baths at each stopping place. This did not daunt Sister Clara. In her uniform, and short veil, and with the small Bill lightly but securely held in her arm, she beat the entire party day after day to the registration desk and had exactly what she wanted of location and service, whatever anyone else got! She assumed not only all responsibility but all explanations, and was so tactful and so good-looking that the men of the party seconded any plan she proposed and persuaded their women-folks if not to concurrence, at least to silence! Perhaps Bill, with his Brownie cap and his broad smile, helped!

Never in all her life had Lillian had such a luxurious experience. Sister Clara was valet and lady's-maid and nurse and advisor and schedule keeper and everything else. The proper clothes appeared — expertly cleaned and pressed and mended and assembled for each occasion. The baby was there to play with, or asleep, as was most convenient. When the happy crowded days of Munich were over, and Sister Clara bade them "Good-bye" at the train, Frank wished he could kidnap her to take to America and Lillian almost shed tears of happiness as she looked at her strong, rosy, little boy who was pounds heavier and much more serene and quiet after his few weeks in Sister Clara's care.

Only a day-by-day review of the beautiful program prepared by the German group can give any idea of the multitude of experiences. Marvelous technical meetings and formal occasions such as the one where the King of Saxony received an honorary degree, and the one when George Westinghouse received a medal for his researches — excursions — and a series of luncheons, dinner and evening parties — Frank completely carefree — making notes of savings, and wasted motions and tremendously impressed by the savings in material and the waste in human effort. "Even the elevator man puts out the light whenever there is no one in the car; but at every stop, he opens the doors outward, steps into the hall, bows, and then steps back into the elevator!"

Coming back on the *Arabic*, Frank had a marvelous time with some Oxford students who proved greatly interested in Motion Study and conducted what was practically a Short Course, all the way across the ocean. The family at home had been fine all through the trip, and the small Andie was taking more and more responsibility and leadership. All the old happy holiday traditions of the Moller household were added to the New England background and the traditions there. Hanging of May-baskets, on May day; dressing up and going from door-to-door in the neighborhood on Halloween; the new England type of celebration for Thanksgiving; Easter egg hunts — all combined happily with the Moller Christmas traditions, and the elaborate celebrations for birthdays, St. Valentine's parties, and Memorial Day excursions. Sometimes Andie's inventions made life a little complicated — the small chickens bought experimentally one Easter were loved to death — carefully buried in the garden with their feet above ground so that the grave could be easily located for mourning, and surrounded by the flowers from the new Sunday hats, including Lillian's, when no fresh flowers were available. As the others proved not behind-hand in initiative and invention, no day ever proved monotonous!

The comfortable little half-house at 71 Brown Street proved too small and the family moved next door, to 77, on the corner, which was almost ideal. Downstairs there was a living room, large enough to be turned into an experimental project if Daddy decided to invite a group from Teacher's College in New York to come up and experiment with micro-motion bed-making. Next to this, the dining room was big enough to include Aunt Anne, Uncle Fred, John and Carol on holidays. Then the kitchen where Grandma happily made pies and doughnuts, with Mrs. Cunningham as tender, and as many small children as tasters as could fit in; and the back porch where the overflow sat, to beg for cookies hot from the oven. On the other side of the hallway, the entire left side of the house, overlooking Angell Street, was turned into an office and workplace, which — supplemented by Taylor Hall at Aunt Anne's a few blocks away — for some years met every possible need. Here one and then two secretaries took over and became whole-hearted co-operators and gradually here all activities of the Gilbreth business centered. Frank became increasingly convinced that there were intensive advantages to a man in having his office in his home, as so many European men have. The Dictaphone made it possible to work any hour of the day or night and branch offices in every industry where he did consulting were decentralized, where that was valuable. The real problem became co-ordination of these branch offices, which spread throughout the country and abroad, with the Providence set-up. And their great advantage was the fact that Lillian could spend so much time and do so much work without being far away from the home and family problems. Also, the two partners could utilize every available moment or ounce of energy to work together and take advantage of any changes in plans which made an extra supply available.

There were certain fundamental problems which were always present. Lillian was — by inheritance, experience, and training — a morning worker. Frank always preferred to do his work at night, and could work on — if he had to —hours and days without stopping. Lillian had to change work frequently and thought it fortunate that her home and family life provided so many interruptions — some necessary and some unnecessary — but none the less welcome. Frank tried to adapt his likings to hers, but soon found the only way they could really accomplish most was to set up the schedule, foresee and provide for handling interruptions, and do his best to keep her on the job. One of his masterpieces had been seeing that she wrote *The Psychology of Management.* He had set up a Gantt Chart, provided Dictaphone cylinders, and checked up on her progress, until the first draft was made, and then helped through every stage, until the book was on the shelf. This accomplished feat persuaded her of the validity of his method and from that time on he had an easier time. With the years, naturally, they developed more and more effective ways of working together. He became a most voluminous writer and perfected the technique of recording his thoughts on his Dictaphone, which he called is "Thotrap," or in his Lefax notebook, or books which he carried with him everywhere. As he carefully indexed the subjects on every page, it was possible to file the sheets easily and put his assembled material in his hands, whenever he needed it. From this, he wrote manuscripts, longhand, on the steamer, or on the train, or wherever he was — every moment he could snatch — and the result he brought back or mailed back to her to be revised; then taken on another trip for additions, or his own revisions, and so on, until the material was ready to be presented as a paper or published immediately.

Fortunately, she had realized even before she married him, that her best job would be as "tender," and that nothing was so important as to make it possible for him to work, and to help him in every way she could. She gathered up everything he had done — from the imprisoned balls and small pincers which he had carved with his jackknife out of his mother's broomstick handles; to the publicity he had published through the contracting years; or that which had appeared about his work in newspapers, magazine, etc. These became a part of the "N" file, or "Notes-File," which he started, and had their own section as drawer after drawer was filled with Management material of all sorts. Photographs, notes, publicity, papers — accumulated with greater and greater speed, becoming more and more bulky, but the mnemonic classification provided adequate filing system and kept things in order. The accumulating books were not so easy to house and the photography equipment was a real problem. Many a trip, Frank started off with luggage and equipment which filled not one cab but two, and his return always meant more things than he had started with. But in spite of Tom's inspired techniques of mixing everything up, surprisingly few delays occurred, and these seldom proved serious. It was certainly annoying to Frank to find, as he occasionally did, that some indispensable piece of clothing, equipment, or data, had been left at home, but it was fun for Lillian to check with Grandma, and Aunt Anne, and the household staff, and catch the first train — often to have a chance to look over the progress of a job, meet the client, and take home new data and a new drive from the experience.

The work at Brown University progressed slowly, but satisfactorily, for the real purpose was not the "Ph.D." which was the ultimate result, but the constant feeding of new material — in the areas of psychology, education, and personnel — into the data to be used on the jobs. Every possible expansion must take place, for the number and diversity of jobs was increasing. Everything must be done, too, to see that domestic affairs ran smoothly. The children's educational program must be carefully planned, for there was Aunt Anne willing to give, or arrange for, piano or violin lessons, and that meant practice schedules to be added to the study for school. Andie took to both piano and violin happily. Ern, who had a fine ear and a sweet voice, preferred improvising to practice; Martha had a baby 'cello; Frank and Bill seemed to prefer rhythms to mastering an instrument. The girls naturally took to dancing school more easily than the boys; all went to Sunday school, though Dad had insisted that should be made optional. He was greatly opposed to forcing religious obser-vances upon the children and felt that if they joined the Church, it must be because they themselves wanted to do this and not because they were forced to. Deeply religious at heart, and with tremendous reverence for God's Works as they showed themselves in the heavens, the earth, and the sea, with a tremendous admiration for the laws by which the universe runs, and the findings of science — he was not a church-goer — and, like Taylor, felt that the minister took an unfair advantage in speaking without allowing his hearers to answer back!

An observer and a lover of out-of-doors, he preferred to spend Sundays, if the weather was fine, out in the automobile. But Sunday morning sleep was a great treat to him, after the many late nights at work. So the children were sent off to Sunday school and were back and ready for play when he got up for the one o'clock dinner which Grandmother had made into such a marvelous experience that even sleep could not compete with it. But, if everything was to run smoothly, Lillian felt she must be on the job. Besides, she could not bear to miss one of his waking minutes, because work kept him from home so much. So that the children fur-nished the one contact, at the time, with the Church and Church school. The girls were dressy little creatures and rejoiced in Sunday furbelows. Like most mothers, she insisted that the boys wear blue serge and white collars, and be all slicked up, for her satisfaction, at least through Sunday dinner, even though this caused considerable agony of spirit. Perhaps she did a little surreptitious influencing of votes at the Family Council meeting to make this possible, but she was so obviously happy in the result and Grandma seconded her so nobly that no protests were made!

One increasingly difficult problem was summer vacation. In many ways, it seemed simpler and easier to stay in the comfortable Brown Street house. On a corner, it had ample windows for all four sides, with a breeze coming through during the hottest weather. The Brown University campus was practically deserted through the summer season and made an ideal and almost private park. A few hours in the faithful car took one to lovely picnic spots with sunshine and flowers and fresh or salt water, and the comfort of supper at home, and one's own bath and bed to finish the day. But a change, of course, is attractive and weekends at Block Island or Narragansett or Jamestown, where the Darts and the Dodges spent their summers, had their attractions. Taking a summer place presented difficulties because so much furniture, equipment, and clothing had to go along. So far as Lillian was concerned, the results were hardly worth the effort. She was still unconsciously, as on the houseboat at Port Washington, trying to impose standards of living inappropriate to the problem at hand, with not always great success. It would have been so much better and easier to present the problem in all its details to Frank for simplification and solution! But an unwillingness to burden him with what seemed unnecessary problems, and a pride in keeping annoying small details out of his busy life, meant that many times she was so tired that it was all she could do to keep from boxing ears all around, or putting all the small fry unceremoniously to bed until a good night's sleep could set everything to rights again. Gradually she came to realize that it was more important to be rested and able to enjoy family parties than to insist on elaborate routine and costumes which had no real value and gave no real satisfaction. It was a much-needed and impressive lesson — that simple clothes, simple meals, and a simple program took less time and effort and gave more pleasure than complicated ones. It meant that the one real problem was simplification!

The year 1914 was a diversified one. The trip to Germany proved to be very profitable, for Frank soon had two fine contracts there underway.

One was at the Auergesellschaft in Berlin, where Welsbach lamps were being made, and the other at the Zeiss Company, in Jena. It was a satisfaction that neither company was making anything that had anything to do with preparation for war. Frank was especially happy over the job with Jena because all his life he had been interested in lenses, as used in microscopes, telescopes, and cameras. Here was a chance not only to get to know more about them, but to get new equipment for the motion study work. He would probably have been glad to have worked without pay or to have taken all his pay in lenses, binoculars, et cetera, though he had no idea at the time that he would take his final payments in this currency because of the difficulty in transferring money to the United States. He made some wonderful friends in the Jena plant, but also enjoyed his stay in Berlin and his contact not only with Dr. Schlesinger and the other engineering friends, but with those who helped him on the job. Chief of these was Irene Witte, who was assigned to him as a translator and secretary, but who proved such an apt student and so intensely interested in management, that she took over almost as fast as he could give. The year was a series of trips across the ocean.

In March, the Moller family stopped for a visit in Providence on their way to Europe. Jane and May Bunker came for a visit also and Mr. Remane of the Auer came to Providence to see the New England Butt Company and to accompany Frank back to the German jobs. These went splendidly and he managed to visit Cologne and Aachen and also to have the thrill of visiting Dr. Lucien Bull at the Marey Institute in Paris. It was a pleasure to represent the American Society of Mechanical Engineers at the dedication of the Verein Deutscher Ingineur in June, before returning home for a busy summer.

For a new project, the first Summer School in Scientific Management was to be held in August. This was an attempt to meet the requests of various teachers of economics, industrial engineering, and related subjects, for information on management, but especially Motion Study, and a small, highly-selected congenial group met for several weeks; visiting the New England Butt Company and hearing lectures and taking part in discussion at Taylor Hall. The unedited notes of the summer session give an excellent picture of progress in the Management field up to this time. The celebration of Mother Gilbreth's eightieth birthday on August 26 was the high spot of the social part of the session. It closed August 28, and on the 29th, Frank sailed back to Germany. The School had been a very satisfactory experience, as the group had become vitally interested in fatigue elimination, and had promised in all the colleges represented to start "Fatigue Elimination Day" with the first Monday in December and to make it an annual event.

Frank had a very happy trip to Holland — one of a series which resulted in a warm friendship with Captain Krol, of the Holland-American Line. It was a treat to see him start a trip, because as soon as he was on deck, all his worries and problems seemed to vanish. He put on his favorite peaked travel cap, which was of an indeterminate tan and green plaid — which the family hated, but he liked — got out his pipe; swung his field glasses and his camera around his neck; and prepared for that enjoyment of a sea voyage which only a wonderful sailor has. All boats had this effect on him — the houseboat and the motor boat in the Port Washington days, and now the sailboat, and even the rowboat, which were part of every summer when he could manage it. Experiences began to be dramatic because of the war. The boat was held at Queenstown and his diary and letters contained full and exciting accounts of what happened to him everywhere. Several of the American organization, including Whitaker, Allen and others, were established on the German jobs, which progressed by leaps and bounds. He worked as usual, strenuously and effectively, but never was too tired to notice everything going on in the cities where he was, or to spend his weekends and rare holidays in the Deutsches Museum in Munich where he and Dr. Von Miller spent happy hours together. The stops in Paris or London meant renewals of old friendships, as well as new sightseeing and contacts. He got home for Christmas, but went back shortly after, and these recurrent, rapid trips went on and on.

The new little daughter who had come to join the family in June arrived as quietly and lived as serenely as she was to go taking part in family, home, and community life. She had lovely blue eyes and golden hair and a feeling for perfection, which the family sensed and appreciated, in a variety of ways. Ever since Frank Junior had been named, his father had vowed that the next girl should be named for her Mother. Lillian had never liked her name and was eager to have the new baby called "Constance." It was the name she had wished for herself, and had urged without success for her youngest sister. But Frank was firm, and little Lill fortunately proved to be satisfied with her name and the reasons why she had it. The larger the family the more care and petting the baby gets! So, perhaps, it was fortunate that no Gilbreth child ever occupied that position very long!

The household ran smoothly, and the work at Brown progressed in spite of many interruptions. The children kept well and happy and during Frank's trips, Lillian used every available minute to complete her work for the degree which she hoped for at the 1915 commencement. Both the partners were encouraged by increased appreciation for their work. Dr. G. Stanley Hall invited them to Clark University, where Frank gave a lecture and they both took part in a seminar. It was encouraging to know that Dr. Hall and Dr. Burnham felt that real contributions had been made in the fields of "Skill Study" and "Fatigue Study." Dr. Poole and Dr. Bancroft came on to visit at 77 Brown Street and discussed the progress in application of Motion Study to hospitals and to surgery. Frank had time to make one of his trips via Italy and to stop at Naples and Herculanium as well as at Milan before he went on to the jobs. He visited hospitals abroad, checking on his hospital studies, and was also busy at setting up the international work for the handicapped. More and more of his time in the United States was spent on this hospital work and the diary entries for 1915 are full of projects in the New York Hospital and visits to the Boston City Hospital. There was time, too, for lectures at colleges and universities in the Midwest as well as in the East.

Lillian spent much of her time at home, but did succeed in making one rushed trip to California to see the family — something which she was to do every year or two as long as the dear parents were alive.

The ordeal of the year was taking the oral examination for her Doctorate, after having had the thesis accepted, and no detail of the experience was ever forgotten. It was a rainy day; Frank was in Europe; she sat for long hours answering questions; was so nervous that her definition of psychology offended one of the examiners, who barked out, "So you have become a behaviorist, have you?"; had no notion how she was progressing, and when the committee filed out to discuss what she had done, and polled their votes, felt sure that she had failed. When kind Dean Barris led the procession back and said, "I am pleased to announce," she never heard the end of the sentence, for she was convinced that he would only have been pleased had she passed! She ran home happily through the rain to cable Frank, and tried to explain to the children why she was excited, and what a "Ph.D." meant.

Commencement Day was beautiful and sunny, and, except for Frank's being on the ocean instead of on the campus, perfect in every way. President Wheeler had come on from California for his class reunion, and seemed in some way to represent not only the beloved home campus, but the friends and family as well. It was a thrill to speak to him, as the academic procession marched through the line of alumni while it reversed itself, but an even greater thrill after the exercises to present the spotless children, whom Helen had herded to the campus, to him, with certainly a "These are my jewels!" feeling, although the words were not used.

When Frank arrived, his first question at the pier was, "Did you get it?" As this was shouted before the steamer docked, the hearers must have been curious as well as amused, but nothing like that ever bothered him at all. Lillian had gotten rid of a considerable number of senseless inhibitions, but she remembered with amusement the day she had happened to meet him in the subway, soon after they were married, and he, sensing her embarrassment, had shouted, "Hello! How are you? Have you got your divorce yet?"

There never was a more inveterate or a more skillful tease or one who took more pleasure in teasing, and even now that so many children had come to share the job of being teased, none proved to be such an acceptable object as Lillian because none found it more embarrassing and more difficult to cope with. He always said she had no sense of humor. She always said she had, or she could not have lived with him!

Each year seemed to bring a greater diversification of projects, all of which were intensely fascinating. While most generous in allowing all his Motion Study devices as well as methods to be used, Frank was interested to see what types of patents he could get in order to turn over his material in a more unified form and with a greater assurance of the work being done effectively.

He could see the extension of use and also the adaptability of the techniques to a great variety of applications. He made a rapid trip to Canada early in 1916 to demonstrate his Motion Study Methods and establish the basis for getting patents there and as he was doing the same sort of thing both in England and in Germany, the prospects for extensive patents seemed very good. This never interested him except as a provision for maintaining standards in the Motion Study work — for his papers before the Engineering Society and at the colleges gave every detail of the progress freely and fully, and his diary notes made it evident — as did his conversations with his partner — that they both agreed the main object was to make these inventions and developments useful as rapidly as possible.

The material was getting a wider and wider hearing as they checked it, not only with the work done in engineering, but with the findings in education and psychology.

Unfortunately, nothing much could be done except trial and error work in the field of "Fatigue" because there were not adequate definitions, or units of measurement, but both the Micro-motion method and the Cyclegraph were already making contributions in the field of skill study and education. Certain devices like the wire model and the stereo-ochronocyclegraphs were developed because of possible serviceability in the field of training, and it was a delight to Lillian to see that her years in the field of education and psychology furnished useful material. Even more satisfactory was the work the partners had done together in this field which made it possible to use everything appearing in the development as a check for the Motion Study work or as a stimulus to it.

It was remarkable how much territory — geographical and otherwise — Frank managed to cover. He dashed out to Milwaukee for a lecture, and then up to Madison to speak for Professor Torkelson and meet the President of the university. He stopped to see Russell Bond in New York and entertained Harold Gould in Providence. He became a member of the American Posture League and of the Simplified Spelling Board. He took a hurried trip to Columbus to visit Professor Sanborn and push the hospital standardization work. He undertook to help Mr. Barrett systematize the Pan-American Union, as a volunteer project. He went to the A.S.M.E. meeting in New Orleans; became interested in the problem of harvesting sugar-cane; and had a great visit with his old friend Sam Wellman. The two were by now so stout that they were called the "Gold Dust Twins." His number of friends in the magazine field grew — French Strother, Mr. Townsend, and Norman Hapgood, among the number. He made a careful trip through the Ford plant and dashed up to Ann Arbor to see the Bursleys and back to Detroit to visit Babcock and see his route board. He went to Philadelphia to see the Bancrofts and the Dodges. He undertook, at the suggestion of, and with the help of Walter Camp, to make Micro-motion and Cyclegraph studies of Gil Nichols and Ouimet, the golfers, in the Providence laboratory. He threw himself whole-heartedly into his work for the Remington Company and the detailed studies of typing which are so carefully and exhaustively recorded in the "N"-file. His job with the Eastman Kodak Company kept him in touch with the latest developments in the photographic field and he never traveled without cameras of all sorts. It caused him great satisfaction when Robert Kent reported that Taylor had been dissatisfied with much of the Time Study data and felt that it must be done over.

In spite of all this work, he took time to run the Second Summer School of Management, which closed on the twelfth of August. He was at a job in Cohoes in New York when Anne Cross phoned him that he had a new son, born in Buttonwoods, Rhode Island, early that morning.

The coming of Fred Moller Gilbreth was in keeping with the lively and original nature with which he was endowed. The family had moved down to the shore and expected to be adequately supplied with trained nurse, doctor, et cetera, before his arrival. But for some unknown reason no one was in the house — when he made his entrance, bawling lustily and apparently quite able to take care of himself — but his Mother, Mrs. Cunningham's young sister Annie, and the hastily summoned neighbor, who was so afraid to meet him that she complicated the situation considerably. Fred had blue eyes and lovely red curls which his father said were "Wasted on a boy!" and he and his Father became pals on sight. The summer was a happy one, in spite of many hot days, for the children loved the water; Grandma had many friends; and things ran so smoothly that Lillian had little to do except take care of and play with the new baby.

As always, Grandma's birthday, August 26th, was kept as a family holiday and Frank only regretted that this new son could not have been born on her anniversary. He was named for Fred Moller, in spite of his strong resemblance to the Bunkers, and became the first of a line of namesakes which increased with the years.

Everything went well with the partners, for the work spread and all the jobs ran smoothly. The hard disciplines of the construction business made handling the new jobs seem easy. Both partners enjoyed the problems presented and the contacts they afforded, and key people in all the organizations where they worked became friends — and many of them life-long friends.

Frank never stopped in New York without seeing Calvin Rice and profiting by his advice. He had several jobs in Upper New York, including one with Pierce Arrow Company, and his visits there meant not only happy, long days and nights in the factory, but visits with Mr. Kennedy and Mr. Cluett at the Troy Club. The Remington job meant visits with Mr. George Dickerman. He sometimes stopped to take dinner with the whole family at the Brown Street house, and the quiet modest gentleman would have been much astonished if he had known that the Gilbreth Family at a Family Council meeting awarded him the prize for the most popular visitor of the year because, "He never talked down to us!" When, in appreciation of the hospitality, he sent a fine new edition of the *Book of Knowledge* to join the reference library in the dining room, his place in the household was established and always waiting for him.

The Remington contract was a fascinating one because of its many ramifications. The section of it which received most attention in the Providence laboratory was the "Speed School"; for the supervisor (Mr. Waters), several of the experts and the most promising beginners came to Providence for a protracted stay and co-operatively submitted themselves not only to tests of aptitude, ability, and skill, but to all the psychological tests which the Brown laboratories could provide. When at the Chicago Business Show in September "our" amateur won, the family, as well as the entire organization, was jubilant.

Frank was increasingly enjoying the social as well as the technical contacts in Providence. He became a member of the Providence Engineering Society and rejoiced when John R. Freeman gave them beautiful rooms in one of his buildings. He also joined the "Town Criers" which was a local service club, and became friendly with its members. The only reason he did not join some of the other clubs like the Art Club was because Sister Anne had a membership and he and Lillian could go with her whenever they chose. Lillian had her own club work to be seen to when he was away. Every other week meetings of the Wednesday Club, with the necessity of debating herself once a year; work in the P.T.A. demanded by the children; and membership and finally Presidency of the Collegiate Alumni, which was the forerunner of the American Association of University Women. It astonished her greatly when she was asked to be President of the local group, but Frank thought it advisable to accept, and she felt she had obligations to any group which tried to be useful to the colleges. It was a little disillusioning to be told, after her election, when she foolishly asked why she had been selected, that she was the only person in the club who was acceptable to everyone because she was the only member so new that she had not become affiliated with any small clique.

The one book which appeared this year was *Fatigue Study*. The two partners had outlined this and accumulated the material with great interest. They realized it could not be as sound technically as the ones they had written or the ones they planned because of the lack of technical knowledge in the field. But it was possible to assemble the material on rest periods, chairs, "home reading box" at the New England Butt Company, the "Fatigue Museum" at Taylor Hall, and the other descriptions of attempts to eliminate fatigue or provide for overcoming it. Because Frank was away so much and was so rushed, this time Lillian drew up the first draft, and never forgot Frank's terse comment when he read it — "It certainly is gabby!"

Well, it certainly was, but at that time nothing much more dignified and exact was possible, and the book seemed to meet a certain need and be useful to a certain group.

Frank and Lillian relaxing in Buttonwoods, Rhode Island (1916)

The book which appeared in 1917, *Applied Motion Study*, was exactly the opposite of *Fatigue Study* — in that it was anything buy "gabby" and that it contained some of the most carefully thought-through and well-documented material which the partners had ever published. It consisted of chapters which had been articles presented before technical societies. This meant a certain amount of repetition and a scientific rather than popular presentation. While some of the literary defects bothered Lillian considerably, they did not bother Frank, who felt it was far more important to get one's material into print and being used than it was to take time to polish and to refine.

A stream of papers for magazines and for meetings and mountains of notes for the "N"-file accumulated, to be sorted and put into place as rapidly as possible. Creating new material naturally seemed to Frank more important than reviewing what to him immediately became old stuff. But the symbol numbers made at least a first grouping possible and that meant that all of the material in the field was at hand, if it was needed.

1917 brought a further and a happy expansion of the work. The U.S. Rubber Company became a valued and an interesting client. The National Surety was another, with many new problems ramifying into the office field. Many lectures at colleges took Frank to Cleveland, New Haven, State College, Columbia, and farther afield. The "Crippled Soldier" work became a major interest, and more and more writing and speaking was done in that area — yet Frank found time to go to the Town Criers' Club either as a speaker or a listener, and even to the John Howland School where the children were, to visit the teachers and to keep in touch with their work. He was increasingly eager to help in every way toward furthering the cause of the Allies in the World War — in March helping subscribe for the first Technical Club Ambulance; going to Dayton to talk with the National Cash Register people about jobs for crippled soldiers; and keeping in touch with all the occupational therapy everywhere which might be useful. It was through this work that he met

Professor Blessing and Major Allen Cullimore. The latter had lost his arm in an accident, and was delighted to show he had overcome his handicap, in order to help cripples overcome theirs. A fine, courageous spirit, he demonstrated even in those early days, the qualities that were to make him a leader in engineering and education.

On April sixth, when this country declared war against Germany, Frank dashed to Washington to volunteer his services following a telegram he sent, in which he said — none to diplomatically — that if they did not know how they could use his services, he would tell them! He dashed from office to office, seeing Howard A. Coffin, Secretary Baker, Captain Ridley, Major Tyler, Captain Black, Major Mitchell, and General Gorgas. He would have liked to have gone overseas at once with the Construction Division, but was willing to do anything so long as he could be useful at once. It was not easy for the family in Providence to give him up to the service, but he was so unhappy at the thought of staying out or delaying, that his wife felt that he must go at once if he felt so tremendously impelled to do this.

Fortunately, he could be at home the day of the "Tonsil Party!" Always liking to do things wholesale, Frank had had all the children tested for "tonsils" and it was decided that all down through Bill needed to have theirs removed —all, that is, except Martha, who was to go to Aunt Anne's to spend the morning. It was April twelfth, a clear morning. The entire lower floor was turned into an operating room and the upper floor into a ward. Martha joyously ate a hearty breakfast with Daddy, while Lillian starved with the other children. Two doctors arrived, with an accompaniment of nurses, and the work started. It was not until Ernestine's tonsils were out that the doctor recognized that she was the only one who had not needed the operation. Thereupon poor Martha was dragged protestingly home, subjected to the either in spite of roars and kicks which almost subdued the entire operating group, and lost not only the tonsils but the wonderful breakfast! Anyone who has tried the experiment of nursing several youngsters through the convalescent period after this particular operation has missed something.

Frank continued with his jobs and the technical meetings always incident to May, but used every free minute to besiege the Washington Group for an assignment in the service. In June, he and Lillian attended the Sagamore Conference, which his old friend, George Coleman, of the English High School days, ran every summer at his beautiful home at Sagamore-on-the-Cape. It was a fine opportunity to check up on progress in sociology and problems in that area. In August, Frank took his mother to Nantucket. It was a great treat to them both for he had put up a big barn there in his early days in construction work and was anxious to have her admire the beautiful stonework which he had never had an opportunity to show off before. They loved the bathing and the sunshine and the quaint old town and driving around on the moors, and it was a treat to them both to be off together again.

The Third Summer School was run with especial emphasis on war-time problems.

Meantime, Lillian had had a unique experience. The California family had been clamoring for a visit, so she decided to take the children West, with the help of Mrs. Cunningham. That meant the four girls — Anne, Ernestine, Martha, and Lillian — and the three boys — Frank, Bill, and the little Freddy. They had ample room on the train and every possible help, yet it was a very fatiguing experience. The children who were in the drawing room always wanted to be out in the car with Mrs. Cunningham, and those who were with her there preferred the drawing room. They experimented with the diner, and with the large lunch basket packed at home, supplemented with malted milk, which seemed to be the favorite at the moment, and which Lillian came to hate for the rest of her life! It was good to get to Oakland, and to be met by the adoring family. It is awful to think what an upheaval that peaceful household had! The day when Grandmother invited the family friends "to see Lillie's little girls" and these petted darlings were put into their best white dresses and

Lillian at work in Providence, Rhode Island, with 8 of the children –
shortly after Daniel's birth (1916)

satin hair-bows only to follow Andie under the sprinkler which was inopportunely going on the lawn and to appear before the guests bedraggled and dripping — the day when little Ernestine went on a "sit-down strike" and refused to go out into any car but Grandma's Packard limousine — the many days when the lively Bill and the faithful Frank got into all sorts of mischief — and the problem of trying to find any time in the twenty-four hours when the co-operative but exhausted family could get any kind of rest!!

The trip back was hot and dusty — for this was before the day of air-conditioning. While undoubtedly Providence was hot, too, early in September — it was good to get back and to find Grandma and Daddy and good faithful Tom ready and waiting to welcome them. On the 17th of September, Daniel Bunker Gilbreth joined the family group. He was pink and white and blue-eyed and very blond and smiling, and everyone's idol at once and the very personal chum and possession of the small Fred who called him "Honey" and never wanted to let him out of his sight! Anne was already developing a great sense of responsibility and took the two smallest boys under her careful care whenever she was home from school. She was making a fine record there and it was undoubtedly due, partly, to her example that the others were all progressing as well as they did.

About ten days after Daniel's appearance, *Applied Motion Study* came from the press and became the second highlight of the month of September.

Frank continued to visit his jobs, including the Pierce Arrow Plant at Buffalo, which was a particularly satisfactory job, because of his great admiration for the Pierce Arrow car. He kept in close contact with his Washington friends in the Surgeon General's office, especially with Colonel Owen, who became his devoted friend, and with whom he talked over every aspect of the Crippled Soldier work.

On November 9th, Colonel Bowman asked him to join the War College Course and co-operate as a Major of Engineers with the General Staff.

In December, he spoke for George Coleman at the Ford Hall Forum — one of a series of such speeches which he made — and which Lillian carried on later. He also checked through there, with Doctor Southard, the project on locating psychiatric cases in industry in which there were both interested. This was a significant undertaking. For years the partners had kept a list of problems in industry which they found it difficult to solve — people capable of promotion who refused to be promoted; people incapable of promotion who wanted to be promoted; people who constantly had chips on their shoulders; people who felt that every supervisor had a grudge against them; and other types. At a conference, they had mentioned these cases to Doctor Southard, who was an old friend of Frank's and a brother-in-law of one of Aunt Caroline's friends. He had felt sure that psychiatry had the answer and with their cooperation had arranged a series of meetings at the Psychiatric Hospital in Boston. At these meetings, patients whose case histories indicated that they had furnished problems in industry similar to those the Gilbreths had listed were interviewed by Doctor Southard, and, later, treatment prescribed was reviewed. As a result of this, the Gilbreths had done some writing and Doctor Southard himself had written several papers. Also his assistant, Dr. Myrtelle Canavan, had become a student at one of the Summer Schools and had proved to be not only a charming and stimulating person, but an expert in motions. Photos, movies, and cyclegraphs of her inoculating a test-tube were among the selected group always in Frank's wallet. So that any meeting with Doctor Southard meant a reunion.

December was a busy month trying to set up the jobs so that Lillian could handle them or Frank could send material wherever he might be, arranging for Lillian to give any papers which might have been promised, or write any other which were not complete, and finally, on the 20th, reporting at the War College to be vaccinated, receive a first typhoid inoculation, and meet his new colleagues.

The next day, Frank was offered a Majority, with one thousand men under him, by Colonel Mitchell. Unable to accept, he suggested his friend, H.P. Gillette, and tried to forget his disappointment at not going overseas and concentrating on the job at hand.

He could not go home at Christmas, but ran down to Philadelphia to spend the day with the Bancrofts. The next day, he got his order to go to Fort Sill, Oklahoma, and cooperate with Captain Garey and Captain Ellis, at the School of Arms and the School of Fire in the making of films to teach the soldiers. He had been tremendously irritated by his few days in Washington, sitting at a large desk, and assigned nothing to do. The fact that his busy mind planned the development of the work, to be sent to Lillian, did not completely satisfy him, so that he was delighted to be on his way. For months he had been thinking of the war problem as involving every man, woman, and child in the country and giving opportunity and responsibility to each. One of his letters had said, "The women must do more than the men. They must take a man's place at work, but the work of those away is not missed. They must relieve unnecessary fatigue from the working classes; they must advance the cause of The One Best Way To Do Work; they must teach the cripple to be an economic success." He took trunks full of data of all sorts with him, as well as a most adequate supply of well-fitted uniforms, and his partner did her best to set things up at home so that everything he might possibly need might be forwarded to him with the least possible amount of delay.

The first few weeks at Fort Sill were a happy experience for Frank, for, as usual, he found a tremendous number of things to do and the people he worked with were very congenial. His long letters home kept the family in close touch. Captain Ellis and Captain Garey became great pals. He supplemented long days of work with lectures and conferences in the evening, and sent to the home source of supply for greater and greater quantities of data. Lillian of course was thrilled to be called "an Advisor on the project" and to get everything she possibly could out of her educational and psychological experience, to add to the engineering data.

Frank must have been worn out, for the changes in water and in food did not agree with him. The final straw seems to have been a box of apples and a large package of home-made candy. He had neglected to drink sufficient water because he did not like the taste of it, and the combination of things he omitted and things he ate proved too much for him. So rheumatism set in, and early in February he was so wretched that he was forced to go to the Post Hospital. Fort Sill still was one of those army posts which had expanded faster than it could be supplied with necessities. Oklahoma is subject to dust storms and was at the time thinly settled.

Major Frank B. Gilbreth (1917)

There was an inadequate supply of bedding and of drugs but especially of skillful nursing. Throughout February he moved from the hospital to his quarters and back again, and on March first, Captain Ellis wired Lillian that he had developed uremic poisoning and advised her to come to Fort Sill. It was not easy to get off. The word came during the weekend, and it was difficult to get tickets and money for the trip. Finally a kind friend motored out to her factory and opened the safe to get the money. It was hard to leave the family and the work.

When she arrived there, March fourth, she found two doctors, and two special nurses on the case besides the consultants, and that pneumonia had set in. For over a month a desperate struggle to pull him through took place. The crisis came very rapidly — the resident doctor had not expected it so soon and Lillian had had trouble getting him to supply the adrenaline that might be needed to help the patient through. Fortunately she had gotten it.

Frank's long patient teaching on how to handle a project, was in the final analysis, the thing that pulled him through. All the way out on the train, his wife had tried to write down carefully what he would have done if it had been his job to pull one of the family through such a critical illness as he was having. She knew that he would keep a careful record of everything that happened; take pains to understand the doctor's orders; provide the best nursing possible; but above all make sure that the patient's comfort and welfare was considered; and that he had, every moment, someone near him who would go on fighting and persuading him to fight, day and night, until the illness was over.

There were many difficult problems to solve. The two doctors in charge of the case disagreed as to treatment — one believing in alcoholic stimulants and the other refusing to use them! No trained women nurses were available and it was necessary to bring them from Lawton and St. Louis — and to change when they seemed indifferent or the patient disliked them. Linen was scarce and had to be carefully guarded after it had been acquired or someone else would take it. Medicines were scarce and some had to be sent for from Lawton or high-pressure used on the hospital pharmacy and the doctors to get a reserve supply. Frank had almost inordinately high ideals of cleanliness and everything he had to eat had to be prepared where he could see it, and kept covered with mosquito netting. Nothing that came from any of the kitchens would he taste. "I've seen too much," was all he would say. Bedding and clothes had to be changed constantly and he insisted on sponge baths and being shaved even though the rheumatism pained him excruciatingly and the doctors and nurses tried to dissuade him. He disliked his first nurse intensely and Lillian sent her off although the doctors said she was efficient and Lillian must take the responsibility of having him left without trained nursing.

But she knew Frank! She knew that while he was conscious he would be so irritated by inefficiency or things which were not up to his standard that he could not rest and relax sufficiently to get better. And she knew that, even if everyone pronounced him unconscious, he was probably registering many more impressions than they suspected, and certainly would be highly resentful of being treated as unconscious if he were not.

Everything was done to cooperate with her. A bed was set up for her next to the patient's, and there she was allowed to stay. What a comfort it was to be able to be on the job constantly! The night of the crisis, she could feel that if everything else failed to rally him, she might be able to pull him through by telling him how necessary he was. The adrenaline doubtless kept the tired heart going until it could pick up again for itself and the friendly nurses, doctors, and friends, all pulling together, were a large part of whatever pulled him through, but someone had to correlate everything and hold on!

It was only after the crisis was over that Lillian was able to get a clear picture of what was going on. There were no private rooms in the hospital, but Frank had been given the quietest corner and an adequate amount of screens were available, at all times, to make a little room for the two single beds, the chair, the table, and so on. The walls, of course, of this little enclosure were only sheets, and as there was no provision for isolation. One of her chief fears was that her patient might contract something besides what he had. She strongly suspected that he had contracted pneumonia from the patient on the other side of the sheet from where he lay, although all the medical people said it was impossible. On the other side of the sheet which was her wall, she could almost touch the next patient, who was also very ill. And going in and out of the ward, she had to pass through a long lane of men, ill with every sort of thing, but all cordial and quiet and interested to know how her patient came on. She knew that Frank would be disgusted if she allowed anything that would give them pleasure to be taken out of their program because of him, so she made this clear to those in charge. There had even been a suggestion of cutting out the usual Sunday afternoon concert, for fear it might disturb him — but she had vetoed that for him also. The things which really might have disturbed him, and all the other patients, like the frequent deaths and the handling of these, could not be quieted down or eliminated. There were few visitors to the ward, except the various doctors. There were practically no nurses except for the orderlies. In fact she heard that in some of the wards there were not even trained orderlies, and that men from the veterinary department had been sent for when the number of patients grew large! Once in awhile, the little man from the "Y" came through, distributing oranges and cigarettes. And always, Captains Garey and Ellis, and the other officer friends came in when they were off duty, to urge her to go for a walk or over to the mess dining-room for a meal. With the crisis past, she could accept a few of these invitations — but she was most content to sit next to her patient, or lie on her little cot where she could make sure that she would be on hand at a minute's notice.

Getting well was a slow, trying process, because the rheumatism made so painful the turning about and other treatments which the recovery demanded. Getting out on the porch was a change, but a severe sandstorm drove everyone in and the monotony of the ward continued. Fortunately, Hamilton, whose patience and light touch were doubtless contributed to by his part Indian ancestry, could be allowed to take full charge of the Major during his convalescence. This was a blessing, as the last trained nurse, who was quite acceptable to the patient, hurt her foot and had to go home, and poor Lillian never could learn not to jerk when she was trying to help the patient.

The notes which Lillian took during these weeks make amusing reading. She was so anxious to do an adequate job that she made her own set of bedside notes to supplement those taken by the nurses. She made all sorts of notes also on what happened and on what the patient said and did. There was little attempt at the time to interpret these notes. It was simply jotting down of what she saw and heard, but they did seem to present many things which indicate his character and how consistently he lived up to his ideas and ideals. Those for the week of Wednesday, April third, read as follows:

> *Supplementary Notes of L.M.G. on Patient's Mental Condition*
>
> *Wednesday, April 3* — Patient has hallucinations which are more or less logical. Hallucinations all have to do with experiences at "School of Fire." Worries greatly over apparent disagreement as to facts. Never varies from his usual standards. Demands cleanliness of person, consideration for others, et cetera. Prefers male attendants. Knows what is comfortable and how he can be made comfortable. Hates to be argued with. Detects lies or insincerity at once. Much disturbed by not being able to locate himself in time and space. Wants continually to know points of the compass; which floor he is on; which side of the room; number of bed; et cetera. Allows no discrepancy in statements of others.
>
> *Saturday, April 6* — Continues to talk of work at "School of Fire" only and in a logical and connected way. Always audible. Conforms to laws of cleanliness, neatness, et cetera. Conforms to all treatments that appeal to him as reasonable. Is increasingly angry because doctors and nurses say he is better yet insist upon keeping him in bed. Has not been told he has pneumonia, as he fears the disease. Takes much pleasure in having spots painted on his hands with iodine in

order that attendants may avoid hurting him when they handle him. Is appealed to by a reasonable attitude in the doctors if they talk to him as a colleague, or a man of sense. Not responsive to the typical "medical man" attitude. Is all this time irrational and remembers nothing during his convalescence of all this experience. Uses all terms, such as technical Scientific Management terms, absolutely correctly.

Monday, April 8 — Talks of children for the first time. Still talks constantly of his work. Is irrational, but always detects discrepancies in statements of doctors, nurses, et cetera — also insincerity.

Tuesday, April 10 — Talks in his sleep on crippled soldier problems. Gives a connected talk beginning "Gentlemen" and ending "I thank you all for letting me tell you." Claims for the first time that he understands Crippled Soldier's problems as he has had a cripple's experience. Advises all at least to go to the hospital to get in touch with the cripple's feelings. Is a logical, articulated talk. Throughout the entire time after the patient has come out of the uremic coma, he talks considerably and appears to recognize people, yet it is to be noticed that during his convalescence he has *no* recollection of his experience before the time his temperature becomes normal. Throughout the entire period that he is at the hospital he is unable to realize that the various members of his body form part of a complete whole. It is remarkable to the observer, however, that he maintains his standards throughout, also the use of his usual vocabulary, and his ability to talk logically and connectedly. After his illness he remembers only those that he knew before becoming ill, having no recollections of Mrs. Fisher, who nursed him for two days; of Colonel Smith and other patients in the ward who visited him; of the location of his bed; of the types of medicines and treatments applied; tests made; et cetera. The patient realizes thoroughly the limitations in his memory of his experience, and is overapt to distrust his own conclusions.

Nothing is so thrilling as recovery from an almost fatal illness and it was a happy task for Lillian to record Frank's progress. Easter Sunday, March 31st, marked the beginning of real improvement. He could sit up in the evening. The next day he could be carried to the porch in a rocking chair. A few days after he could take a few steps with crutches and the next day after that he could put on his clothing. He had insisted all through his illness in having a pair of his trousers hanging over one of the screens, ready in case he wanted to put them on. Now, after a month of waiting, on they went! The doctor coming in, was asked when he would discharge the patient, and allow him to go to Washington. He replied, "When you can walk the length of the ward and back!" That was a terrific ordeal, but Frank snatched his crutches and made the trip in spite of weakness and pain, for whatever else he lacked, he did not lack determination!

It was very difficult to have the discharge papers properly signed and countersigned, and finally, on April 9th, Frank and his wife started off without them, but with the promise that they would be waiting for them on their arrival at Walter Reed Hospital in Washington. Accompanied by Hamilton, who refused to be separated from his Major, they started off — stopping in St. Louis long enough to chat with one of the nurses and cheered by a few minutes talk with Frank and Elizabeth Chapman, at Columbus.

When they arrived in Washington, they went immediately to Walter Reed Hospital. No papers were there. But Frank was admitted, and it was a happy moment for his wife when he was safe in bed. She had no idea where she could find a place to stay, herself. But a friendly officer, Captain Schauffler, sensing the difficulty, recommended a nearby rooming house where his wife had stopped, and that problem was solved.

The next few months were for Lillian a series of trips between Providence and Washington. The children had kept well and happy but there was much to be done for them and of course the office work was far behind. Poor Frank found the endless series of delays almost unbearable. He wanted to return to Service but it became increasingly obvious that this would not be possible for a long time, if ever. Having, with difficulty, reconciled himself to the painful truth, he then wanted to be honorably discharged from the Service so that he might take up his civilian work again. But this too proved something requiring much delay. His one consolation was working with Colonel Owen on the Crippled Soldier work and spending every minute he could get at the Army Medical Museum. He had himself wheeled about the hospital and visited the occupational therapy ward. He came to the conclusion that the things taught were taught rather because the teachers had been trained to teach them than because they furnished interesting and adequate occupational work for the patients. Undoubtedly his experience here made an important contribution to the Crippled Soldier work.

Lillian did everything she knew to keep him interested. She sent or took him piles of data. She tried to interest him in writing papers. He tried valiantly to snap back into his old interests and his old speed, but he was still in great pain and it was difficult to talk, to sit, to lie down, in fact, to do anything. Colonel Owen spent time at the hospital and pulled every string to get privileges for Frank to be at the Museum, and the faithful Youngers, who lived nearby, spirited him to their house for delicious dinners and even more stimulating talk whenever he could get away. But it was a hard, difficult period. Finally, permission to leave did come, and it was decided that Frank should go home to Providence, then as soon as possible, down to Nantucket to see what the sun and the sea could do for him.

It was a marvelous occasion — that arrival at home! Little Freddy had changed more than anyone else and become a companionable boy instead of a baby. Even Dan was crawling everywhere and rioting with the others. Girls and boys had all the accumulated experiences of six months to talk over and all the charts they had filled out and work they had done, to exhibit. Mother spent happy hours concocting all the favorite dishes to feed him up. Oatmeal, cooked for ages, just as he liked it — doughnuts and apple pies and rice puddings and "Baked Indian" and gingerbread and so on in endless procession! The Town Criers and all the Providence friends streamed in and out but, — in spite of every-thing and no matter how hard he tried to put up a good front — pain, lack of strength, and uncertainty as to whether he would ever feel like himself again — made life a hard problem.

It was no easy job for Frank to travel to Nantucket though his wife did everything she could to make the trip easy and happy, but the moment the dear old island came in sight he seemed to feel better. He climbed into one of the funny old carriages with some difficulty and was driven all over the town while they looked for a house. He wanted it near the shore — big enough to hold everyone — and she insisted that it should be inexpensive and easy to keep in order. Finally, they located what was really just a little shack down near the bathing beach. It had originally been a paint shop of the lighthouse keeper. When the channel coming into the harbor changed, Dr. Coleman had bought the whole property, sold the house — moving it off on another lot — and rented the shack to an artist, who persuaded him to do it over again with a skylight and other things that his work called for. Nearby were two small "bug-lights" which had been the lighthouses, also a part of the doctor's purchase. His practice, except for summer visitors, consisted largely of people who had little money, so he would say to a patient, who regretted that he could not pay his bill, "Never mind, just leave me this chair or table, or some piece of furniture, when you are gone," and paste on a little label inconspicu-ously, to establish his property right. Not only the house, but the two towers were crammed full of a conglomeration of all kinds of furniture and furnishings — no two things alike, none real antiques, or of any great value, many needing repair!

From the first glimpse it fascinated both Frank and Lillian. He kept saying, "Of course, it's too small, but isn't the location perfect?" and she kept thinking, "If only he can be happy here, nothing else matters!" Finally, after endless discussion, it was decided to buy the place, just as it stood, and to plan for the changes and additions which would gradually make it more and more livable and attractive. It cost eighteen hundred dollars, and never did any money bring such fine returns.

Cheered by the purchase and the plans for a long rest on the beach, Frank returned to Providence and the work there, while the family scurried up to Nantucket to get everything ready for him. It was a miracle they ever managed to fit into the place that summer, but "The Shoe" as Frank had named it, seemed to expand in a wonderful manner, and after all, small girls, and especially small boys, can be packed in like sardines! Both towers were reserved for Daddy, and the little one, close at hand, was turned into a work place. The larger one, some distance off, made a quiet place to rest or read or even spend the night if one needed complete peace and quiet. The heterogeneous furniture had a certain quaintness and charm. Tom did some repair work — which was not artistic, just utilitarian! Nobody minded any lacks because everyone was so happy to be there. Only a few neighbors, and these far enough away not to be disturbed by joyous clatter; a sand pile across the road; the beach only a short walk. Surely the simplest life was the happiest!

Frank was in his element, planning everything. Wardrobes were to consist of three bathing suits apiece and one outfit for going up into the town. Meals were to consist of breakfast when one wanted it, dinner at noon, and supper almost any time and any place, preferably on one of the beaches, and a picnic with a fine bonfire and a chance to cook over it. All management techniques, which had unfortunately lapsed a little with Daddy's long absence, to be revived and improved, and many new ones to be introduced.

When Frank first joined the family he was so lame that when he tried to get up from the beach not only the small boys but friendly neighbors had to haul him up, for though he had lost much of his weight, he was still very heavy. But the first beach neighbor who offered to help proved to be Dr. Harry Schauffler, brother of Captain Schauffler, of Walter Reed

Hospital days, and soon the hour at the beach became a gathering of friends and as many hours at "The Shoe" as he had strength for became similar gatherings.

Frank started in, enthusiastically, to teach the children. He rented boats to row and to sail and gave lessons which the small crew learned with interest and satisfaction. Lillian was petrified with fear lest he fall out of the boat and be unable to get back. But she soon learned that he must be allowed to take over the direction of his life again, and even encouraged to feel he could do anything that he wanted to do. That final stage in the nurse-patient relationship, when the patient is more and more independent and the nurse less and less needed is not an easy one. It must be carefully handled, but it is indispensable to complete recovery.

On the beach, Frank had the children gather shells and blades of grass. These they arranged according to size, while he showed them how this illustrated the law of statistical regularity. At home, in "The Shoe" he put up a chart showing one square meter divided into millimeters, and told them it contained a million divisions. Every one's height and age was recorded on the jamb of the door leading from the dining room to the little hallway that went to the kitchen. The whitewashed walls were decorated with all sorts of Codes and the Management Symbols. Every game anyone knew was enthusiastically played and many new ones were invented. Each summer was to see elaboration of all this until the children, refusing to let anything lapse or change, would cry, if this was suggested, "It's tradition!"

The little boys made endless boats. These were only pieces of planking roughly chopped to approximate hulls and supplied with broomstick smoke-stacks, a screw-eye in the front and a piece of twine, and a boat could be hauled around the sand pile for hours, from one carefully constructed pier to another, and back to "The Shoe" in the evening, to be docked under the boys' camp beds. Frank seemed absolutely happy near his beloved sea and the small children became small amphibians with the greatest of ease! Their Mother and Grandmother worried about them considerably — Frank, noticing this, made a set of rules which he and the children thought priceless. They started something like this:

> "No child may go in the ocean more than three times
> a day or stay in more that eight hours at a time."

> "No child may go on a boat of any kind who has
> not learned to swim."

and so forth.

When they were in a boat, they had to know and follow seamanship rules, to keep busy if possible, to keep everything shipshape, to obey the Captain absolutely, and to be prepared for any emergency. Grandma loved the sea herself, so far as watching it and taking a quiet dip were concerned, though she was never happy when she or those dear to here were out on it. Lillian really never got over being homesick for her mountains and never did like or trust the sea completely. But she tried to put up as good a bluff as she could! She could never make up her mind whether it was better to go along on the sailing trips, feeling more or less seasick, and always sure that the boat would tip over, or to stay at home on shore, and watch the weather, and agonize as to what might happen. But it was fun to see Frank looking so much better; the children so happy and rosy; and the little house fitting its purpose so well. It was no job at all to put it in order in the morning; the sand or water which returning swimmers dripped everywhere did no harm and was easily brushed out; the simplest food tasted delicious and everyone was content!

Margaret Harwood, the astronomer at the little Maria Mitchell observatory, and her friends were a great source of enjoyment. These fine young women stopped in to go swimming with the family or invited everyone up to Maria Mitchell House and Observatory to see the flower show; read the books; or look at the stars. Margaret was guide, philosopher, and friend, and shared her experience and her visitors with equal generosity. Both were endlessly interesting — for she spent her winters at the Harvard Observatory and Shapley, Kings, and other astronomers and their families included Nantucket in their summer jaunts. The children adopted her as "Marnie" and no one and nothing ever bored her. It was really hard to leave everything and go back to Providence, when, all too soon, Labor Day came.

By September, Frank was able to take up his work with new strength and new confidence. The honorable discharge had come through, and he must be content to do what he could to help in the War, through working for defense industries and continuing the Crippled Soldier work. He signed a contract with the California Loading Company and spent much time in that plant in Old Bridge, New Jersey.

In October, some of the Moller family came East and Frank and Lillian met them in New York and enjoyed their visit in Providence. Baby Dan was baptized on the twentieth, while they were there. The old jobs went well and new ones were added. It was a pleasure to work for the Regal Shoe Company and renew the contact with Frank's old friend, Elmer J. Bliss, its President. Frank and he had done some interesting war work in developing the best method of fitting shoes to the soldier. The micromotion method had proved useful in making records and the cyclegraph proved the most effective way of detecting malingerers. These of course could not limp at a uniform rate and the stereochronocyclegraphs record made this very clear.

On November eleventh, Armistice Day, concluded the War, brought great happiness to everyone, and meant — for the partners — a careful review of their work program in the lights of its new demands.

Frank spent every free moment at the Army Medical Museum in Washington and went to Chicago to see L.W. Wallace and Mr. Segur on work which could be done by The Red Cross Institute for the Blind.

On Thanksgiving Day, Anne and Fred Cross, and Carol, joined the Brown Street group for dinner. John, who was in the navy, could not be there, but Cousin Georgianna Pendleton, a relative on the Gilbreth side, came down from Boston, and so did Gertrude Moller, who was taking a course in occupational therapy and training for work in this field in Boston.

It was marvelous for Lillian to have one of her sisters so near. Gertrude spent many weekends in Providence and Frank never failed to get in touch with her on his New England trips. He was big brother to all the Moller girls, from the first day he met them. It was a wonderful treat to the children to have Daddy at home the entire Thanksgiving weekend. He took Anne, Ernestine, Martha, and Frank with him for a visit to the Regal Shoe Company. Anne was about thirteen, Frank about seven — the others in between, and they all had a wonderful time.

Things went so smoothly at home that both partners went on to New York for the A.S.M.E. meeting. That was their big annual treat. They never missed it if they could help it. It was such a thrill to stay at the Astor and go to every meeting and event — something to look forward to a whole year, and then remember until the next year came around. This year Eva Powell was visiting in New York also, and there could be a grand reunion and many reminiscences. The thrill of the month for Frank Junior was to be allowed to make the trip from Providence, alone, carrying the microchronometer which Dad needed; to stay with him at the Murray Hill Hotel; and come back with him in time for Christmas at home. Gertrude had become very ill, and Elinor and Mabel had come on to be with her and take her home. They spent Christmas day in Providence with the family, as she was recuperating, and insisted that they have and give that pleasure, so that for the whole family as for the world, the Christmas season meant peace and happiness.

The next year [1919] opened in the same happy way. As long as the Moller sisters were in Boston there were visits back and forth. Frank, in his search for every possible illustration of motions, became interested in work with the epileptic, and made several visits to the State Epileptic

Hospital to make films and cyclegraphs. One visit was enough for his wife, and she had the nightmare as a result of it, for many years.

The Pierce Arrow job went splendidly and the children were much excited over the possibility of getting a Pierce Arrow car. On February fifteenth, Frank sailed for England for the Red Cross Institute for the Blind and the Surgeon General's Office.

He was fortunate enough to catch the *Baltic* and renew his friendship with her Captain Finch, also to have as a steamer mate, Sir Arthur Pearson, the blind founder of St. Dunstan's Institute, England. He visited the Butterworth's and made several investigations and a report at St. Dunstan's. He called on Lloyd George, and Captain Evans, his brother-in-law, and on Beatrice and Sidney Webb. He found the Webbs interesting but eccentric. He had a fine visit with the Spooners, in their comfortable home. Professor Spooner was for years head of the Mechanical Engineering Department at the Technical University and a great friend of Mr. Butterworth's. He was generous in every sense of the word and Frank proved very congenial. His book on mathematics and his plans for a book on "Fatigue from Noise" proved congenial subjects of conversation, as did Frank's own books and photographs. Frank went up to Manchester and lectured there at the Institute of Technology, then caught the *Baltic* back from Liverpool. Before the month was over he had landed, gone home, been on the Pierce Arrow job, down to Old Bridge, and was back in Providence.

A whole set of new projects, as usual, was simmering in his brain. At home, he was busy teaching the children the Roth Memory Course, and planning with them how he would buy the automobile and drive it back home. In the laboratory, he and Lillian spent hours working on *Motion Study for the Blinded* with black shields over their eyes and a table cross-sectioned to make placing of dinner service and equipment and other life-projects of the blinded simple and interesting. He debated the advisability of writing a correspondence course in Management and of course, as always, wrote endless notes and manuscripts.

May was a busy month. The partners went over to Montclair, New Jersey, to see an old house which he thought would be fine for the family. Frank had made a careful job of discussing the pros and cons of leaving Providence. Much of the work was in New York and now, — that the New England Butt Company, pioneer installation was complete and beautifully maintained — and that Lillian had her Ph.D. — there was no reason for staying in Providence. New York was the center of activity in the Management field and transportation from there anywhere in this country and abroad was a simple problem.

He had spent months in making a survey of all the suburban residential possibilities, including Westchester County, Long Island, and New Jersey. The decision finally was, that for them, New Jersey was the best solution — because of greater ease in getting to Washington and the Midwest — but especially because of better schools for the children. Having decided upon New Jersey, he then carefully checked one town after another and decided upon Montclair. This had been called "the engineer's town" because so many engineers lived there — not only those who worked in the New Jersey plants, but many whose officers were in New York. It was at the end of one spur of the Lackawanna Railroad — the ferry service from Hoboken made the trip to downtown New York pleasant and the Hudson tubes made uptown New York a fairly easy problem. Aunt Lizzie Fliedner and her children lived there. So did Calvin Rice, who for so many years was one of Frank's most trusted advisors.

So, out to Montclair he went, to meet and interview the Superintendent of Schools, Dr. Bliss; the Principal of the high school, Mr. Dutch; and some of the Principals of the lower schools. All were splendid people with high ideals, and the school buildings and curricula modern and progressive. Checking with real estate people showed that not many suitable places were available. The two which finally seemed best were very different and it was between these two that Lillian was to help him choose. One was a fine new house large enough for the family life, but with no space for the accumulation of data and an office. It was on a lot large enough to set off the house, but with little place for sports. The other was a run-down old place at the edge of town which had once been part of a beautiful estate. It had belonged to an Englishman named Bradley who had built upon it a fine old rambling house, a barn, green-houses, and all facilities for keeping horses and dogs and hens, and even cows, if one desired. He had turned part of it into a deer park and it was one of his own stags which had finally gored him to death. His wife had remarried, his daughter was grown, the only son had flown across the German lines and never been heard from. Part of the land had been sold, and the house rented for some years, but it was a beautiful house, and one which could be restored, with time and patience and some money. Frank compared the two very fairly, and then said, "Would you rather take the new place and see it deteriorate, or take the old place and try to bring it back to life?" There seemed only one answer and the old place was selected. Frank named it "Mostulab" — a contraction of "Motion Study Laboratory", but the name was never used except in letters because it was so hard to pronounce. It seemed a shame that it was not used, as were the names for the Nantucket lighthouses, "Micromotion Study" and "Cyclegraph" which the children had shortened to "Mic" and "Cyc."

Encouraged by Lillian's agreement that the place was fine in every way, Frank decided to buy the Pierce Arrow car and on May twenty-seventh, did complete the purchase in Buffalo. On the same day that he received title to it, the twenty-ninth of May, he had word, as he noted in his diary, that "Boy #5 was born at five a.m." Lillian had decided that the next boy should be named for Frank's father, John Hiram. Frank did not like the name "Hiram" and decided that he wished all the children had their mother's surname for a second name. So the blonde little boy with the sweet smile was name John Moller — not only for his father's father, but for his mother's grandfather, John Moller of New York. As always, the children were wildly happy over the new baby and Ernestine adopted him at once for her especial charge. Anne was always quite content to have Fred and Dannie, who became even more inseparable with the years. Almost the same height, though very different in coloring and temperament, they got on beautifully. Frank and Bill, of course, constituted the older boys. There was even a greater difference here in look and temperament, but they got on very well, too. The new little brother was slim and fine-featured and looked like Ernestine, who was very proud of that fact. Everyone was delighted that he had come in ample time so that he could go along to Nantucket with the rest of the family, easily and comfortably.

Proud of his new possession, Frank drove the car home, having considerable trouble on the way, probably more because the roads were inadequate, than because of any fault of the car. It had been used, but beautifully kept-up, as the owner was an invalid and drove very little, and that very carefully. The children greeted it with shrieks of joy and could hardly wait to show it off to all their friends.

Not content with all the other projects he had in hand, Frank decided to have his tonsils out, and on June twenty-third, this was accomplished. He insisted on walking over to the doctor's office, scorning to go in the taxi with his wife, who had insisted on being there while the operation was performed — which he thought very foolish and unnecessary. He refused anything but a local anesthetic and walked buoyantly into the operating room, insisting on mirrors being placed so that he could see everything going on. When one tonsil was out, he was so anxious to show it to his wife that she was obliged to look at it, although she left rather hurriedly. Out came the second one, and out walked he, saying proudly, "It was nothing at all," but she noticed he did not decline the ride home in the taxi. By morning his poor throat was badly swollen and it was days before he could eat or talk with comfort.

Mrs. Cunningham, Tom, and Grandmother went on up to "The Shoe" with most of the children, and on the second of July, Frank took Lillian, Ernestine, and the baby John, up in the big car. Ernie was proud and happy to be the one selected to take care of the baby. The children all looked fine, except poor Bill, who had been terribly sunburned, and whose head was all puffed out, and his eyes entirely closed. That poor lamb went through one series of accidents and adventures after another, for he had to try everything at least once. On July seventh, Frank noted that he was fifty-one years old, and on the twelfth, he wrote that he had been thirty-four years in business on that day.

He had not very much time in Nantucket that summer because the jobs were so interesting and so exacting, but he was well and happy, and his letters and diary were full of comments and jokes which amused the family. His clients always became his friends and he always lived in their problems as if he had been one of the organization himself. He enjoyed knowing all their problems and making suggestions not only for plant operations but for selling and advertising. There were photographs showing that he took the six older children to visit the Winchester Laundries that summer. They looked very correct and well-dressed in their city clothes; but at Nantucket, as usual, they lived in bathing suits and were completely happy. Many of them were becoming old enough to enjoy paper and pencil games. The perennial favorite seemed to be the geography game. Someone selected a letter of the alphabet and then each one wrote down all the geographical names he could think of beginning with that letter. The one who had the longest list of names which no one else had thought was the winner. No one would deign to accept a handicap, and it really was a hard game for the younger ones. But they always insisted on playing and refused to have anything made easier for them.

Another type of game which Mother and Grandmother looked at with doubtful approval was the "gambling game." This type was started in Nantucket and added to and developed all through the years. Frank insisted that the only way to take the proper attitude toward gambling was to learn every type of game of chance there was; to keep careful record of what happened to you; and gradually to realize that "you can't possibly beat the game!" So he and the children tossed coins and shook dice and played cards and set up every game of chance he had ever seen or remembered. It was a fascinating amusement. Dad was as excited and played as enthusiastically as the smallest of the children and begged as persuasively that dinner be delayed or bedtime be postponed. Careful

scores were kept and charts were made and winnings collected. The big
jar of pennies was replenished with everybody's haul when the fun was
over. Every platitude Frank ever knew was ready to meet all objections.
"You're only young once!," if it was time to go to bed. "The better the day,
the better the deed!," if it happened to be Sunday. Star jobs, like being
the banker or the croupier, went about in rotation. But always at the end,
Dad took over that job, and always at the end he had everybody's money.
He pretended that it was an educational project and he only did it
because of the lessons it taught the children. But even the youngest child
knew that Dad loved every minute of it and loved it himself all the more
because of that!

Leaving "The Shoe" and going back to Providence was not so much of
a hardship as usual because of planning for moving to the new home in
Montclair. The children talked of little else and the letters Frank wrote
home on his trips were full of it also. He insisted on driving most of the
children down in the big car when moving day came, early in November.
It seemed a big undertaking to Mother and Grandma as they watched
him start off, the car overflowing with children, wraps, luggage, and
lunch! But he did not seem to mind any of it; and they always seemed
to behave better when off "alone" with Daddy! He had great fun with
them when they got to Montclair, for he stopped the car at several funny
old places and pretended each was the new home. But finally they
arrived at 68 Eagle Rock Way and this time the children did not wait
for denial or confirmation. They recognized all too happily the many
things he had described, and swarmed out of the car to claim the place
for their own. It was set far back from the street with a beautiful lawn
in front of it, with Japanese maples and tall beautiful old trees everywhere. To the side was a still wider lawn — just the place for baseball
and football. In the back were the rose garden, the vegetable garden, and
then the greenhouses and the barn, which was now to be the garage,
until Dad should make it over into his workplace for photography. The
house had porches all along the front and the lawn side. The one on the
side was large, screened, and well-stocked with chairs and a swinging

hammock couch. There was a wide hall, and to the right — the big dining-room with the beautiful brown and gold damask paper and beyond — the pantries, and the kitchen that was to be Tom's domain for so many years. To the left of the hall, the big old drawing-room was to be transformed into the office. Here there was room for the double desk at which the partners worked, shoving manuscripts across the table to one another for revision; for the "N"-file; the technical books and all the other books that went to make the working office and laboratory. Then came the fine old living room with bookcases around two sides, a fireplace on the third, and built-in cupboards with cushions on top so that one could sit and look out on the porch and the gardens or look in at the bookcases and the fire. Upstairs, were six bedrooms, big enough to stow the family away comfortably. On the third floor were the store rooms and rooms for the family helpers and a big room ear-marked for the oldest boy. It was to be used by the oldest boy for years — as one after another went to college, to work, and to set up a home of his own.

By Thanksgiving, the family was well established, and looking back on 1919, showed it to have been a very happy year: Fred Moller, a Captain and back home after the hard years at the front in France; Frank Gilbreth, himself again except for a heart which seemed to be behaving beautifully; Lillian and the children, well, busy, and happy; plenty of work; a new book on the shelf — *Motion Study for the Handicapped;* and the new little John Moller as a member of the family. Only Grandma seemed more tired than usual and had increasing spells of feeling miserable. It was very hard for her to resign herself to being less active than she had been accustomed to be, or to giving up the delicious food which she knew how to cook so well. Increasingly, when Frank was away, she would make excuses to rock in her big chair, or lie down with one of the children who was taking a nap or going to bed early. But when he was at home, no matter how she felt, she insisted on doing anything he wanted to do and keeping any discomfort she had to herself.

One of the things which gave Frank increasing satisfaction during these years was the fine publicity which appeared in many magazines. He managed to stay at home more in 1920 than in 1919, partly because in spite of her valiant efforts, he could see that his mother was growing weaker and weaker and he wanted to enjoy every minute that he had her to the full; partly too, because many of his jobs were within a short distance; also because he had so much writing to do, and so much investigating in his laboratory.

George Iles, a writer friend who published in Canada as well as in the United States, wrote splendid articles about the Gilbreth work and proved a devoted friend. The Society of Industrial Engineers continued to support and develop the Fatigue Committee and welcomed papers on Fatigue. Frank delivered one at the Spring Meeting in Philadelphia in March, and was greatly encouraged by its reception. The Safety Council became interested in the various aspects of his *Motion and Fatigue Study* as they reduced accidents and prevented hazards. Hamilton Holt printed much Gilbreth material in the *Independent* and the British papers seemed as interested as those in the United States.

It was of course not to be expected that some difficulties on the jobs would not develop. The California Loading Company was a case in point, ending in a lawsuit which was settled at the last moment, out of court, in the Gilbreth's favor. Poor Frank was spared at least this, because his beloved mother was becoming steadily more ill, and he could not and would not leave her, even to complete so profitable a settlement as this.

He had made up his mind definitely that she could pull through, for years more of happy life, and felt it was his job to find something to cure her. Having every confidence in the doctor, he did not experiment in the medication. But he did bring home every imaginable thing to eat and to drink, so that the usually simple household menu became varied and elaborate, although poor Grandma could not relish anything. Brandy and whiskey and every sort of wine and soft drink brought him a certain amount of comfort in the purchase and presentation. But the dear old lady could not respond to any of his attempts and it was evident that she was ready to go, if only he would reconcile himself to this. The last few days he never left her for a moment. Lillian signed the papers for the lawsuit; met Sister Anne who arrived for the last farewell; and then tried to carry Frank through the bereavement. It was a major calamity in his life, for his mother had been not only his staunch supporter but his beloved companion and devoted friend all through his life. He realized after awhile that it was better for her to go than to live on unable really to enjoy life. He seemed most comforted by the suggestions that he add the devotion which had been her share to that he already was giving the children and that her birthday become a perpetual family holiday, to be celebrated joyously through the years. He was happy too that she had some time in the new home — Thanksgiving, Christmas, Easter, and even part of the beautiful May with the garden full of lilacs and lilies-of-the-valley.

His whole family realized how hard her going had been on him, and Cousin Fred Bunker, who had been always a chum of his and a devoted friend of Lillian's ever since she met him in Boston, before her first trip abroad, planned a beautiful surprise for him. He was at the time on the Governor's Council in Maine. Through his suggestion, Frank was offered an Honorary Degree at the University of Maine, at its forty-ninth annual commencement, on the seventh of June. He had registered for Massachusetts Institute of Technology, but never gone; he had never even thought of going to the University of Maine. But they seemed proud and happy to call back this son of the state which they represented, to honor him and his work. The children were thrilled that "Daddy was to be a Doctor, too," and Frank and Lillian set off on what was to her a milestone in their lives, and a thrilling experience. She had taken along the beautiful black silk gown her Mother had given her when she took her own Doctorate at Brown and had ordered the right size mortar-board, so that Frank might be properly appareled. But at the last minute he "struck" at wearing what seemed to him to be a woman's gown — in spite of the fact that she told him truthfully that there were no sex distinctions in the academic regalia. So in his "citizen's clothes" as he phrased it, and without the gown, he marched up with the honored guests, while she mourned quietly sitting in one of the pews with Cousin Fred. The rejected gown and mortar-board were folded in her lap. A Weston cousin, who happened to be there, came by and said, "Is that Frank's cap and gown?" Was it an angel or a devil who prompted her to say, "Yes"? At any rate, he took it, passed it over to an academic officer, who soon was saying to Frank, "Your cap and gown are here," putting them on for him so quickly and neatly that he could do nothing about it. He gave his wife one fierce glare, which she was careful not to see — then carefully inspected the academic group, to discover to his intense and quite evident relief, that he was dressed exactly like every one else. He never mentioned the matter afterward, and neither did she, but they both knew who won that battle! She could remember very few she had won — although one other very satisfactory one came to mind. She had been giving her first talk at Teacher's College for a class run by Miss. Gunther and Frank's old friend, Ray Balderston. She was a little nervous about the assignment, especially when he threatened to come up and listen to the talk. Finally she had said, "If you do come, I will stop wherever I am and you will have to finish!" That had been too much like a dare for him to resist, so come he did, and looked at her as much as to say, "Now, what do you propose to do about this?" Rather suspecting some such thing might happen, she had told her Gunther-Balderston friends to back her up. This they promised to do. So she continued the talk calmly, "I told Mr. Gilbreth when he threatened to come here and listen to me that if he did that, I would stop and he would have to finish the talk. He has come, I have stopped, and the rest is up to him!" Of course he finished the job and did it beautifully. So she scored one that day, and added another at this June commencement.

The family went down to Nantucket and was settled happily in the little house before Lillian had time to realize another baby was coming, and that he should be adequately prepared for. This time she had decided to make a break in the usual routine and go to the little cottage hospital. There were advantages in being at home, especially in that one could take up family and household responsibilities more promptly. But she was tired. Grandma, had, until the last few weeks, preferred her to any other nurse, and while the care was cheerfully and affectionately given, it was exacting. But Fate, or the Stars, or something, had decided that this baby was to be born at "The Shoe" itself and born there he was, on July Fourth.

She was always sorry afterward that she had not been able to register completely all the details of his coming. "The Shoe" had been made much larger and more comfortable, with a porch built all around it, but some way or other adequate lighting of "Dad's and Mother's room" had not been planned for. So that the little room, which held all the children's clothes — stacked in bins and on hangers according to Motion Study principles, and the pride of the family — had to be covered with sheets and turned into an adequate place for a new baby to come into. He came easily and quickly and with the same cheery technique with which he was to lead his life. This time it was his Mother's turn to select the name, and she chose Robert. It was the name of her father's fine old Scottish partner and seemed not inappropriate for a Gilbreth who was a Galbraith and one of the clan MacDonald. She would have like to have made "Bunker" his middle name, but Frank remained firm in wanting the "Moller" included. So, Robert Moller he became — and of course "Bobby" to all the family. He was Martha's boy and she received him with open arms and a loving heart. He looked very much like Frank Junior, and had the same lovely disposition. The family grieved that Grandma could not be there to welcome and enjoy him. It was surprising how well the dear "Old Shoe" took this new assignment of having a baby born and started on his life in its shelter. Tom — who patiently stripped every child's bed every morning and washed at least one complete outfit per child per day, year in and year out — laughed at the idea of a small baby's outfit being any extra burden. Mrs. Cunningham was more than ready to dispense with the trained nurse, whom it was difficult to house, as soon as the doctor would allow. She proved a far more efficient and comfortable nurse than most of the hospital-trained ones Lillian had had. The baby was good, smiled days and slept nights, and seemed to enjoy life thoroughly. Best of all, Frank could be at home and take the children for long happy trips while the new baby and his Mother napped or got acquainted. Lillian never forgot the happy day when she could be pulled, in her favorite little walnut rocker with the cane back and seat, into the dining-room. Her Mother had sent her a beautiful Canton tea set, in honor of her birthday, and the coming of Bobby. It was really far too choice for "The Shoe" but she longed to have this lovely new treasure where it could be a beauty spot, year after year. So Frank had put up a set of little shelves with hooks for the cups and wires to hold the plates and saucers upright, and here she was, in her new blue dressing gown, surrounded by the happy children, enjoying seeing her china in place.

Another treat that came only when the babies were small and she first came back to the dining-room table was sitting on Frank's right, with no jobs of serving or passing — free to look at him and the children — and enjoy having no responsibility!

Usually Grandmother had done the serving, but now Andie took over the job so capably that her Father was comforted and proud to think he had such a reliable standby. The children had arranged themselves so that each older one had a smaller one to look out for and somehow the occasion became a red-letter day in a very happy summer.

Frank spent much time at Lever Brothers, where packing soap was one of the main projects. Finally, he had sent over some boxes and a big supply of soap cakes, so that the children could make some experiments. It was fun to turn the whole "Shoe" into a Motion Study Laboratory. The children felt they were making a real contribution. Frank enjoyed this, as he did the days in Cambridge and the visits of many friends, including L.W. Wallace, Frank Sanborn, and Charles Lytle. Mr. Wallace had been in his first Summer School and Frank Sanborn — a classmate of his early school days — had been in another of the Summer Schools, so they were appreciative of the applications they knew and of the new techniques which were constantly being added. Mr. Lytle was an intelligent and interested observer also, and was to use all that he saw in his writings and teachings later, and proved a cooperative and appreciative friend.

Everyone was interested in the Fourth of July baby. The *Lever Standard* on the Cambridge job, published an announcement:

> *Young Major Gilbreth arrived at the Nantucket home of Major and Mrs. Frank Gilbreth on July 4th. Besides notifying George M. Cohan that he is no longer the only "Yankee Doodle boy born on July the 4th" we wish the young Major long life and prosperity.*

September came all too soon, and the family went on its way back to Montclair and to introduce the new baby to his winter home. In October, Frank made another trip to England, to dine with the Industrial League and Council at the House of Commons and to be the principal guest speaker. At this meeting his work for the re-education of the crippled soldiers was stressed. He also met and became deeply impressed with Mr. Tom Shaw, M.P. The two proved to be very congenial and Mr. Shaw assured Frank that the British workers would welcome Scientific Management if they were allowed to be a part of the group making the decisions.

He spent a day or two in Paris, but was back in November for the meeting of the Society of Industrial Engineers in Pittsburgh, and to give a paper on "Some New Factors in Industrial Education" — also to preside over the Fatigue Elimination Committee, which was the pride of his heart. *Popular Science Monthly* was writing up his work, and Fred C. Kelley, who prepared some of the articles, became a valued and stimulating friend.

1921 proved another year of great activity. All of the different types of participation in the war and its results were carefully gathered together and filed so that they might be available if needed. The California Loading Company job had given splendid opportunities for making beautiful and detailed process charts. These covered loading of point detonating fuses; of 155 m.m. boosters; of bouchons; and of hand grenades. They were useful not only as records of how the work was done, but as the most complete demonstrations of the adaptability and serviceability of the "process chart technique" to record the various operations, in great detail and indicate the type of activity being done.

The most stimulating overseas project was an exhibit at Olympia, England. This came about through cooperation with Professor Spooner, who not only made the contacts but supplied young engineers who could help with the work. Frank took overseas complete equipment to set up a booth illustrating all the techniques of the Motion Study work. The family were thrilled to receive the photographs showing King George, Queen Mary, the Duke of York, and Princess Mary, visiting the exhibit one day and the Prince of Wales making the visit on another. It was exciting to have Daddy come home and explain that the one mistake had been the mercury lamps which cast such a horrible green light on the royal visitors that they were not encouraged to stay long! It was a fine lesson for the children, too, to note the correct clothes and deportment of the royal visitors and to realize what a responsibility royalty really was.

The partners spent much time working in and through the technical societies — for this was the year of the hot controversy in the Taylor Society, on the "Stop-watch versus the Micro-motion Technique." They had been invited to give a paper on some such topic as "Fundamental Factors in Planning and Control." Frank of course immediately saw an opportunity to present a full and even pugnacious exposition of the Micro-motion method. This certainly was fully justified because of the disparaging things which had been said about it by some of the Stop-watch proponents, publicly as well as privately.

The result was a long meeting to present the paper and the many and heated discussions. This was followed by other meetings and the preparation of a second paper which the Director of the Taylor Society felt prolonged the controversy without settling it. It was therefore never published and the Gilbreths always felt that they had not had a complete opportunity to say their final word. It was really a milestone in the acceptance of their work for Frank demonstrated that he would never give up fighting and a review of all the material presented on both sides shows that the pros and cons were well and clearly stated. From that time on, impartial evaluators could balance the pros and cons and ultimately an integration could result.

One source of enormous satisfaction to Frank was the award of an honorary membership in the Society of Industrial Engineers to Lillian at the Spring Convention in Milwaukee. This was a complete surprise and a tremendous thrill. Mr. Hoover had been the first "Honorary Member," which made the honor of being the second even more worthwhile, so far as both Gilbreths were concerned. Best of all was the warm-hearted satisfaction of the members of the Society themselves and the real pleasure they seemed to take not only in Lillian's happiness but in Frank's evident and very vocal surprise and satisfaction. Of course she knew that he had always over-stressed her contributions which naturally had influenced this group of his devoted friends to their kind and appreciative gesture, but that made the membership none the less valuable to her.

The May bulletin of the Society has much to say of this happy event, but one paragraph merits quoting:

> *After the applause subsided, Mr. Emerson called Mrs. Gilbreth to the platform and presented her to the audience. She bowed her thanks and beckoned to her husband to come to the rescue and voice her appreciation. Frank B. came forward, valiant and smiling, but when he faced the audience and made an effort to speak, for once in his illustrious career words failed him. By his expression we knew what he was striving to say and so accepted with applause his speech without words.*

The Nantucket summer was, as always, a happy one. Tom considered himself an expert, because he had taken a fine piece of wood about one foot wide and four feet long and made it into a table by supplying four legs which exhibited his usual faulty craftsmanship, but at least salvaged the wood. When "The Major" came home and saw this, he found that by tipping it across his chair, he had a new and serviceable work table. He saw that more adequate legs were substituted and properly braced, and wooden pockets across the front kept papers from sliding down on the reader; and he called this "The laziest man's table." This was adapted and copied and proved not only useful and interesting, but a good illustration of fatigue elimination by a simple device.

"Fatigue" was becoming more and more a matter of major interest, although little more scientific material upon which to base the material was available. Frank continued to work with the Posture League; with the National Safety Council; with every group he could find, interested in fatigue. He and his wife wrote numerous papers in this field, which the faithful Society of Industrial Engineers and other groups presented and published. He was always on the lookout for simple convincing illustrative material which would interest people in Motion Study and make them motion-minded. In the home laboratory, careful records were made of him, writing his name; then re-writing, with every other letter left out. The stages in the learning process — until the time had been reduced to one-half of what it was originally — were set down for use in teaching in the industries and out.

There was an increasing realization by the partners that Motion Study was primarily a matter of teaching. The Summer Schools of Management had been a help in realizing this, and it was a matter of great pride that every person who had attended during any year was making fine use of what he had gotten. Young Bill Dealey — the only person, except for Cooper, not at the time a teacher — had put his material, with the help of a friend, into a paper which, because of its vocabulary and its subject, interested the educational field. He and his sister, who was a psychologist and who married one, seemed to be remembering and using what they had gotten with great effectiveness. They were to be pioneers in carrying through some material Frank had presented on "The Need for Redesigning the Typewriter Keyboard, According to the Principles of Motion Economy" — although this he did not know at this time.

It was interesting to go over the typewriting studies and see how much they had contributed in many ways — interest of industry in psychological tests, and the general serviceability of psychology; indications for need of a redesign of the keyboard, because of the unequal distribution of effort to the two hands; invaluable suggestions for adapting typing for the handicapped; information on the relative time of "get ready, do it, and clean-up," on machine operations, indicated by the large amount of time it took to put paper and carbon into the typewriter and remove them as compared to the key-stroke times; data on the learning process and on skill and on what constitutes an expert.

Frank and Lillian could and did spend hours analyzing the material and testing its serviceability. At the start of their partnership they had realized that their background and training had led them to emphasize different things. Being more observant, he had always seen and recorded differences — her emphasis was primarily on likenesses. This was, perhaps — partly at least — because in her endeavor to understand a completely new field, she searched desperately in the fields she knew, for help and parallels. Frank was quick to see that there were possibilities in locating likenesses and in transferring one field of experience to another. The therbligs, of course, which analyzed a work cycle into fundamental elements, made such transfer possible and easy. Much was done during this time to utilize such material in this field as was available, and to indicate where more work needed to be done.

Feeling that the Society of Industrial Engineers deserved his whole-hearted support, because it supported him, and also that it furnished a valuable medium for extending interest in Methods work, Frank offered a week of his time in the fall for an extended speaking trip, and certainly made fine use of every hour of it. In December, he presented the paper on *Process Charts* at the American Society of Mechanical Engineers meeting so that the year closed with a record of contributions to all the leading Management Societies, which were stimulating interest and discussion.

1922 again proved to be a marvelous year. Frank made numerous trips to Europe — all of them happy and profitable. His letters, the diary of publicity, and the photographs show one series of interesting and stimulating contacts after another. Through Doctor Volmer he met wonderful people in Holland. He never had a happier experience on any job than he did that of the Gebruder Stork in Hengelo. This fine old family manufactured machinery to handle tobacco. Frank reveled in being in the plant, and in visiting the family at their home in the country. The plant itself was in beautiful surroundings, and the personnel relations were as fine as the operating techniques. The photographs of the organization at work; and on a picnic; the well-kept day nursery with its rosy-cheeked children and immaculate surroundings delighted Frank, who could not write and tell enough about his happy experiences.

From February twenty-fourth to the twenty-seventh, he was visiting Prague, as an ambassador of good will from the Engineers of America and as a first step in planning the International Congress of Management to be held in the summer of 1924. The record of his few days there was full of marvelous experiences. He was met at the border by a representative of the government, and considered a guest of the country as long as he was there. He spoke at the University to the manufacturers, and to the Academy; and lunched with the President Masaryk; and had every facility put at his disposal for sightseeing in the historic buildings, in industry and through the beautiful old city. It was a red-letter visit and a milestone in his career. It meant to him a "green light" on preparing to take his wife to the Conference when the time came. It impelled him with a desire to put freely at the disposal of this democratic country everything that had been done in the Management field, but especially in the field of Motion Study.

He went to Berlin in March, and had a long conference with Miss. Witte. She was faithfully translating everything sent to her into German and conserving what she knew to be the principles of scientific management and of the Gilbreth work. Otherwise his visit to Germany was disappointing as he felt there was a tendency to adapt everything to their own ideas and to make changes which were really "inventing downward."

Between trips he dashed back to the work in the United States, which went splendidly also. There seemed to be a greater utilization of the Motion Study findings in new fields than ever before. It was encouraging to see the work for the handicapped going on; with the eyesight conservation group utilizing what was appropriate for their work. There seemed greater integration in the Management Group and the meeting of the Taylor Society at Philadelphia in March was a happy experience. The Gilbreth's paper on *Super Standards* was whole-heartedly accepted and it was pleasant to present it under the friendly chairmanship of Professor Willetts.

The British group seemed to misunderstand the meaning of *The One Best Way* and Eric Farmer wrote voluminously, criticizing Motion Study techniques and objectives. This attitude spread through the Industrial Psychology group. They had always shown a tendency to change vocabulary and to disparage American Methods work as compared with the British, and especially that of the Institute of Industrial Psychology.

At home, papers for the Academy of Political and Social Science followed one another in rapid succession, and the related groups in economics and sociology showed an increasing interest in the findings of Industrial Engineering.

The summer at Nantucket was a specially happy one. As a new baby was expected, Lillian decided to go down early, and to enjoy the comfort of the little Nantucket hospital. She had a happy week there before the family arrived. As the new baby had not arrived, she went to "The Shoe" but was back in the hospital on June twenty-second, when the baby arrived, easily and happily, at seven o'clock in the evening. Frank was on hand this time, though he missed many of what he called "The coming-out parties." This time, through Dr. Grouard's cooperation, and the fact that little was going on in the hospital, he was accepted as chief assistant, and had a marvelous time!

Lillian had hoped for a baby girl, and felt that, as there had been six boys, and that quota was accomplished, she had a right to another small daughter. Every girl in the family shared this hope. The boys were loud in making it clear they did not. Daddy was non-committal. Never was a baby more wanted and loved than the small Jane. It had been decided that she should be named for her father's favorite cousin, Jane Bunker. But he had been insistent on the Moller name, so Moller was substituted, for Aunt Mabel's Goddaughter. Each Moller girl had happily taken over the place of Godmother. Gertrude had Martha and Dan; Ernestine had the Gilbreth Ernestine and Bob; Elinor had Frank Junior; Josephine had had the little Mary and now had Lillian; Mabel had Bill and now was to have Janey; Grandma Moller had Anne and Jack, who later was to become Aunt Ernestine's adopted Godson. Fred Moller had Fred Gilbreth.

This was the first time that Frank had really been free so far as time and worry were concerned. He could be at the hospital several times a day, strolling over in his summer "whites" with bouquets of his favorite "Queen's-lace-handkerchief," which he had picked along the road. He could sit and chat and admire the new baby. Her eyes were darker than Anne's but blue; and her hair blonde. In fact she had resemblance's to all her brothers and sisters, who spent their visiting time trying to find these resemblance, and wishing they could snatch her back to "The Shoe" at once.

Her Mother could hardly bear her out of her sight, especially after an adventure which ended happily, but might have been a serious one. One morning, as the nurse brought her from the nursery to her Mother's room, she said, "Last night, the police brought a prisoner here because of course you know we have no jail. She is going on trial this morning."

"What was the offense?" asked Lillian.

"Oh, she murdered her illegitimate child a while ago," was the nonchalant reply.

"Where did she sleep?" asked Lillian.

"Oh, next door to the nursery," was the indifferent answer.

"And who was on duty to see that nothing happened?" was the next question.

"Oh, she didn't make any trouble," was the answer!

Lillian wondered what would have happened to the poor distraught creature and the baby, if the baby had squawked in the night! It might have been a critical situation. The baby did not squawk, nothing happened; the prisoner did not come back — but Lillian felt a little happier when they could move over to "The Shoe!"

Frank had a wonderful time with the children that summer. He had put over the project for the Winchester Laundry, of burying the outmoded equipment for home laundry. He and the children paralleled the experiment by burying the family wringer, washboards, and flat iron — which Tom reluctantly loaned and dug out as soon as he had an opportunity!

The work went on satisfactorily. Czechoslovakia continued to express its appreciation by translating the Gilbreth books and preparing through the Maearyk Academy of Labor to utilize material as fast as he could send it to them. Kenneth Condit, of the *American Machinist,* undertook to write a long series of articles which could be serviceable not only to this country but abroad. The work went well with Lever Brothers, Krementz, Heller & Merz, the United States Rubber Company, and other work going satisfactorily.

1923 was another happy busy year, for the Condit articles went splendidly and new clients and jobs were added. A survey at Filene's; visits to Bridgeport Brass Company; the Evans Laundry; Barber Asphalt; American Radiator — not only a diversity of jobs but of industries and areas.

Frank's circle of friends grew, and among them were many of his clients. If he went to Boston, it was almost a reunion with E.A. Filene, the Shapleys, the Dreiers — as well as all the old friends. And so it was everywhere on all his trips.

Anne had started to Smith the fall of 1922, and she and her Daddy were both thrilled when he could stop off to visit her; meet her instructors; and take her and her chums to dinner.

The American Society of Mechanical Engineers Ordnance Meeting in April — visits to the college friends at Michigan, Purdue and the other colleges — starting Lillian off to California for the celebration of Pa's golden wedding on May twenty-first — made the spring months busy and happy ones. There was not so much time spent by Frank at Nantucket that summer, because work was so demanding, and he had set his heart on having both Lillian and himself attend the 1924 conferences in Europe. One was to be the Power Conference in London — the other, the First International Management Congress, at Prague.

The Gilbreth family at "The Shoe" in Nantucket (1923)

The one real worry was that Frank's heart troubled him considerably during his stay in Nantucket. Dr. Grouard warned him that it was not in good order, probably never had recovered from the strain put upon it at Fort Sill, and must be watched carefully. He supplied necessary stimulants and said Frank should never be without them. One or two sharp attacks frightened Lillian so that she packed the stimulants for every trip, and saw that Frank was never without them when he was at home. But with the fall and winter, the attacks became less violent, and finally seemed to cease entirely. However, the possibility of heart impairment and its results had never been out of either Frank's or Lillian's minds, after the Fort Sill experience, and they both realized that everything must be done to prepare for an emergency.

This did not mean any great change in their procedure. Frank had always thought about what would need to be done, in case anything happened to him. He had carried adequate insurance, and had incessantly attempted to teach his partner everything which she might need to carry on if he were not there to do it.

1924 bid fair to be the happiest year of any they could remember. The jobs went well. So did every area of the work, but especially the planning for the trip in the summer. This was a source of endless pleasure and careful planning. Frank finally worked out a day-by-day schedule for the trip, in greatest detail. It seemed to both partners that perhaps the time was coming when instead of going from client to client they might set up a school, with the clients sending their men to be trained. This would insure selection of the best person the client had for the training, with every check-through on smoothness of installation and adequate provision for maintenance. The publicity of the last years would all build into this, especially Condit's fine articles. It would mean completing the jobs underway. This seemed feasible as they would have to be nearing completion while both partners were in Europe if things were to run satisfactorily. Fortunately, the time schedule was not difficult to make, because Andie would have finished her second year in college, and could handle the family in Nantucket with the Nantucket friends on call — and Aunt Anne free to come if she were needed. Ernestine would graduate from high school on the 13th of June, the children would leave immediately afterward. The partners could sail on the nineteenth, with the official party, be in London for the World Power Conference, and be in Prague from July twentieth to August first. They could return from France on August seventh, to be back in New York on the fifteenth, have a little time in Nantucket, and bring the family home in time for school and college in September.

John Cross came home in March, on the *Nevada*, having done a fine job and being happy in the Navy. He stopped for a visit with the family and Frank had time to see Sister Anne's pleasure in having him back and even do a talk at Moses Brown, John's old school, to everyone's great satisfaction.

In May, Frank went to Purdue to give several talks; then on to Ann Arbor, to Harvard, to Lehigh, to Columbia — and his diary showed day-to-day planning — up to the sailing of the steamer. One great satisfaction came from a trip to the Life Extension Institute — the report said that his heart seemed in fine condition and likely to give him no trouble. Lillian was trying to surprise him on his birthday — which could be spent, they planned, in London — by a short account of his life which she hoped to expand into a biography. She dictated it on the Dictaphone when he was away from home, and scrupulously paid for the time of the secretary who transcribed it by doing equivalent hours of work in the office herself. She called it *The Quest of The One Best Way*. It was typed and ready, early in June. She was greatly tempted to give it to him, but decided it would be more fun to keep it for a surprise.

As always, the family looked forward eagerly to a graduation from high school. Ern's was to be the second and her Daddy was very much pleased at her good record. She had done especially well in English but had had a difficult time in Mathematics. In fact he was so annoyed with one Mathematics teacher who thought she had a vacuum where her mathematical ability should be, that he insisted on the school psychologist giving her a psychological test, and exulted when this proved her real ability! He and Lillian, and such children as could get tickets, went to the Exercises, and were proud of their graduate. Cousin Jane went too, then came home for the ice-cream party and the celebration.

Frank, who had had long and exhausting trips, slept late the next morning, while Lillian gathered a big bunch of syringa for Ernestine to carry to her Class Day. He finally got started on the day and decided to go to town to have the passports [vise'd] and do some last shopping for the trip abroad. He stopped at the door, as usual, for some last chat. As usual, Lillian brushed off some specks of dust, to have him say, as she gave the inevitable last touch, "The pat of finality!" In a few minutes he telephoned from the Lackawanna Station, as he often did, if he remembered on his trip to the train some final things needing to be done at home. He told her that he had missed the train, by a good many minutes, and she said, "Never mind. It must be almost time for the next one," to which he replied, "Good old optimist." He then said that he had forgotten his passports, and she asked him where he thought they could be. He said, "In the usual place, of course — in the drawer back of the desk." She asked him to wait, while she checked there, and he said, "All right. I'll wait." When she went back, there was no one on the line, so Central reported, and she decided that the train had come in and that he had left the telephone booth to take it.

There were many things to be done, and it was some time after that one of the neighbors came in — pale and distracted — to tell her that a policeman had stopped at her house and asked her to go to the Gilbreth's and tell them that the Major had dropped dead in the telephone booth. His own doctor had been called, and could assure her that he had not suffered — that probably he never knew he was going — and that certainly his last word had been that to her, when he said, "I'll wait!"

Perhaps it was fortunate that the children were coming down with a combination of measles and chickenpox, and that the whole household procedure had to be adapted to their needs. Aunt Anne came on, neighbors and friends did everything, and that evening Frank was brought home in his beloved uniform, to stay until the services could be held.

It was a beautiful summer evening and the scent of syringa in the garden came through the house. As it grew dark, a violent thunderstorm broke. Their father had taught the children not to be afraid of them, but to enjoy them. In spite of everything that had happened, the wonderful, beautiful, and startling electrical display held them spell-bound. Finally, small Bill spoke up and said, "Gee, I'm sure that Daddy is there! Isn't it exactly like him?" — and everyone agreed that he was there, perhaps participating and certainly enjoying.

Frank had had very definite ideas as to the type of services he wanted. A military note — no flowers — no music — his brain to go to Harvard — to be cremated — to have his ashes scattered "To the Four Winds of Heaven" — no mourning — the work to go on — nothing to be made difficult for anyone — the children to be made to feel that Death was as simple as Birth, and as natural.

His wife carried out these wishes, as she knew them. She telephoned Sister Anne; she telephoned Myrtelle Canavan at the Harvard Medical Museum; she telephoned Aunt Lillian. As the California family could not get there in time, she telegraphed them and urged them not to come on, as she wanted, if possible, to carry through Frank's summer plans. Everyone responded marvelously; Dr. Black, the Minister, understood what was needed, and the local American Legion Post took over managing the home service. Such children as were well came to the home service — and Aunt Anne stayed with them while Aunt Lillian, with her namesake, went to the Crematory and arranged for the trip up the beautiful Hudson so that the ashes might be scattered and find their way to the sea. Myrtelle Canavan came on herself, so that that part of Frank's wishes might be carried through.

The devoted family and friends thought of everything where thought was needed. Fred Cross took over handling the insurance settlement; Wallace Clark offered to take her in as a partner, or, when she thought that Frank would prefer her to carry on under the Gilbreth name, to stand by financially, or in any other way. The Sanders suggested that their Elizabeth — who had been Anne's classmate at high school, and was now her classmate at Smith — accompany her on the European trip, as Andie would have to take care of the children.

The Moller family reluctantly decided to do as she asked, and to postpone their visit until her return from Europe, and through everyone's cooperation, when the party sailed on June nineteenth, she was a member of it, with all plans for the summer in line to be carried out as Frank had wished.

The dear children prepared a special copy of *The Ambidextrous Magazine* for their Mother to read on the trip, with stories, drawings, and everything they could think of that might please or interest her.

She had an opportunity during the trip over to check on many things, and to do some careful planning. She remembered that when the beloved "Pa" Moller had died in 1923, Frank, who had grieved for him like a son, had said, "Now you and I are on the firing line!" She realized that now he would say, "You are in the firing line, Boss, and you must conduct yourself accordingly!"

She realized, too, and it comforted her — that she had the best this world offers — beautiful memories, the children to work for, and faith in the future. As she saw it, the first job ahead was to carry out Frank's plans for the summer. Everything that could be done had been done to make this possible. The children were prepared for the Nantucket summer, and were more than anxious to free her from anxiety by accepting Andie's supervision and Andie was proud that she could take over the job. It had been arranged months before that every member attending the Prague conference should represent each Society in which he held membership.

Those Societies which had given Frank special assignments had transferred this to her, and she had adequate credentials to do his work as well as her own. The papers she and Frank had prepared were to be presented under their joint membership, and fortunately he had revised and approved them all. Warm friends — who were part of the group — would make the readjustment of the program as easy as possible. After the trip was over and the schedule filled as adequately and accurately as possible, would be the time for future planning.

Elizabeth was a great comfort and everyone helped Lillian find work to do. The papers to be presented at the London Congress had all been preprinted and were on the boat. To fill her time adequately, she read and briefed them all, and could hand over to her colleagues who were to discuss them material which saved them a considerable effort. At the same time, she was educating herself on the Power Congress program. In London, she and Elizabeth were house guests of the Spooners. While their deep mourning for Frank was in some ways difficult to endure — in others, it was a very real comfort. The paper, as she presented it, went over well, and it was not as hard as she had anticipated to take part in the technical and also in the social events. This was largely because she had Elizabeth as a companion, and did not want to deprive her of any good times. They even visited the kind, deaf, old Lord Leverhulme, on his beautiful estate, and Libby made quite a hit, with her gay ways and excellent dancing. It was something to be remembered, to see Lord Leverhulme dancing with her and to hear him shout, quite unconscious that he was raising his voice, "It can't be much of a treat to you to dance with an old codger like me!" — while the matchmaking Mamas on the sidelines discussed his liking for the young American — and Lillian understood why Frank was so fond of him.

There was time for a stop in Berlin and a meeting with the Matschosses and the Schlesingers before the party went on to Czechoslovakia. Not all or even a large portion of the American group who had gone to London went on to the Management Conference. Lillian was comforted that the

Freemans decided to go, because of their old friendship and the fact that she knew what a help and support to her they would be.

Nothing could have been more appreciative or touching than the welcome of the Czechoslovakian group. To them it was a personal tribute, that Frank's widow had been willing to make the trip. They made her feel constantly how real and deep was their sympathy and appreciation. It was, comparatively speaking, not difficult to give the papers, or even preside at the final formal session. Even being made a member, along with some others, of the Academy Masaryk, as Frank had been, was no serious ordeal. But the Memorial Service for Frank which they insisted on having, and conducted as they would have conducted it for one of their own leaders, was a harrowing experience.

A black pall, mourning everywhere, eulogies — all of the things which could be avoided in Montclair had to be endured now. Only trying to help Frank's most intimate friends, like L.W. Wallace and Robert Kent, who had to speak through what was obviously a terrible ordeal for them also, pulled her through.

A few days in France, for Elizabeth's benefit, and the comfort that comes from the perennial beauty of Paris, and they were back on the steamer, and en route home. There was time now to make decisions as to what came next. It was a satisfaction to look at the work plan and schedule Frank had made for the trip, and to see that everything had been carried out exactly as he planned. Beyond that, she could do no detailed planning, and it would not be fair, ever, to try to shape future proceedings by his past decisions. One could only say, "If he were here, what would he advise?" and then, "How nearly can I plan to do this?" She felt sure of certain things — he would not want her to move the family to California. He had always felt that the children should be brought up as strenuously as possible, given great responsibility, and allowed to take over the direction of their own lives, as soon as they felt adequate to do this. The beloved California family were certain to urge that Lillian and

the children move near them, and that life be made as easy for the entire group as possible, but the wise thing would be to stay in the dear home in Montclair, if this was feasible. And, if the children concurred, to go on as best she could with the work. That planning could not be done until she had had a talk with them!

It was vital that the children's education be continued on the level where it was, and that they be kept as happy as possible. That was the thing of greatest importance — her first job never to be neglected. She must prepare to carry it on as long as they lived, but especially to keep the family together and to see that each child had a college training, at least, and beyond that, if he wanted it.

Lillian (seated, center) with the entire assemblage at the 1st CIOS meeting in Prague, where she went to deliver a speech originally scheduled to be given by Frank. (Shortly after Frank's death, 1924)

The second responsibility was to Frank's work. This should continue under the Gilbreth name. While she could not possibly expect to develop it as he would have done, she must do her best to see that what had been accomplished was not lost, but was conserved and added to, as that became possible. The third thing to be considered was the research to which he was so devoted. This probably could not be pushed at once. But responsibility for this, and a constant search for opportunities, must never be neglected.

If she was able to see that the work itself was conserved and developed, in time, surely, research in that area could be continued.

She landed and went to Montclair for a day or two of visits with Elizabeth and her family — to find that the home was well cared for and ready for the family's coming back in the fall. Fred Cross and the cooperative insurance companies had seen that Frank's policies were paid into the bank and there was no immediate financial problem. A stop in Providence, to thank the devoted Fred and Anne Cross, who had stood by so valiantly, and then on to Nantucket and the children! Andie had done a marvelous job, and the faithful Tom and Mrs. Cunningham kept everything running smoothly. It was wrong to grieve for the past, with the children so strong and well and cooperative. The beauty, peace, and serenity of Nantucket, and the happy memories of "The Shoe" were all she had known they would be, and the children were so happy in their presents and in having her there that of course she must be happy too.

There was time for long conferences and explanations that one or two choices were open to them:

They could move near the family in California, and go to school or college in or near the University of California. Lillian could take care of the home and the family, and perhaps do some writing, but must give up the business, as California was not yet ready for Consulting Management work and Specialists in Motion Study.

Or, they could stay where they were, and go on as nearly as possible, as Dad had planned. But this meant several things: it meant, in the first place, taking a chance financially, and using some of the insurance money to carry the business until Lillian could test out whether clients would accept her as a consultant, or not. It also meant that she must devote more time than ever to the business, and that the children would have to adapt themselves to this. Most of the jobs were in such a state that they could be completed by members of the staff, who then could terminate their connection with the company. After this, Lillian might try out the project she and Frank had had in mind — to have a School of Management. Only she would not undertake anything so ambitious as this. She would call it a series of courses in Motion Study. This would enable her to be at home more than she otherwise could, and perhaps to start the colossal job of organizing Frank's material so that it could be permanently serviceable.

The family unanimously made the second choice and went back to Montclair to try to make the adjustments. The beloved Pierce Arrow was sold at once, with the stipulation that it would be sold out of town, for they felt it was more than they could bear to see it, and perhaps watch it, deteriorate.

Anne decided to transfer, for her junior year, to the University of Michigan. She and her Dad had agreed that a year in another part of the country was a fine experience, in anyone's college course. Uncle Joe Bursley was Dean of Men there, and he and Aunt Margery would share their home with her and make her feel a part of family life. Ernie would go to Smith, and the others continue their work at the High School or at nearby Nishuane.

School opened, and the family routine re-established itself. The plans for finishing the work on the jobs in hand went through. Lillian started to plan the Motion Study Course, which was to start directly after the first of January. The Moller family came — several of them — and as Lillian knew, urged the moving West. But they were understanding and patient, and agreed that she should try her experiment, if that would bring her greatest comfort. Her Mother offered to loan her anything she might need, and to accept repayment as readily as she made the loan. None was necessary at the time, but it was a comfort to know that every help was available and ready.

The Society of Industrial Engineers asked to print *The Quest,* which Frank had never seen, although the children were sure he suspected it was being written. Lillian added the few final lines:

Final Word
Suddenly, on June 14, 1924, Frank went, not abroad,
as he had planned, but "West," as soldiers go.
The Quest goes on!

Frank Bunker Gilbreth (1924)

and the foreword:

Foreword

Out of the World of men you came,
To open gates for me,
Into a world of Happiness,
I had not known could be.

Into the world of stars you go,
And other gates swing wide,
What tho our little day is done?
Eternities abide.

and Mr. Dent, and Colonel Sheehan, and the rest, took over putting the manuscript through the press. When it was finished, every member of the Society had a copy, and half the total "printing" was sent to her, for distribution. It was of tremendous comfort to be able to send this to Frank's friends.

There had been three numbers printed of the little magazine, *The GOB-WAY,* and material for the fourth had been organized by Frank. His old schoolmate and devoted friend, George Coleman, wrote a closure for this one; as Lillian decided it should be the last:

> "My hat is off to the memory of Frank B. Gilbreth, my old schoolmate, a devoted husband, a father extraordinary, robust man of the world, human dynamo, fearless fighter, transparent friend, and creator of THE ONE BEST WAY TO DO WORK. And he came upon THE ONE BEST WAY of passing over into the great beyond. A multitude of friends and clients will keep his memory green.
>
> "His wife Lillian M. Gilbreth, his comrade in all his interests, will carry on his work in all its phases. But it is felt that this little publication, of which this is only the fourth issue, is so peculiarly personal, to him, that no attempt should be made to continue it."
>
> — George W. Coleman

Kenneth Condit offered to carry through the series in the *American Machinist* exactly as it was originally planned. The American Management Association gave Lillian an honorary membership as a tribute to Frank, Calvin Rice started to plan the most appropriate way and time for her to become a member of the American Society of Mechanical Engineers. Frank's university and college friends everywhere asked her to take over the lecture assignments which he had been accustomed to cover. President Elliott and Dean Potter urged her to continue the custom of a Gilbreth lecture at Purdue every year.

Announcement of the first Motion Study Course brought few registrants, but these excellent ones, from companies who allowed Lillian to select personally the member of their organization who was to be a student. Joe Piacetelli was willing to ask for a leave from the Barber Asphalt Company to come to direct the laboratory part of the Course, and the Barber people were willing to spare him.

Then came Christmas, and Andie's homecoming, and the usual traditional celebration to put through. Andie was in the "Seventh Heaven" because she was engaged to Robert Barney, a young staff instructor in the University of Michigan Medical School. Try as she did to enter into her child's happiness, Lillian felt that her staunchest supporter would be taken from her, and disgraced herself by bursting into tears instead of smiles when she heard the news. But she managed to live that down, and put the holiday celebration through, only to be overtaken by flu, which knocked her completely flat, physically and emotionally. But flu or no flu, life must go on, and the Course started, even if the children did have to push her upstairs, and the students pretended that they did not notice what a thin and shaky teacher they had. There was really only one way to take now, and she must take it. There was really only one consolation, and that was work! And, knowing, as she did, that bringing up the children, and doing the work in Frank's field, were jobs no one else could do, was the greatest incentive possible.

1925 was a busy year. Frank's habit of keeping full diary notes still persisted and the record shows a persistent attempt to fit into Lillian's program the things he was accustomed to do. Days were not long enough to handle things adequately, but the family, the friends, and everyone cooperated — which, of course, was the only thing that made the schedule possible at all. The Motion Study Course progressed smoothly, and weekends gave opportunity to fit in lectures at the colleges or at technical meetings. Montclair's being so near New York made evening meetings there possible, and there were always friendly Management men who could come in and take over the Course, for a day, if an out-of-town trip was necessary.

The children's home and school life went smoothly. Anne was happy at the University of Michigan and Ernestine seemed to be enjoying Smith. Congenial friends, old and new, made a little group which she enjoyed thoroughly. The younger children got on well at high school and at Nishuane, and there always had to be time for P.T.A. meetings, and for speeches wherever a teacher or principal wanted a talk. In March, Lillian went up to Providence to visit Anne Cross and debate at the Wednesday Club, stopping in Framingham on the way back to visit the Dennison plant and dear Helen Douglass Ladd and her husband Paul. Later on that month, Cornelia Parker spoke at Ford Hall and Lillian had a chance to be there also. Frank's friends everywhere asked her to take his lecture dates or planned new ones for her. She went to Penn State, to visit the Sacketts, and meet Mr. Beese — who was later to be a colleague at Purdue. Any trip through Philadelphia meant stopping off to see dear Mrs. Dodge and visit with the other Philadelphia friends.

April eleventh shows a notation, "My Andie comes home," and by this time, Lillian was rested enough to show herself as happy over the engagement as she really was! In May, she had an opportunity to visit Andie as well as the Bursleys in Ann Arbor, and get to know Bob Barney, who was to be her first and very beloved son-in-law. On the way back, she stopped for her first speech at Purdue, and to meet all the

Elliotts and Potters who were to become such dear friends. Later in May, came a trip to California, and a chance to celebrate her birthday — which would otherwise have been so sad — with the beloved family.

Such trips gave fine opportunities to check with previous clients and to make contacts for new work. Back, in June, to see Martha graduate on the twelfth — and to write in the diary on June fourteenth, "Frank has been one year on the New Adventure," and to make for herself a check-through as to how many of the projects he had left for her to accomplish could be considered well started, at least. On the twentieth, the family went off to Nantucket, but Lillian and Ernestine stayed in New York to

Lillian with all of the children except Anne, who was away at college (1925)

sell, for several weeks, at Macy's. Lillian decided she must know more about customer and sales person's reactions and fatigue. The family thought they would feel happier if one of the children stayed home with her. So Ernestine insisted that she try for a job also, and the two started off to work together. Ernestine was a "contingent" and on the payroll. Lillian had no formal connection as far as pay was concerned, but Mr. Percy Straus had said she might sell anywhere she chose, and need only hand over such report of her findings as she desired. It was a fine and courteous gesture, and a splendid opportunity!

Ernestine did a fine job, and used her family experience to help her judge sizes, et cetera, in the children's department where she sold. After a day of mentally measuring small customers, or their mother's descriptions of them, against six brothers, her Supervisor in the boy's underwear department asked the management if she could stay where she was, as she "showed outstanding aptitude." It was a fatiguing, difficult, experience for so young a girl, but it gave her something which contributed toward her great success as a buyer at Macy's, years after. Lillian found her experience extraordinarily valuable also. But neither of the two were sorry when the month of work was over, and they could join the rest of the family in Nantucket.

It was, for Lillian, a series of trips, shuttling back and forth between Montclair and Nantucket, that summer. There was much to be planned, as the new Course opened early in September. Being the second Course, it ran more smoothly and easily than the first, and the children seemed to fit happily into their school program. Janey was now at Brookside at the Nursery School, and following the family pattern of insisting on saying her say. She was home with a cold for a few days and when Mother told her it was necessary to stay there until she could no longer expose the others, she immediately asked, with an anxious look, "What will my School do?" Andie was back at Michigan, Ernestine at Smith, and Martha taking a post-graduate course at the High School — the others there or at Nishuane.

The support of the friends, individually and in the technical groups, continued. The Society of Electrical Engineers asked Lillian to speak at as many of their meetings as she could. John Younger had her invited to address the Society of Automotive Engineers, at their Production Meeting in September. The Metropolitan Section of The American Society of Mechanical Engineers had her speak at the November meeting. George Coleman invited her to speak at Ford Hall; the Taylor Society at their meeting at Colgate University turned over the evening session to a talk on *Recent Developments in Motion Study,* which gave her an opportunity to present the progress of Frank's work. Most gratifying was the acceptance of a paper in the December meetings of A.S.M.E. on *The Present State of Industrial Psychology* for it was this group which Frank considered most important. Looking back on the year 1925, one becomes convinced that many of these things could not have been adequately covered — surely there was tremendous understanding and sympathy and cooperation to make the outcome as satisfactory as it was!

1926 started with an adequate registration for the Motion Study Course and everything well set for a busy year. It was a tremendous satisfaction to Lillian that her family, her friends, her colleagues, her clients, and the public — all realized that what she was attempting to do was to carry on Frank's work. The clippings which she continued to paste into the diary showed that not only his work, but his personality, remained. It became evident that what he had often described as the aim of his life, to increase "Happiness Minutes" everywhere, could be furthered by the development of his work!

In January, Mary Anderson, of the Women's Bureau, called a Woman's Industrial Conference. This, for Lillian, who was a member of it, was the start of many years of contact with the Women's bureau. For some time, she and Miss. Mary Van Kleeck of the Russell Sage Foundation were designated as technical experts, without salary, and consulted whenever this was useful.

In January, too, Andie's engagement to Robert Barney was announced, and the plans for the wedding began to be made. Anne had done a fine job at Michigan, and Lillian remembered with mixed emotions the happy news of her having made Phi Beta Kappa. Bob had created a considerable stir at the Sorosis House by dashing in to embrace and congratulate her publicly! Carol Cross, who was staying with the Gilbreths, and making life happier and easier, had received the telegram — she and Janey met the after-dinner train on which Lillian was returning to Montclair, tired and hungry after a hard day's work. Carol said, "I have news for you." Lillian, still nervous about calamities which might come suddenly, was overcome when she heard the happy news that she sat down in the gutter and burst into tears! Janey — much disturbed — said, "What has Andie done to Mother? I am never going to do anything bad to her like that!"

It was interesting how expanding activities brought one back to old contacts. Such was a talk for the A.S.M.E. Section of the Engineering Club of Plainfield. There were not many of the old neighbors still living in Netherwood and it was with mixed emotions that Lillian spoke in the old surroundings. By this time, *The Quest* had been generally distributed, and it was doing its part in keeping Frank before old friends and new.

It was pleasant too to begin annual trips to Purdue and other campuses and to find that Mr. Condit's articles were so useful in establishing a background. Tom Dreier, Joe Chappell, and other writers continued to quote Frank and to make the public feel that his influence went on. This also was a great help. The articles she was asked to write showed her that his many interests and contacts would furnish fine opportunities for helping his work grow. They were in the fields of vocational guidance, fatigue, skill — as well as Motion Study, and its diversified applications.

In March, the American Management Association not only asked for and presented her paper on *What's Ahead for Management?* but the adequate discussion and the fine reprint helped to establish the validity of the work. The American Woman's Association invited her to become its Honorary Member from New Jersey and continued this appointment throughout the years. The fact that she was the only Engineer, showed how few as yet had entered the profession, but also was a help in establishing her place, where she most wanted it to be — among the Engineering Group. The work she had been doing with the Prisons Group at the Reformatory in Bedford was resulting in a text on *Opportunities and Training for Women in Reformatories* which was to prove useful. She remembered the stormy day, the December after Frank went, when Robert Kent, Julia Jaffrey, and she had planned this project, in the Montclair Laboratory, where Frank had worked so unceasingly and so happily.

There was increasing interest also in the application of Motion Study in the household. This was encouraging, as that had always been a subject of tremendous interest to Frank. Even the church group wanted to talk in this area, and both men and women attended the meeting and joined in the discussion. Equally satisfactory were the contacts with the Personnel group, and the realization that so much of Frank's data was useful and interesting there.

In May, the faithful Society of Industrial Engineers invited her to speak on *Fatigue in Industry and the Home* at their Buffalo meeting. This gave an opportunity to correlate the principles and techniques in the two fields, which was very serviceable. Again, as always, the friends and the laboratory assistant handled the Course so smoothly that Lillian was able to be away when that was necessary, and at the same time to gather and present material in the most serviceable way possible to the group receiving the training. The graduates of the previous courses had all made good, and organizations were sending other representatives to carry the work into other plants. Each group became more diversified, and gradually, oversea students joined the American group.

The General Federation of Women's Clubs took up "Fatigue in the Home" at state and national meetings, and began that type of cooperation with Lillian and her endeavors that lasted through the years. The same thing was true of the Home Study group, the Nursing group, and the Home Economics group, and the others working in the area of the family and the home. This year, especially, that aspect of the work developed. The technical groups of colleagues continued their year-in and year-out cooperation. These now included the American Association of Engineers — one of the correlating groups which was proving very serviceable. June brought the thrill of Anne's commencement — the first of the eleven to graduate from college. She graduated "with distinction" and her Mother almost died of joy and pride. So did the brothers and sisters who celebrated at home as they could not get to Ann Arbor. Martha finished her post-graduate course at High School and was ready to enter the New Jersey College for Women in the fall.

In June, Lillian and Carol Cross sailed for London — and then to go on to the International Welfare Congress — (I.R.I.) — in Switzerland and the American Association of University Women's meeting in Amsterdam. The family as usual went to Nantucket, with Anne in charge — keeping things in order and making plans for her September wedding. Lillian had enthusiastically devoted every free minute to working on things for the hope chest, for she loved hand sewing, and this hobby was to prove more and more satisfying through the years. It was good to re-visit dear Professor and Mrs. Spooner, and to have "Meg" shop with her, at her favorite linen stores. These were ones patronized by British women, and out of the general run of the tourist trade. It was good, too, to stop at Liberty's to shop the beautiful flowered linen which only they make — sun-proof, wash-proof, durable, and beautiful.

The I.R.I. meeting proved interesting and it was gratifying to be asked to give the opening address. The five days in July devoted to the subject, "The Development of Scientific Management in Industry," proved stimulating because of the many viewpoints presented by the delegates from different countries.

Most interesting of all, perhaps, was the Amsterdam Conference of the International Federation of University Women, because there for the first time, Lillian had an important opportunity to present problems and solutions of the Management field to this group, in a talk entitled *The Reconciliation of Marriage and Profession.* The unwavering interest and support of college women everywhere through the years was to be a tremendous asset.

One aspect of this was an increased interest in the problems of the home, and in men's place in solving them. This led to work on Model Kitchens for various industries and newspapers, which proved highly stimulating and profitable.

The children's summer in Nantucket went through splendidly and Lillian was much pleased at commendatory reference to her namesake in the Nantucket paper. Little Lill and her chums had started an "F.T." Club, which gave a play and held a sale, and contributed $22.50 to the Hospital Fund.

The *Montclair Times* equally recognized Frank Junior's achievement as a conductor of a camp band at the Scout Camp. He and his chum Fred Kidde had had a marvelous time, working on their own hut, with the encouragement and help of Fred's father, an expert woodchopper, and a grand pal.

In August, Lillian left the family at Nantucket to go to the Silver Bay Conference at Lake George and have the pleasure of being on the same program with James Emory, Arthur Young, President Hutchins of Berea, and other leaders in the field of human relations.

Of course, the big event in the family life was Anne's wedding, on September eighteenth. Ernie was the one attendant. Bob Barney's father and mother and younger brother came on, and the two families established a congenial friendship, to grow and develop with the years. It was a lovely day, and the wedding could be held in the garden. Poor devoted

Anne's wedding photo (September 18, 1926)

Tom furnished the one excitement. Bobby quietly prowled around trying to see as best he could. Tom, fearing he was going to step on the bride's train, snatched him off and tried to run into the house with him. Only Bob Kent's quiet intervention calmed things down! It was a beautiful wedding and no one could be unhappy about Anne's going to Cleveland, because everyone had become so devoted to Bob Barney. The Gilbreth children looked forward so eagerly to visiting him and Andie, in their little new apartment.

In October, Lillian did some radio work, to find that it went very smoothly, and that she enjoyed it thoroughly. An amusing experience was one at the "Psychological" Dinner held in New York in October. Of the speakers, two, Miss. Dorothy Marston and Lillian, were women — the other two, Henry Link and George Dorsey, were men. The chairman gave both men their title of "Doctor" but carefully called Dr. Marston "Miss." and Dr. Gilbreth "Mrs."! The two women exchanged smiles, that even in this advanced group, men had the preference. But the Taylor Society presented one of her papers on *Waste Elimination as it Concerns the Human Element*; the American Society of Mechanical Engineers Management Division presented *Eliminating Waste in Selection of Personnel*; Ohio State invited her to do a paper; and the *Iron Age* and other technical papers showed no discrimination. The Home Economics group continued their support and Mr. Macon and the faithful *Iron Age* reported fully and adequately everything she chose to give them.

A great thrill of the year was the visit to this country of many overseas friends who took part in the discussion at the "International Evening" of the Taylor Society in December. Mr. Harold Butler, of the Labor Office; Dr. Mauro of Italy; Dr. Spacek of Prague; Miss. Bevington, of the Institute of Industrial Psychology in London, and Mr. Manning from the same group; Mr. Vander Leeuw of Holland; — but, above all, the devoted Irene Witte, from Berlin! Each of these made a separate visit to Montclair, to meet the Motion Study group and the family and to pledge support to the Motion Study movement.

This was the last year that Lillian kept new clippings, to any great extent. She felt, as she looked them through, that few of them had real significance as reflecting the spread of Frank's work and that the files of papers written — technical and other; magazines; and programs of meetings — would furnish an adequate record.

From this time on anything in these "Memories" must of necessity be less detailed, but perhaps for that very reason a better indicator of the progress made.

1927 proved very much the same sort of year as 1926. Lillian started it off with a series of out-of-town lectures in New England. These always gave her an opportunity to stay with Fred and Anne Cross, and often a chance to be at a meeting of the Wednesday Club. In January she was appointed by the County Supervisor as a member of the Essex County Board of Vocational Education. This meant keeping in close contact with both the Boy's and Girl's Vocational Schools. It was interesting to try to put Frank's findings at the service of this project. A visit to the Homemakers' Conference at Cornell was the first of a series of such visits, for Miss. Van Rensselaer and Miss. Rose had been Frank's friends as well as hers and any meeting was always an occasion.

It was a pleasure, in February, to be appointed by the A.S.M.E. as representative on the Committee for Exchange Professorships with Czechoslovakia. Lillian knew how very much Frank had wanted her to be a full member of A.S.M.E. This she now was, and she realized, with the years, the value such a membership had. February brought the annual convention of the National Retail Drygoods Association and an opportunity to talk to the Store Managers' Division on "What the Customer Wants." The fact that Jean Lies had been a member of the First Motion Study Course and had found her training very useful made increasing contacts with the retail group available. Another pleasant February occasion was speaking for the Deans of Women at their meeting in Dallas, Texas. Lillian could be there only twenty-four hours — but every minute of her stay furnished an occasion for hospitality, including the most interesting and attractive breakfast party she had ever attended.

Another interesting experience was talking for some of the fashionable New York Women's Clubs — like the "Fortnightly Forum" and "Sorosis." It was a new phase of metropolitan life, and very interesting to observe, although she had no desire for the leisure-time-program as a part of her day-by-day schedule.

Through Roy Wright, who, with his wife, Eliza, became close family friends, Lillian was invited to speak to the New York Railroad Club. Such invitations gave exceptional experience in meeting a variety of people, handling discussions, and answering questions. The children were well and happy. Frank was taking part not only in high school activities, such as being Advertising Manager for the school paper, but also in the Hi-Y Club, and in boy scouting. Janey had a marvelous visit with Andie, to be petted not only by her new brother but by his entire family. Father and Mother Barney were devoted to children and would have enjoyed having Janey spend her entire visit with them.

In March, a significant project in the Homemaking field was undertaken at Teacher's College. Emma Gunther and Lillian had had it in mind ever since Frank's early lectures there. The plan was to set up a series of meetings, extending over a number of weeks, to invited significant organizations to send representatives, and to invite leaders in the field of Scientific Management to present the material. The response was almost over-whelming, for the entire group came each day and stayed through the entire meeting, and the speakers gave generously of their time, interest, and information. It was the first attempt to place the material assembled by the Scientific Management group in detail before the Home Economics and Homemaking groups, in order that there might be com-plete transfer of all material available for home use. The fact that there were no fees, no salaries of any sort, and that the slight expense of the meetings was contributed by Teachers' College — who put its facilities at the disposal of the group and gave the undertaking sponsorship — was significant. The outcome of the project was highly satisfactory.

In April, Lillian had a chance for one of those quick happy trips to see the California family, with a series of parties, including one at Oakland Forum, where Cousin Annie Florence was making a fine contribution to the community life. This trip gave opportunities for stopping in Iowa and in Minnesota and picking up expense money by a series of lectures. There was an opportunity this year, too, to speak on the Stamford Campus, and on her own campus — University of California — at the Twenty-fifth Annual Alumni Luncheon in Faculty Glade. It was a satisfaction also to have the *Home Maker and Her Job* come out and receive favorable reviews. It had been written longhand, coming home on the steamer, the summer of '26 and then put into readable shape for a waiting publisher. Lillian wondered if Frank would not have thought it "gabby" like *Fatigue Study* but felt, even so, that perhaps one of the advantages of such a style was that it made easy reading of the material for the non-technical reader.

No Gilbreth child finished school in the summer of 1927, but Lillian — through the years — was usually a part of some Commencement. This year her contribution was slight. Dick Hall, the son of some near neighbors and friends, had died very suddenly and tragically. His devoted father and mother, as a memorial to him, gave a convalescent home to Dartmouth, which was called Dick Hall's House. Lillian had written the verse which was put over the fireplace and, while she could not attend the Class Day opening, felt herself in some way associated with the consolation the parents got from their gift and the appreciation it received. Directly after this, she went abroad to preside at the Summer School which the I.R.I. was to hold at Baveno, Italy, on the subject near to the Gilbreth's heart — "Elimination of Unnecessary Fatigue in Industry." This time, Dorothy Wright was her companion for the trip. The Conference lasted only a few days and the group was not large, but the friendships started there went on through the years, especially that with Professor Pear of

London, who had done outstanding work in the study of skill. Baveno was a beautiful place and Dorothy and Lillian enjoyed every minute of their stay there.

The 1927 Motion Study group had proved especially interesting because of its members from overseas. One of the great stores of Belgium had sent a student who did excellent work and introduced Motion Study through a whole chain of stores upon his return to his job. Another — Dr. Franz Hahn — whose splendid Ph.D. background made it easy for him to absorb the material rapidly, was to do fine work later on, and become a partner of Ross Allen and Irene Witte. Through these students and the friends made abroad, at the technical meetings, like Frau Dr. Zueblin Spiller and Dr. Friedrick, and the old friends who never became indifferent, the introduction of the Gilbreth ideas throughout Europe went forward smoothly and acceptably. The graduates of the Montclair Motion Study Courses and the members of the Gilbreth organization throughout the years had become organized into a "Gilbreth Research Group." Data were interchanged, and research supported. This was a great help and satisfaction, and also enriched the current Motion Study Course. In the fall, the American Gas Association invited Lillian to speak at one of their General Sessions at their Chicago Convention. The occasion stood out as a high spot of the year, for she was the guest of the Association all through the trip and the Convention, and never was a guest more graciously or bounteously entertained.

Opportunities like this meant contact with an entire industry, for the papers were presented before representatives from every part of the organization, and were printed and circulating through the Association's own magazines and their excellent publicity representatives.

1928 showed some new developments in the work. The Motion Study Course still went on in the spring, but it was supplemented with reports for clients which Lillian made as President of Gilbreth, Incorporated. Such was one on "Personnel Policies" for Sears Roebuck. The contacts with the Philadelphia office, and Mr. Lessing Rosenwald, the Vice President, proved pleasant and stimulating. He always seemed to have plenty of time not only for business, which was handled expeditiously, but for showing and talking over his beloved etchings, which was handled, by preference, more leisurely. Lillian found she greatly enjoyed making such surveys and writing up the reports and was glad when other opportunities presented themselves.

The summer brought two graduations, for Frank finished Montclair High School with a very creditable record and decided to accept an invitation to go to St. John's College in Annapolis, in the fall. Colonel Garey, one of his father's chums at Fort Sill, who had resigned from the Army, and who had taught at Johns Hopkins, was now the President of this little, old college and was doing most interesting things with it. Frank, who was planning to follow in his father's footsteps, and be an engineer, felt that a year in a literary college was "marking time." But his mother felt sure he was too young and too inadequately prepared for technical work, and longed to have him have all the general foundation and culture possible. Besides Colonel Garey was so cordial and so insistent, that it seemed ungracious not to go to him for at least a year. Within a few days of the high school graduation, Ernestine graduated from Smith. This was a great occasion for her Mother and for her. She had belonged to a happy, close-knit group of girls, and all the parents made a point of attending the several days of commencement exercises. The mothers got on very well, for each one looked at her own child and thought of nothing else. But the poor fathers were not especially congenial, and became bored long before the diplomas were handed out. Lillian enjoyed every minute and packed her child and all her belongings into the car, for a long happy ride on the beautiful College highway and time to make plans for "What next?"

This was the year that Mr. Hoover was the Republican Candidate for President. Lillian and Eliza Wright organized and devoted much time to the Women's Branch of the "Hoover for President" Engineers' National Committee. It was a tremendous thrill to have one's candidate elected, and when the telegram from the Engineers' National Committee came:

> "The National Committee is tremendously proud of its Woman's Branch which has indelibly written a new chapter in the history of national politics. Please accept our congratulations."

the women's joy was unbounded. They planned to attend the Inauguration in a body, and also to organize an Engineering Women's Club, in New York City, which might give the congenial group an opportunity to continue to meet and to work together.

The entire Gilbreth family shared in the celebration, and as Lillian wrote to Mrs. Hoover, "We started it in this house with Bobbie showing me a 'The Home is for Hoover' sign he had put on the goldfish bowl, and Janey bringing up a doll's carriage with a Hoover sign on it."

But the big event of the year was the coming of the first grandson! Robert E. Barney, Junior, was born in Cleveland in February. Lillian was not there when he came, but dashed out as soon as Andie was ready to have her, introduced mention of him in every letter and article she wrote, and dedicated her second edition of *The Home-Maker and Her Job* to him. One would have thought there had never been a grandson before!

The experiences of 1929 were even more exciting. The Hoovers' being in the White House meant contacts there, and it was a tremendous thrill to get invitations and boxes of flowers from there, and to be asked to go down and talk "Girl Scouting" with Mrs. Hoover. That was a real experience, for "The Lady" refused to hear any reasons why any one should not have time for her beloved Girl Scouting. The visit ended with a promise on Lillian's part to cooperate on some specific appropriate project when that should appear.

The Dennison people asked her to do a series of talks on "Selling from the Motion Study Standpoint." This was a great pleasure because of her admiration for Mr. Dennison, for the company's policies, and for the fine personnel of the organization. She went to Boston, Chicago, and Washington, as well as New York, giving several talks in each Dennison store, and apparently doing what had been wanted. There was also a project of making a survey on the "Green Line" lunch rooms. This was equally satisfactory, because Mildred and Rowland Johnson, who headed the organization, were so interested, so cooperative and so ready to accept the findings and carry them on through the years that followed. Not so satisfactory, but of great financial value, was the work with the Katherine Gibbs Secretarial Schools. This meant lecturing and surveys of the New York, Boston, and Providence schools — and intensive devoted work it was on Lillian's part. But Mrs. Gibbs did not prove the satisfactory "boss" that later women clients were to be, and Lillian was relieved when the year's work was accomplished!

There was a satisfactory development of the pioneer contacts with the "blinded," for the New York State Committee asked help on a problem. This was to discover why the things they made did not sell. The result of this was a luncheon meeting, to which the buyers of the merchandise were invited. After a chat, over luncheon, they checked over the merchandise displayed in a nearby room. In a few moments they had discarded the unsalable material, indicated what could find ready sale, and made invaluable suggestions!

The summer brought a marvelous opportunity to be a delegate to the World Engineering Conference in Tokyo. The children insisted that Lillian accept this, and W.W. Macon, of *Iron Age* and a faithful friend of many years' standing, commissioned her to write a series of articles on the trip, which would pay all travel expenses. The family departed for "The Shoe," and Lillian for a day or two with the California group and the thrill of their farewells as the Congress party sailed out of the Golden Gate. It was a wonderful trip, with entertainment at Hawaii, and at Japan itself! Lillian proved to be the one woman delegate from any country, which meant more invitations to speak at colleges and meetings than could be crowded into the short stay. But it was an exceptional opportunity to meet old friends and to present Frank's work to engineers, industrialists, and every other group in the communities, including women, and the schools for girls. With typical courtesy and gratitude of the Oriental people, Lillian was showered with lovely gifts which were to be prized for themselves and for the memories, throughout the years to come.

She got back to find the children fine and ready to go back to school or college. Ernestine of course would to into business, and had already a place in an advertising agency, which proved much less interesting than she had hoped. The wish of her heart had been to live with three of her

Lillian in Japan visiting the Ueno family (1929)

classmates in a New York apartment. Lillian was criticized by many of her friends for consenting to this project, for they felt that girls should fit back into their homes when they left college, but Ernestine was so very eager for the experience that it seemed cruel to deny it to her. The four girls had been chums all the way through college — one was musical and another a research worker, the third and Ernestine in the business field. So that they did not talk shop during their free time! The apartment was in the Village, and small and difficult to keep clean, but the girls were perfectly happy and the constant stream of guests seemed to have a wonderful time. Among these, Charles Carey, a young man from Wellesley, Massachusetts, in the heating and ventilating business, proved specially congenial to Ernestine, and the family soon realized that a serious attachment was developing. Martha was enjoying her college life, and taking part in many activities. She showed special aptitude for handling the class budget and became a sort of perennial treasurer of every project that came along. Frank had enjoyed his year at St. John's so much that when it was over, he said to his Mother, "Do you know where I'd go, if I didn't go to Michigan?" When he added that it would be Oxford University, she was sure that the year in the literary atmosphere had been no mistake! He transferred to Michigan, joined Bob Barney's fraternity, to everyone's satisfaction, and was soon very busy and happy on the new campus. In November, Frank Gilbreth Barney was born in Cleveland, and to the satisfaction of having another grandson, was added the tremendous thrill of having him named for his grandfather!

1930 brought many changes in Lillian's life. In the first place, it was becoming apparent that while Motion Study courses in the Montclair Laboratory might always be profitable, the technical schools were becoming increasingly able to take over this type of training. It was satisfying to feel that the clients who had sent students had approved of the results. As Lillian reviewed the long and distinguished list she was grateful and happy for the fine type of cooperation she had had! But if it was possible for industry to have its needs met through the colleges, that was the efficient and right way to have the work done. So she decided to give up "The Course" at the end of its seventh year, and do everything possible to stimulate, cooperate with, and participate in these courses in the colleges — now at Massachusetts Institute of Technology, New York University, et cetera. This decision was made easier because of an adequate supply of consulting work, which seemed to increase month by month. Miss. Mary Dillon, the competent and endearing President of the Brooklyn Borough Gas Company, asked her to design an efficient kitchen, to be exhibited in New York and later to become a part of the Coney Island set-up. There never was a finer, more cooperative client and every hour of the experience was a pleasure and a thrill.

Industrial projects and reports continued to present themselves. The Girl Scouts asked her for a short survey which she was glad to make, as a volunteer project. It, and the friendship of Mrs. William Brown Meloney, editor of the Magazine of the Herald Tribune, brought her a contact which was to develop into a marvelous opportunity to do consulting work of a specialized kind. Mrs. Nicholas Brady, the widow of the Public Service Magnate, was devoting a large part of her income and her interest to charitable projects and wished advice as to how these should best be handled. She was anxious and insistent upon paying most generously for this service and her sweet and spiritual nature and appreciative attitude made what otherwise might have been a difficult assignment a source of great pleasure as well as profit.

Ernestine and Charlie had become engaged and were married on the thirteenth of September at home, as Bob and Andie had been. Dear Ernestine was so busy with her job, now at Macy's, and so happy in her engagement, that she had no time to get ready for the wedding, but fell in with every plan suggested, and smiled serenely while her Mother's wedding dress, which had been worn by Andie, was fitted to her, and while plans for announcements, wedding breakfast, et cetera, were decided upon.

It is difficult to take up the years that follow — in chronological order. Perhaps their experiences lend themselves more easily to being grouped under functions, rather than dates.

There is a variety of material to refer to — copies of a great number of technical and non-technical papers — reports made on jobs — and accounts of various types of work as they appeared in the press. But there are not record books of publicity, copies of letters, or any of the wealth of material which made writing up of the earlier years in some detail a possibility.

The family life developed smoothly and satisfactorily. During the years, the dear mother in California passed on, and so did Fred — the oldest of the three brothers — leaving a wife and two lovely children. Of the Brown family, by 1941, Auntie, Tillie, and Elsie had gone on. Tillie had not married, Annie Florence had not married, either. Both sisters had devoted themselves to work for their community. Elsie married but had no children; David married Bess Eby — a schoolmate of Lillian's — and had three boys — the oldest, Dave Junior, had married and had twin girls; the second, Jack, was married also; but the youngest, Bobbie, remained a bachelor. Everett had married Winifred Osborn — who was at college at the same time that Lillian was — and of his three children, Winnie had married, but had no children; Everett Junior had married and had two little girls; and Jean had married and had had a small boy. Aunt Lillian's Delger had married a neighbor on 29th Street, and had two boys; Uncle Edward's Pearl had had no child by either of her marriages; and Fred's small Timothy was the only grandchild of that branch of the family.

Of the Moller family, in 1941, two brothers and six sisters remained. Bill and his wife, Elsie, had moved to Texas. Frank, Dollie, and Frankie — more like three chums than father, mother, and son — were living in a beautiful Piedmont home. The four devoted "Girls," Gertrude, Ernestine, Elinor, and Mabel — had not married, but were filling their lives with useful activities and proving the most devoted sisters and aunts in the world. Josephine and Van, who was "Big Brother" to the entire family, were happy in their three lovely children; Joe had married John Whipple, as an outcome of a three-generation family friendship, and their son, the small "Gilbreth" was the center of family life. It had been an enormous thrill to Lillian to have him named as he was! Fred — one of brother Fred's three namesakes — Fred Gilbreth and his own Freddie, being the other two — had gone into the Army after a fine record at school and at work — Margie — a student and a musician, was like Janey and Bobbie, still in the midst of their training.

Of Frank's family, his beloved sister Anne had gone on — John and Betsy and Betsy Anne, the one daughter, were living in California, with John still in the Navy. Carol and Norman — her husband — and the small Norman Junior, John, and Carol Anne — were in Detroit.

The Gilbreth family were gradually working out their pattern of going from high school to college — graduating — and taking jobs — and starting homes of their own.

Anne and Bob's two boys had been joined by Peter Charles in 1932. Bob's practice grew and in spite of its many demands he managed to save time to take up one piece of research after another to be reported to medical groups and included in their "Proceedings." There never was a finer or more beloved "head of a generation" than Bob Barney, and Lillian looked to him not only for affection, but for advice, and was never disappointed.

Andie not only ran a perfect home, but did a great deal of community service, including work in the hospitals, parent-teachers' association, and other educational and citizenship organizations.

The three boys were all dark and handsome and strenuous. They led their family, their neighborhood, and the school, a lively life. The Montclair boys nicknamed them "The Cleveland Indians" and delighted in their pranks, both at home and in Nantucket, but they were honest and straightforward and interesting and stimulating. Bobbie showed rare mechanical talent; Frank was the most musical of the three; and Peter had a sense of order and responsibility rare in a boy of his age.

Ernestine was to furnish the first family illustration in her generation of a family and a career. After her short experience in advertising, she continued at Macy's through the years. She became a buyer very quickly, and developed her work in the Adult Games Department till it was the outstanding department of its kind in the country. It delighted her Mother to see her constant improvement not only in operating but in the personnel end of her work for she became the big sister as well as the Head of her department. Her little daughter was born in 1938, and named for her grandmother, and was called "Jill." She looked like her father and had his ease and serenity — but she resembled her Mother too, and adjusted gracefully to her home, the family, and clan, and her nursery school.

Martha went from college to the New York Telephone Company on the recommendation of the Controller of her college, who said he never had had a student treasurer keep such records as she had kept or show such aptitude for that type of work. She could have remained there indefinitely, but found that the ceiling for women in her area was too low to interest her. So, having prepared herself at New York University with Professor Porter, in Motion Study, she undertook its installation in the Montclair Library. It is no easy thing to apply the discipline of such an orderly technique to the operating and personnel procedures of a non-profit making institution. The work naturally did not progress as fast as she had hoped, but both the Chief Librarian and her Mother were delighted with her achievements. She married Richard E. Tallman on June eighth, 1940, and their home became another family center of activity. Dick was a fine fellow — tall and good-looking, with an interesting background and training, and a love of the out-of-doors and of reading which made him an ideal companion for the strenuous Martha.

Frank — having gathered all the honors in his chosen field at Michigan, and become editor of the *Daily* and of its summer edition — supplemented this with doing practically everything on a small paper in a little down near Detroit, for the summer, and getting a job at the *Herald Tribune* in New York. Recommended by Stanley Walker, its editor, he took an opening on a paper in Charleston, South Carolina, which not only brought him valuable experience but an opportunity to know Elizabeth Cauthan, the sister of one of the other young men on the paper. They were married on September 28th, 1934. Frank — with Sis's brothers — set up a paper of their own, but were too inexperienced to swing it, although they all had and got a fine experience. He became a member of the Associated Press and the small family moved to Raleigh, North Carolina, and established a home there. The work went splendidly and Frank became Head of the Raleigh Division.

"Betsy," Elizabeth Cauthan Junior, was born in 1937 — a capable small person and very good to look at. "Sis" was fortunate enough to have her Mother with her for some time, so could take up the secretarial work of which she was so fond and develop another successful "Marriage and Career."

Bill met the right girl before he finished college and he and Jean Irwin were married in 1936. With a heart as big as the world, Jean — who had lost her own Mother — adopted Lillian and the entire Gilbreth family, and made her small home — like Sis's and the Gilbreth girls — a family center. Bill made a splendid record his last year and had no difficulty getting a job with the American Radiator Company. He was in the Research Division and all his experience at college and during the years he had worked between college years, was useful to him, and helped him to do a good piece of work. When the department of his company was transferred and combined at a different place he secured an equally good opening with the Detroit Edison Company and left this for a fine job, which he located and landed in New York, with one of the oil companies. Little Lill, her grandmother's second namesake, of her generation, was born in '38. She looked exactly like her father with his same persistence and his same enchanting grin, and they had a lively time, and a very happy one! It was one of those households where something interesting and exciting happens every minute!

Lillian with two of her sons, Frank Jr. and Bill (1945)

Lillian Junior went through Smith serenely, graduated creditably, and got herself a job at Macy's. They were more than pleased with her work but she found it tiring and uninteresting, and transferred herself to an insurance company at Newark. Here she could set up her own workplace and methods and carry on her activities in her quiet, quality, perfectionist way. In 1935, she married Donald Dodge Johnson — a Princeton graduate and a Montclair boy, with a serenity of spirit rare in an athlete and student. The family adopted Don on sight and followed his happy business and home career with pride and pleasure. In the Safety Engineering department of one of the Dupont plants, he worked himself up to the top with great persistence and an effortless technique, which held the family spell-bound. Lill asked for no career except a home and a family! The coming of Dodge in '37 and Julie in '40 were events looked forward to and rejoiced in by the entire family. Here was another lovely happy home where the family could gather. Dodgie had a beautiful serene spirit, and his record as family favorite was exceeded by no one of his generation. Little Julie, placid and smiling, was his own peculiar possession, but shared generously with the adoring family.

Fred bounded through high school with exciting set-tos with teachers and principals, but settled down at Brown for four years of serene, steady and happy life. Mechanical engineering proved to be just what he had hoped. He enjoyed his fraternity, as Frank and Bob Barney had, before him, and was very active in it, not only in membership affairs, but as waiter, steward, and manager. His Mother loved to visit him to talk with "Brother Warren," the elderly gentleman who lived at the house, and with Edna the cook, who felt that no one appreciated the curly red-headed Fred as much as she did! He graduated, got a job with Ross Allen, who had worked for and with Fred's Father, transferred to Macy's for retail experience and then to Merck and Company, in Rahway, New Jersey, where he rapidly got into the stride of Methods work. His strong feeling for home and family was a source of endless support and joy to his Mother, and his love for all the "small fry" was an "Open Sesame" to all the homes of the next generation.

Dan pursued a far more peaceful course through the high school and went to the Wharton School in Philadelphia with the blessings of Mr. Ferguson, the Principal. He and Bill Onderdonk, who had lived side-by-side since their small-boy days took the same course; both became Betas and continued their friendship through the years. The Wharton School proved a splendid place for Dan, who majored in retailing, and found both the technical and general work to his liking. He also, like Fred, was active in his fraternity, and became its Business Manager during his last year. As excellent opening at Bambergers's Department Store in Newark was ready for him, and he did fine work here — growing up to be Assistant Buyer in record time. But the long hours, the monotony, and the general set-up of the Department Store did not satisfy him, and he was glad to transfer to one of the insurance companies. His education, personality, and his experience, proved just what was needed and he seemed the right person in the right place. In December 1940, he married Irene Jenses, who had been a schoolmate and a "best girl" during high school days. With an interesting background of Scandinavian culture, combined with a sweet personality, education, and some secretarial experience in industry, Irene took over husband and home with serenity and competence — another home center, with host and hostess who delighted to entertain not only family, but the big happy group of youngsters with whom they had grown up.

John did beautiful work all through school and re-elevated the family standing in Latin! He had thought of Harvard, but a trip to Princeton with Donald marked him as a "Princeton man" the rest of his life. Never did any one enjoy or love his college more! He majored in Industrial Relations and the family looked forward with pride and assurance to the use he would make of his training and his life.

Bobby — slowed down by a post-flu heart condition in his early childhood, which meant a year out of school — developed a philosophy of life which seemed to his Mother almost to compensate for the discipline of that experience. Of the eleven, he, perhaps, had the most family feeling and interest in all the details of the family development. Every new in-law was welcomed by him as a real own brother and sister so that he had his peculiar unchallenged place in each household. It was perhaps natural that political economy and sociology, even at the high school, were his major interests and that his Mother was convinced that his deep interest in humanity and his warm heart would bring him to — and prepare him for — fine service in the world.

He prepared for, and was accepted by Brown, but the heart specialists recommended a milder climate, so that he actually entered at the University of North Carolina, and identified himself with its interests and activities with a fine spirit. It meant much to him and to Frank, Sis, and Betsy, that he could spend weekends and short holidays with them! Janey — in spite of all that the family might try to do to hide it — was, of course, the center of interest and attention of every one. As a small child, her Mother used to rock her and sing a foolish doggerel:

> We love Anne and Ernie, away off in Smith —
> We love Frank and Martha, though they're inclined to tiff!
> Bill, Lill, Fred, Dan, Jack, Bobby — we love them one and all—
> But Janey! She's the baby!
> And we love her best of all!

She finished her nursery school and went to Nishuane with the older boys, but Brookside, where she had had her nursery training, always remained interested in her, so she was awarded a scholarship there and avoided the strenuous junior high days of the public school, much to her Mother's pleasure. She forged to the head of her small class, along with one or two brilliant boys. Just at the end of the last year she broke her leg and graduated with it in a cast inscribed with autographs and messages from her classmates and not at all disturbed by her appearance. Representing her group, she had persuaded Dr. Black, the minister, to give the graduating address and was not unduly upset when he included an account of her methods of persuasion! Her Mother remembered the day she had met the Standing Committee at the Church, and Dr. Black had teased her by saying, "There is one member of this group who makes me very sad," and then reassured her by saying it was because she was the last of the Gilbreths to join and he regretted there were no more. She had a happy time in high school, although the sorority life proved demanding and the unduly busy social life made keeping high standards of scholarship difficult. Just at this era, "pairing off" was the fashion, and as Janey never was one to take life lightly, this also furnished emotional problems! She and Bobby graduated together, because, of course, he had had to lose time because of his illness, and it was not only a thrill to Lillian but to the entire family when she have the graduating address at the joint graduation. Everyone who could get there, went. It was a beautiful night and the entire family was excited and happy. One year at Sweet Briar proved a pleasant experience but when Janey transferred to Michigan in the fall of 1940, it was evident that she had found the right place. She joined "Sorosis" as Andie had done. She wore the pin of dear "Aunt" Margery

Brusley's youngest nephew. She followed her sorority and fraternity sister and brothers by taking on activities and she rejoiced her Mother's heart by promising — as Bob had also — to try her best to graduate before making other plans.

So much for the family, as of June, 1941!

As for the work — it had developed in many areas. Consulting work in the industries went on, with reports and without. Interesting work was done for International Business Machines, and its President, Mr. Thomas Watson — which furnished stimulating, though occasional, projects through the years. Much other work was done which records do not show, because it was advisory and confidential. The work for Mrs. Brady Macauley never became formal enough for records to be kept on file. Lillian was never to forget the happy mornings spent in her beautiful apartment overlooking the park in Paris, or wherever Mrs. Brady happened to be, going over her many interests and projects — among them were the Carroll Club and Girl Scouts. The Carroll Club was put on a basis which was to be more and more self-supporting and all the appropriate techniques of management were installed, including budgets, operating schedules, and personnel procedures. It was a fascinating combination of volunteer work with the necessity of persuading a generous donor that it must become more and more democratic in very way.

Even more stimulating was the work with the Girl Scouts where the same necessity — but on a much larger scale — of combining a large volunteer group and a small professional group in an adequate project called for every bit of experience and judgment Lillian could muster. She threw herself into this with all the energy at her disposal adding her own volunteer work to the professional work she contributed through Mrs. Brady and her projects. From this, came intensive study of professional/

volunteer relationships all through the social service fields and ultimately the *Code for Volunteers* which was to be generally accepted and proved useful. By 1941 there was a possibility that conferences on volunteer opportunities for women would spread from the Purdue Campus through educational institutions.

In another area, significant progress was made, and that had to do with the home. The "Model Kitchen" for the Brooklyn Borough Gas Company and Miss. Dillon was followed by various projects at the *Herald Tribune* for Mrs. Ogden Reid and Mrs. William Brown Meloney. These were supplemented and added to by Eloise Davidson and through her and the Institute, the *Herald Tribune* and *This Week,* the fundamental principles of "Effectiveness in the Home" spread through the country.

"Better Homes in America" through Mrs. Meloney's initiative, included not only a Gilbreth Kitchen, but a "Clothery" — a new combination of laundry and sewing-room, and a nursery. The "Little House" on Park Avenue in New York existed only a few months, but it was visited by many people and described not only in a beautiful booklet but in a great number of magazines and papers. A "Motion-Saving Household Desk" was developed by Lillian and, through the cooperation of Mr. Watson, became a part of the I.B.M. exhibit at the Chicago World's Fair.

Through her 1935-1941 appointment as Professor of Management at Purdue, with part-time spent in the School of Home Economics, Lillian was able to introduce both operating and personnel material into Home Economics thinking. Several fine undergraduate and graduate students, of Master's and Doctor's Degree caliber, worked out projects in this field and there was every indication of interest in the outcome.

As for work in the area of Public Service, it was a pleasure to serve as a "Dollar-a-Year" woman under President Hoover in the Employment area. Asked by Colonel Woods, who headed the committee work, to

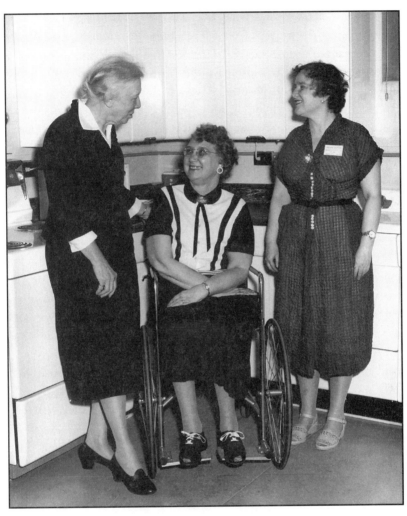

Throughout her life, Lillian's work with the disabled was an
important aspect of her work. Pictured here at the Conference on
the Handicapped, University of Connecticut (1953)

undertake the area of work with women, she had the pleasure of inviting
her beloved college friend, Alice Dickson, to work with her, and the two
made such contributions as they could, through the women of the country.

Several years on the Essex County Vocational School Board, proved useful, as did a happy service on the New Jersey State Board of Regents. As the only woman on a small board, Lillian enjoyed not only an opportunity for service but warm friendships and happy meetings with trained and devoted minds. It was a pleasure to work with Miss. Quigley, the stimulating and competent librarian of the Montclair Library, on the use of space in the small, cheery, but inadequate building — and to work with the principals and teachers of various schools the children attended, wherever this seemed possible. A rare remembered compliment came from a quiet little colored Mother who asked the principal of Nishuane to ask Lillian to be a repeat-speaker for the Parent-Teachers' Association "because she was the only speaker we understood."

Lectures and work in the academic field grew with the years. Purdue especially, wanted more and more time until finally Lillian spent one week there every other month. She found there the answer to one of her big problems — which was — where to give Frank's technical library and the papers. She and the children decided to offer these to Purdue — as the Moller family had given Annie Moller's Indian Basket Collection to the University of California. Purdue accepted the gift, and offered Lillian a full professorship in Management, while she should be getting the collection in order. She was allowed to draw up her own contract, with a week off every month for her consulting work in Montclair. Her time was divided four ways: between General or Industrial Engineering, Industrial Psychology, Home Economics, and the Dean's Office as "Consultant on Careers for Women." Through cooperation in all four areas, the plan worked out, and through the devoted assistance of a helper who came, almost providentially, to work on the small Gilbreth Library, at the end of '41, everything was in shape. This meant indexing of books and material; preparation of all the material which would make it possible for an adequate biography of Frank to be written, and things in such shape that student's, on the Campus, and — ultimately — everywhere — could make use of Frank's long intensive years of work.

As for international work, only home and family responsibilities prevented this from being almost continuous. As the one woman delegate, not only from this country, but from any country — Lillian had had rare opportunities to see and to speak all through Japan and to receive such appreciation of Frank's work that she returned home stimulated and ready to work harder than ever. The meetings of I.R.I. and of the International Management Congress meant happy trips to Europe — strenuous but very worth while. Two visits to Sweden — one as official delegate from "Better Homes in America" added an international background to her Housing experience.

One opportunity came which she reluctantly refused. This was to become a member and, finally, the Methods Expert for the Church Group which spent a year in the Orient checking on missionary activities. It would have been a wonderful experience, and the children felt that she should have it — but she felt that nothing would ever compensate for a year at home with them, and was never sorry that she had made the decision.

Honorary degrees and other honors were all too generously conferred. Most gratifying was the founding of the Gilbreth Medal by Frank's beloved Society of Industrial Engineers. This was named for Frank and her and their profiles were on the Medal itself. Through the years that followed she was invited to be Chairman of the Awards Committee, and was happy as President Hoover, Joseph Roe, Allen Mogensen, David Porter, and Ralph Barnes were added to the list of recipients. No honorary degree or other honor could be as great as this opportunity to have Frank's work adequately remembered each year with the Medal's Award. Each recipient represented a separate and a very great satisfaction — President Hoover, the prestige and standing and humanitarian and service aspect — Professor Roe, its academic standing and the spread of its prestige in the universities and colleges — Allen Mogensen, its Public Relations aspect, its dynamic power and its usefulness in a variety of fields — Dave Porter, its high ideals and selflessness, its teaching value, its careful devotion to

Lillian on a visit to a factory in Puerto Rico (1955)

perfecting people and techniques — Ralph Barnes, its research, its combination of theory and practice, its applicability to a diversity of problems. All together, they spelled — to her — to the profession — and to the world — the value of Frank's work, its usefulness and adaptability, and the constant extension of its scope and its usefulness.

As, in the summer of 1941, Lillian attempted to look backward and around and ahead — in spite of the sad state of world affairs — she had much to rejoice in. All the children were well, busy, and happy, and anxious to be of use in the world. The Montclair home and the Nantucket home were completely free of any obligations — the "Little Shoe" would remain with the family, and open its doors summer after summer, to one generation after another. Dear old "68" in Montclair would be taken down, as it had served its purpose. Lillian and the unmarried ones would find a home center, suitable and easy to maintain, and from it — it was to be hoped — the remaining spinster and bachelors would leave to found homes of their own!

Frank's work had become so much a part of the teaching of schools and colleges that it would serve its purpose and develop with the years. The research so near to his heart would be carried on by other people — other groups — and other places — but it would go on — and that was the only thing that mattered!

THE QUEST OF THE ONE BEST WAY — which was his life ideal, work, and passion — would go on!

— *Lillian M. Gilbreth*

Index of Illustrations

Lillian M. Gilbreth Honors and Awards

Academic Degrees

Earned Degrees:
1900   University of California – B. Litt.
1902   University of California – M. Litt.
1915   Brown University – Ph.D.

Honorary Degrees:
1928   University of Michigan – M. Eng.
1929   Rutgers University – Dr. Eng.
1931   Brown University – Sc. D.
1931   Russell Sage College – Sc. D.
1933   University of California – LL.D.
1945   Smith College – LL.D.
1948   Alfred University – LL.D.
1948   Purdue University – Dr. Industrial Psychology
1949   Temple University – L.H.D.
1950   Stevens Institute of Technology – Dr. Eng.
1951   Colby College – Sc. D.
1951   Milwaukee-Downer College – Sc. D.
1952   Syracuse University – Dr. Eng.
1952   Mills College – LL. D.
1952   Lafayette College – Sc. D.
1953   Princeton University – Dr. Eng.
1953   Washington University – Sc. D.
1955   University of Wisconsin – Sc. D.
1956   Skidmore College – LL. D.
1959   Pratt Institute – Sc. D.
1959   University of Massachusetts – Sc. D.
1960   Western College for Women – L. H. D.
1964   Arizona State University – LL. D.

Memberships

AMERICAN ASSOCIATION FOR THE ADVANCEMENT OF SCIENCE –
Member

THE AMERICAN COLLEGE OF HOSPITAL ADMINISTRATORS –
Honorary Fellow

AMERICAN INSTITUTE OF INDUSTRIAL ENGINEERS (AIIE) –
Member, Honorary Member

AMERICAN MANAGEMENT ASSOCIATION (AMA) –
Honorary Member

AMERICAN SOCIETY FOR ENGINEERING EDUCATION – *Member*

AMERICAN SOCIETY OF MECHANICAL ENGINEERS (ASME) –
Member, Fellow, Honorary Member

ARMED FORCES MANAGEMENT ASSOCIATION, Washington, D.C. –
Honorary Life Member

AUSTRALIAN INSTITUTE OF MANAGEMENT (AIM) –
Honorary Member

BRITISH INSTITUTE OF MANAGEMENT – *Honorary Member*

COMITE INTERNATIONAL DE L'ORGANISATION SCIENTIFIQUE
(CIOS) – *Member*

ENGINEERING INSTITUTE OF CANADA – *Honorary Member*

HOSPITAL MANAGEMENT SYSTEMS SOCIETY – *Honorary Member*

INSTITUTE FOR SCIENTIFIC MANAGEMENT OF POLAND – *Member*

THE INSTITUTE OF WORK STUDY PRACTITIONERS, England –
Honorary Fellow

INTERNATIONAL ASSOCIATION OF PERSONNEL WOMEN –
Honorary Member

THE INTERNATIONAL UNIVERSITY CONTACT FOR MANAGEMENT
EDUCATION (IUC) – *Member*

THE IRISH WORK STUDY INSTITUTE – *First Honorary Fellow*

L'ACADEMIE INTERNATIONALE DE L'ORGANISATION SCIENTIFIQUE –
Member

MASARYK ACADEMY, Czechoslovakia – *Member*

METHODS TIME MEASUREMENT (MTM) – *Member*

THE MIRIAM HOSPITAL, Providence, RI –
Life Member of the Corporation
NATIONAL ACADEMY OF ENGINEERING – *Member*
NEW JERSEY HOME ECONOMICS ASSOCIATION
(affiliate of the American Home Economics Association) –
Life Member
NOVA SCOTIA ASSOCIATION OF MANAGEMENT SERVICES –
Honorary Member
PHI BETA KAPPA
SOCIETY FOR ADVANCEMENT OF MANAGEMENT (SAM) –
Honorary Member
SOCIETY OF PROFESSIONAL MANAGEMENT CONSULTANTS –
Honorary Member
SOCIETY OF WOMEN ENGINEERS (SWE) – *Honorary Member*
SYSTEMS AND PROCEDURES ASSOCIATION, Motor City Chapter,
Detroit – *Honorary Member*
VEREIN DEUTSCHER INGENEUR (VDI) – *Member*
WOMEN'S ENGINEERING SOCIETY, London, England – *Member*
THE WORK STUDY ASSOCIATION OF SOUTH AFRICA – *Patron*

Medals and Awards

1931   Gilbreth Medal Award

1944   Gantt Medal awarded jointly by ASME and AMA
to Dr. Lillian M. Gilbreth and Frank B. Gilbreth
(posthumously)

1949   National Institute of Social Sciences Medal

1951   Wallace Clark Award

1954   Washington Award, Western Society of Engineers

1954   CIOS Gold Medal

1957   Engineers of Southern California, Award of Merit

1959   Montclair State College dedicated "Lillian Gilbreth
Home Management House"

1959   Industrial Management Society named Dr. Gilbreth
"Mother of the Year" on Mother's Day

1959   Cullimore Medal, Newark College of Engineering

1959   Systems and Procedures Association of America Award

1961   Frank and Lillian Gilbreth Industrial Engineering Award
(AIIE) to Frank B. Gilbreth (posthumously) and
Lillian M. Gilbreth

1961   Human Relations Award, New School for Social Research

1962   "The Frank and Lillian Gilbreth Conference",
Annual Conference and Convention of AIIE

1962   New Industrial Engineering building at University of Rhode
Island named "Gilbreth Hall" for Frank B. Gilbreth and
Lillian M. Gilbreth

1962   The Association of Management and Industrial Engineers
of the Philippines Award

1963   Association Interprofessionnelle pour l'Etude du Travail Medal

1964   The Women Chemical Engineers of the Philippines,
Certification of Distinction

1965   The Central Business District Association, Detroit,
National "Salute to Women Who Work" Award

1965   National Rehabilitation Association, President's Award

1966   McElligott Medallion, presented by Association of
       Marquette University Women to Lillian M. Gilbreth
       and Ernestine Gilbreth Carey "for professional excellence
       and personal integrity"
1966   Chicago Association of Commerce and Industry,
       Management Training and Communication Division,
       Testimonial plaque presented by 12 Professional and
       Technical Societies
1966   The Hoover Medal
1967   The Institute of Work Study Practitioners, England,
       first recipient of the Frank B. Gilbreth Medal
1968   Order of The Precious Crown —
       3rd Class, Emperor of Japan
1984   Release of the U.S. postage stamp honoring Lillian M. Gilbreth

Books

Co-authored with Frank B. Gilbreth
Time Study
Fatigue Study
Applied Motion Study
Motion Study for the Handicapped

Written by Lillian M. Gilbreth
The Psychology of Management
The Quest of the One Best Way
The Home Maker and Her Job
Living With Our Children
Normal Lives for the Disabled (with Edna Yost)
The Foreman and Manpower Management (with Alice Rice Cook)
Management In The Home (with O.M. Thomas and E.C. Clymer)

Dr. Gilbreth also contributed chapters on *Non-industrial Applications of Industrial Engineering* to both the 1st and 2nd editions of *Industrial Engineering Handbook,* edited by H.B. Maynard.

Articles and Papers

1959 Proceedings, 11th Annual Industrial Engineering Institute, University of California, Berkeley – *Long Range Planning*

1960 ASME 50 Years Progress in Management – *Management's Past, A Guide to It's Future* (with W.J. Jaffe)

1962 Advanced Management, Office Executive – *Work and Management*

1962 The President's Forum, President's Professional Association – *Message to Management*

1963 The Journal of Industrial Engineering – *World Wide Industrial Engineering*

1964 Advanced Management Journal – *Integrity, The Touchstone of Good Management*

1964 Proceedings, First International Conference of Women Engineers and Scientists – keynote, *Focus For The Future*

Presidential Committees

Dr. Gilbreth has served under Presidents Hoover, Roosevelt, Eisenhower, Kennedy and Johnson on committees dealing with civil defense, war production, aging, and rehabilitation of the physically handicapped.

Teaching

Before World War I, Lillian worked with her husband, Frank B. Gilbreth, conducting *Summer School of Management for Professors of Engineering Psychology and Economics,* Providence, RI.

During World War I, while Major Frank B. Gilbreth was on active duty at General Staff College, Washington, D.C., Dr. Lillian M. Gilbreth prepared Industrial Engineering material which was used by her husband and his colleagues in their teachings.

Director of Industrial Engineering Seminars at Montclair, NJ
    1924-1930

Professor of Industrial Engineering at:
    Purdue University
    Newark College of Engineering
    University of Wisconsin

Member of educational teams sponsored by U.S. Federal government sent to:
    Japan
    Philippines
    Taiwan

Lectures

Lecturer before technical groups, civic groups, service clubs, rehabilitation teams, colleges and universities, in U.S. and abroad, including: Australia, Canada, England, Germany, Holland, India, Italy, Japan, Mexico, New Zealand, Philippines, South Africa, Sweden, Switzerland, Taiwan, and Turkey.

Frank and Lillian Gilbreth Collection
PURDUE UNIVERSITY LIBRARIES

The papers of Frank and Lillian Gilbreth reflect the working activities, and family life, of the Gilbreths, pioneers in time and motion study and scientific management. Included are diaries, business and personal correspondence, publications by the Gilbreths, conferences, meetings and seminar information, photographs, audiovisual materials, awards, diplomas, and work flow charts. The bulk of the collection is the Gilbreth's information file or "N-file," which covers materials from the early 1900s to 1924. There is correspondence received by Lillian M. Gilbreth on business matters during the 1960s, as well as some genealogical materials.

The largest part of the Gilbreth Collection is the N-file, which contains information on the early principles of scientific management and their application in both the manufacturing and personnel areas. There are case materials, photographs, family matters, applications to business and industry, materials on the home, sports, and other matters. There is a printed index and topical card files to the N-File, available for researchers. Photographs in this collection cover the activities of Lillian M. Gilbreth, in the 1960s along with early photographs of Frank B. Gilbreth.

Audiovisual materials include records, audio tapes, videotapes, movies and other materials. Of particular interest is the videocassette entitled, "The Early films of Frank Gilbreth." There are some interviews with and about Lillian M. Gilbreth on audio tape.

Among correspondents whose letters are included are Bernard M. Baruch, Herbert Hoover, William J. Jaffe, Robert W. Johnson, Fred Kersting, George C. Marshall, the Meninger family, Andrew A. Potter, Walter Scott, Anne Shaw, and Dorothy Stratton.

The Gilbreth Collection is housed in the Special Collections Department of Purdue University Libraries in Stewart Center, West Lafayette, IN.

Gilbreth Memorial Fellowship

The Gilbreth Memorial Fellowship recognizes academic excellence and campus leadership. This scholarship of $2,500 is available to graduate students enrolled in any school in the United States and its territories, Canada, and Mexico, provided the student is pursuing an advanced degree program in industrial engineering or its equivalent.

The Fellowship is administered through the Institute of Industrial Engineers' Foundation. Candidates for these awards must:
1) be active members of the Institute of Industrial Engineers ;
2) be enrolled full-time in graduate or undergraduate industrial engineering programs;
3) have an overall point-hour average of 3.40 on a scale of 4.00 (graduate students must have had a 3.40 average as undergraduates to qualify); and
4) have at least five full quarters, or three full semesters, of school remaining from the date of nomination (November of proceeding year) to be eligible for consideration for a full scholarship or fellowship.

The nominee's scholastic ability, character, leadership, potential service to the industrial engineering profession, and need for financial assistance are all considered by the Scholarship Fund Trustees when selecting the scholarship recipients.

Students may not apply directly for scholarships. They must be nominated by their department head or faculty advisor. For further information, see IIE's website at http://www.iienet.org, or call IIE Member and Customer Service at 1-800-494-0460 or 770-449-0460.

The Gilbreth Network

The Gilbreth Network is an informal group of people, brought together by their common interest in the lives and work of Frank and Lillian Gilbreth. This Network seeks to:

- Provide those currently doing research with the names of people doing similar work, to share resources and material.
- Offer assistance to students preparing graduate and post-graduate papers.
- Provide information on new books and articles, as well as newly discovered Gilbreth material.
- Gather any previously unknown Gilbreth material to share with membership and see that original documents are sent to proper archives for preservation.

There is no cost to belong to the Network. Small contributions to the costs of postage and photocopying will be greatly appreciated. If large documents, such as a Gilbreth Bibliography, are developed, a fixed, small fee will be needed, reflecting only copying and postage costs.

The Quest is the quarterly newsletter of the Gilbreth Network. It contains general information of interest to "Gilbrethites," sources of information and articles from our members.

If you know of others who may be interested in the Network, either send them a copy of this material and application, or have them send a request to the Network Coordinator.

> Gilbreth Network
> c/o David S. Ferguson, CSP
> 113 Kay Ct.
> Cloverdale, CA 95425
> (707) 894-3854
> E-Mail: dferg@metro.net